WORKING WITH TRANSACTIONAL ANALYSIS

This unique book, incorporating both theory and practice, provides an invaluable guide to the assessment of dreams in transactional analysis (TA).

Grounded in the latest neuroscientific research, it offers both neophyte and experienced TA practitioners a pathway to incorporate a client's dreams within individual and group therapy, exploring key issues including trauma, dissociation and nightmares, dreams of change and transformation, dreams of healing, and transference and countertransference in dreams.

It will support therapists through the very first steps toward the analysis of more complex interpersonal dynamics and dream analysis in a group setting. Also discussing the direction of future research in the area, as well as an overview of an experiment on dream analysis during the recent pandemic, this will be key reading for anyone working in the field.

Anna Emanuela Tangolo, psychologist and psychotherapist, supervisor and transactional analysis teacher of the European Transactional Analysis Association (TSTA-P), is director and founder of the PerFormat school in Pisa, Genoa, and Catania. She has published *Psychodynamic Psychotherapy with Transactional Analysis*, and *Group Therapy in Transactional Analysis* with Anna Massi, both in Italian and English (Routledge), and directs the journal *Percorsi di Analisi Transazionale*, as well as the publishing series *Percorsi*.

Francesca Vignozzi is a psychologist and psychotherapist, supervisor, and teacher (PTSTA-P) in training at the European Transactional Analysis Association. She is the deputy director of the PerFormat school in Pisa, Genoa, and Catania. She has published the book *Comprendere la psicoterapia* and is the author of several articles and scientific contributions on psychodynamic transactional analysis.

INNOVATIONS IN TRANSACTIONAL ANALYSIS: THEORY AND PRACTICE

Series Editor: William F. Cornell

This book series is founded on the principle of the importance of open discussion, debate, critique, experimentation, and the integration of other models in fostering innovation in all the arenas of transactional analytic theory and practice: psychotherapy, counseling, education, organizational development, health care, and coaching. It will be a home for the work of established authors and new voices.

NEW THEORY AND PRACTICE OF TRANSACTIONAL ANALYSIS IN ORGANIZATIONS: ON THE EDGE
Sari van Poelje and Anne de Graaf

GROUP THERAPY IN TRANSACTIONAL ANALYSIS: THEORY THROUGH PRACTICE
Anna Emanuela Tangolo and Anna Massi

RADICAL-RELATIONAL PERSPECTIVES IN TRANSACTIONAL ANALYSIS PSYCHOTHERAPY: OPPRESSION, ALIENATION, RECLAMATION
Karen Minikin

REVITALIZATION THROUGH TRANSACTIONAL ANALYSIS GROUP TREATMENT: HUMAN NATURE AND ITS DETERIORATION
Giorgio Piccinino

WORKING WITH DREAMS IN TRANSACTIONAL ANALYSIS: FROM THEORY TO PRACTICE FOR INDIVIDUALS AND GROUPS
Anna Emanuela Tangolo and Francesca Vignozzi

https://www.routledge.com/Innovations-in-Transactional-Analysis-Theory-and-Practice/book-series/INNTA

WORKING WITH DREAMS IN TRANSACTIONAL ANALYSIS

From Theory to Practice for Individuals and Groups

*Anna Emanuela Tangolo
and Francesca Vignozzi*

Translation by Martina Del Romano

Designed cover image: Photo courtesy of Franco Bertozzi

First published 2024
by Routledge
4 Park Square, Milton Park, Abingdon, Oxon OX14 4RN

and by Routledge
605 Third Avenue, New York, NY 10158

Routledge is an imprint of the Taylor & Francis Group, an informa business

© 2024 Anna Emanuela Tangolo and Francesca Vignozzi

The right of Anna Emanuela Tangolo and Francesca Vignozzi to be identified as authors of this work has been asserted in accordance with sections 77 and 78 of the Copyright, Designs and Patents Act 1988.

All rights reserved. No part of this book may be reprinted or reproduced or utilised in any form or by any electronic, mechanical, or other means, now known or hereafter invented, including photocopying and recording, or in any information storage or retrieval system, without permission in writing from the publishers.

Trademark notice: Product or corporate names may be trademarks or registered trademarks, and are used only for identification and explanation without intent to infringe.

British Library Cataloguing-in-Publication Data
A catalogue record for this book is available from the British Library

Library of Congress Cataloging-in-Publication Data
Names: Tangolo, Anna Emanuela, author. | Vignozzi, Francesca, author. | Del Romano, Martina, translator. | Cornell, William F., series editor.
Title: Working with dreams in transactional analysis: from theory to practice for individuals and groups / Anna Emanuela Tangolo and Francesca Vignozzi; translation by Martina Del Romano.
Description: Abingdon, Oxon; New York, NY: Routledge, 2024. | Series: Innovations in transactional analysis series | Includes bibliographical references. |
Identifiers: LCCN 2023047820 (print) | LCCN 2023047821 (ebook) | ISBN 9781032418346 (paperback) | ISBN 9781032407708 (hardback) | ISBN 9781003354666 (ebook)
Subjects: LCSH: Transactional analysis. | Dream interpretation.
Classification: LCC RC489.T7 T365 2024 (print) | LCC RC489.T7 (ebook) | DDC 616.89/145–dc23/eng/20231207
LC record available at https://lccn.loc.gov/2023047820
LC ebook record available at https://lccn.loc.gov/2023047821

ISBN: 978-1-032-40770-8 (hbk)
ISBN: 978-1-032-41834-6 (pbk)
ISBN: 978-1-003-35466-6 (ebk)

DOI: 10.4324/9781003354666

Typeset in Times New Roman
by Deanta Global Publishing Services, Chennai, India

TO OUR MOTHERS, FERNANDA AND PIERA
WHO DID SO MUCH TO STIMULATE
OUR IMAGINATION
AND OUR DREAMS

CONTENTS

Acknowledgments		*ix*
Foreword		*xii*
WILLIAM F. CORNELL		
A presentation in two voices		*xvii*
	Introduction	1
1	Dreams in psychology and psychotherapy	3
2	Neurosciences and dreams	26
3	Transactional analysis of dreams	46
	Suggestion: The history and culture of dreams	61
4	Our method of dream analysis in different settings	65
5	Dreams in individual psychotherapy	85
6	Script dreams, recurring dreams	104
	Suggestion: Kafka, insomnia, and dreams	124
7	Trauma, dissociation, nightmares	130
8	Change and transformation dreams	151
9	Dreams of healing	170

CONTENTS

10 Transference and dreams — 185

Suggestion: Cinema and Fellini — 204

11 Dreamwork in group therapy — 209

12 Countertransference dreams — 225

Suggestion: Cinema sci-fi, anime, and graphic novels — 245

Afterword by Paolo Migone — *251*
Index — *254*

ACKNOWLEDGMENTS

Our first thanks go to William Cornell, editor of Routledge's Innovation in Transactional Analysis series, who has supported and followed our work for years and chosen to publish it in English, as well as to Paolo Migone, our supervisor and friend who has followed our studies on psychoanalysis.

As we have repeatedly written, many of the ideas in this book have germinated in a climate rich in stimulation and fertile exchanges which is the group of teaching colleagues in the PerFormat School of Psychotherapy. To them go our heartfelt thanks for supporting and encouraging us at every stage of this book's life. In particular, we thank Anna Massi for the fruitful discussions since the early days of the project, Marina Zazo and Patrizia Vinella, with whom we share responsibility for the training of future therapists.

We are deeply grateful to those who have actively collaborated in the realization of this project, namely Silvia Rosa, our editor and cultural historian who has accompanied us since the beginning of our research, Martina Del Romano, an impeccable and efficient translator. We do not know her personally, yet she has been a firm reference for us during these months of book gestation. Many thanks to Carlo Serrati for his professional and generous supervision of the chapter on neuroscience and dreams. For the reading of this chapter in particular we are also grateful to our colleague Brunella Bartalini—with whom we share trips to Albenga, one of our psychotherapy school locations.

To Franco Bertozzi, our photographer and supporter, a heartfelt thank you for the gift of the cover photo from his trip to Morocco.

We express our deepest thanks to our students in the School of Psychotherapy, who continually stimulate us to think, study and question ourselves, and to our patients for the trust and generosity with which they let us into their most intimate and private room, the room of their dreams.

And finally some more personal thanks:

From Francesca

I'm especially grateful to Giulio Biagioni who provided me with a double fundamental support: first in guiding me in the search for scientific articles and second in sharing the night watching of beautiful and challenging dream films.

Special thanks to Sandra Trifirò, tireless companion of my dreams, for all the times in the last few months that she patiently waited for "the last sentence."

From Anna Emanuela

Thanks again to Franco Bertozzi who listens, suggests, and advises my every literary and scientific production, always offering me a divergent and innovative point of view.

And to Marco Bertozzi, director and film scholar who made me discover and love Fellini's "dream in images" and dreams.

To the women of my family: my grandmother Amina, my aunt Gabriella, my mother Fernanda, and Elena, my sister, because from them I have learned the art of dream telling, an activity that accompanied us each morning as we prepared to face the day.

They who are awake have a world in common amongst them; but they that are asleep are retired each to his own private world […]
>
> Heraclitus

FOREWORD

William F. Cornell
Series Editor

Without dreaming, our capacity to think, our inner worlds, become dreary, mechanical, detached from the realms of reverie and mystery. Without the capacity to think, our dreams may pass through us as meaningless flights of nighttime fancy or even grow into compelling, near-psychotic visions of one's self and the world. In many cultures throughout human history, dreams are seen as gifts of the spiritual realms, fodder (or perhaps warnings) for one's soul. In dreaming, we witness our night-time slippages into the world of fantasy, hope, and sometimes horror. Our dreams occupy liminal spaces within the realms of the desired, the forbidden, the conflicted, the psyche's emerging potentials. Contemporary models of dreaming do not limit the field of dreams to the night and sleep. As Ogden observes:

The frontier of dreaming, as I am conceiving it, is a psychological field of force over-brimming with freeing, taming, ordering, turning-back-on-itself, impregnating, "versifying" impulses (2005, pp. 8–9).

Both forms of dreaming—that done in sleep and in waking unconscious dreaming—generate a living semi-permeable barrier separating and connecting conscious and unconscious life (2005, p. 48).

Since Freud's monumental *Interpretation of Dreams*, the effort to receive dreams as meaningful communications from the unconscious has been central to almost every model of psychodynamic psychotherapy. And yet, until this book by Anna Emanuela Tangolo and Francesca Vignozzi, there has been no systematic approach to working with dreams within transactional analysis.

As the editor of the Routledge "Innovations in Transactional Analysis" series, I was thrilled to receive Tangolo and Vignozzi's proposal for this book, one which would fill in a serious gap in the literature of transactional analysis. This book not only fills in a gap in the TA literature but offers a remarkable, comprehensive approach to "dreamwork" that will engage and inform psychotherapists and psychoanalysts regardless of their particular theoretical model.

But as editor of this book series, as I read the incoming chapters of this book, I found myself wondering why a theory of dreams has been so absent in transactional analysis. To have some sort of answer to this question, it was necessary to return to Eric Berne's own writings. Before Berne began to develop transactional analysis as its own model of psychodynamic psychotherapy, he had been trained as a classical psychoanalyst. Although he became disenchanted with psychoanalysis (and psychoanalysis became disenchanted with Berne), he wrote *The Mind in Action* (1947), an overview of psychoanalysis written for the layman. Here Berne writes of the unconscious and dreams from a classical, analytic perspective:

The chief tensions present in the unconscious minds of most people are unsatisfied oral wishes, unsatisfied anal wishes, and unsatisfied wishes for the later period of life after the fifth year. They are usually both libidinous and mortidinous, loving and hateful (p. 109).

During sleep, the Ego is largely out of commission [...] During sleep, the Superego is partly out of commission. Therefore, the dreamer does things in his dream that he would never dare to do nor perhaps dare even to think of doing in waking life (p. 118).

The manifest dream will be a compromise between the tensions of the Superego and the unsatisfied wishes of the Id, and the analysis of the dream will lead back to the latent thoughts which arise from those two forces (p. 119).

The Mind in Action was republished in 1968, after Berne had become famous for *Games People Play*, then under the title of *A Layman's Guide to Psychiatry and Psychoanalysis*, keeping the original book largely intact and followed by an extensive introduction to transactional analysis with chapters by Berne and other leading practitioners during the "birth" of transactional analysis. The psychoanalytic and TA sections read like two separate books within the same covers. The TA section makes no reference to the unconscious or dreams or to integrate Berne's earlier presentation of psychoanalysis. There is, however, a significant addition with respect to dreams in the 1968 *Layman's Guide* to the original 1947 text, as Berne observes:

There is now evidence to show that even ordinary emotional experiences have to be "digested" in some way through dreaming in order for the individual to feel well. A person deprived of the opportunity to dream may become quite confused; many psychoses are preceded by a period of prolonged lack of sleep, and hence the opportunity to dream. It may be said that the mass of "undigested" emotions which results has some effect in bringing on the psychosis (1968, p. 136).

In Berne's books on transactional analysis written over a decade, there is but one direct reference to dreams in his final book, *What Do You Say After You Say Hello?*, while writing about sleep, noting, "Thus it happens that people who are deprived experimentally or punitively of the opportunity to dream eventually go in a state resembling psychosis" (1972, p. 267). In spite of Berne's immersion in classical psychoanalysis when he wrote of dreams, Tangolo and Vignozzi note that Berne's own voice mirrors a much more contemporary attitude toward dreams when he wrote:

It is a common error to suppose that *finding out* the meaning of the dream is the important thing. This is not so. The meanings must be felt, and these feelings must be put into proper perspective with other past and present feelings of that particular person, for the interpretation to have any effect in changing the underlying Id tensions, which is the purpose of the procedure (1968, p. 136).

It is impossible to consider the meanings of dreaming without some option of the unconscious, and in Berne's development of transactional analysis, he turned his back on the analytic emphasis on the centrality of unconscious experience (Cornell, 2008). As contemporary transactional analysis has re-incorporated notions of unconscious experience, it has done so primarily through an emphasis on relationality, as evidenced within the dyadic dynamics of the transference-countertransference relationship and enactments. Dreamwork, as developed here by Tangolo and Vignozzi, brings attention back to unconscious forces within the contexts of intrapsychic conflicts and desires. While this book offers a detailed accounting of working with dreams within a transactional analysis context, the authors draw upon a broad spectrum of psychoanalytic authors and dream researchers. Their emphasis on the felt experience of dreams is consistent with the reception of dreams and reverie in such analytic theorists as Bion and Ogden. This is a book that will speak to psychotherapists of all disciplines with an interest in dreams.

Tangolo and Vignozzi open and ground *Dreamwork in Transactional Analysis* with chapters that offer comprehensive overviews of psychoanalytic and neuroscientific perspectives on the nature and functions of dreaming before beginning to articulate their approach to dreamwork as transactional analysts. It is, perhaps, no accident they convey a sense of "dreamwork" rather than the more common conceptualizations of dream analysis. "Analysis" implies a stance of a view and assessment from the outside—the dream as something to be looked at from a thoughtful distance. Tangolo and Vignozzi enter the oneiric world from a place of curiosity and respect. The dream is at work on behalf of the patient, and patient and therapist are at work in the unfolding of the dreams and its potential signs and challenges:

Our method is essentially to welcome a client's dream narrative as a gift that brings something new into therapy, a perspective that adds something to the usual narratives of daytime experience. Welcoming it, without the immediate pretense of understanding its meaning, is the first duty of the analyst, and the client (as well as the group, if the telling takes place in a group setting) is also involved in this experience. Thus, listening to a dream means accepting the gift that the most emotional and deepest part of ourselves—or someone else— makes to our rational mind, a gift that we accept as we accept the story that a child may decide to tell us (Chapter 3, p 46–60).

They suggest that the investigation of a dream is like "getting to know a city by getting lost in its alleys," a kind of wandering, wondering, discovering, risking getting lost:

Working with dreams requires giving up the search for linearity, causality and scientific evidence and being able to stand in uncertainty, to move in complexity, in the presence of multiple parts (Tangolo & Massi, 2022, p. 141).

Their discussion of Berne's inception of transactional analysis is both respectful and critical. In so doing they echo Ogden's (2022) recent differentiation of ontological psychoanalysis, attending to the emergent future, from the more traditional models of epistemological psychoanalysis that focus on history as causal factors—the ontological grounded in experiential understanding, the epistemological based in interpretation. Tangolo and Vignozzi critique Berne's overly deterministic (and rather pessimistic) script theory, captured by Berne's image of sitting at a piano believing one is playing his own tune when, in fact, the music is generated by a piano roll. Berne's was an epistemological model, with treatment based on game and script interpretation. Tangolo and Vignozzi argue:

> In any case, liberation is external, which means that interpersonal support is needed in order to encourage change and free the person from their fate, which is more often tragic than "winning." As transactional analysts we have had to emancipate ourselves from this view, which is so deterministic and reductionist as to be pessimistic and, above all, far removed from the results of research carried out over the past fifty years in developmental psychology (Cornell, 1988).
>
> (pp. 151–2)

The authors present a detailed approach to the dreamwork in both individual and group psychotherapy, stressing as much the exploratory environment that needs to be created, in which the shared *experience* of the dream precedes the effort to discover or ascribe meaning:

Exploring means proceeding slowly, following the breath, the gaze, and the bodily tensions of the dreamer, who may be sweating, contracting, squinting and looking beyond, and still coming to terms with unknown dimensions of their self that may perturb them.

It is like being in the company of a child while they watch a scary movie or listen to a story or play with their monsters. One has to stay close by, sometimes a step behind, to allow the dreamer to move forward and find a passage first (Chapter 4, p. 65–84).

Tangolo and Vignozzi stress the transformative potentials of dreams. Drawing upon Quinodoz's (2002) writing about "dreams that turn over a page," they describe how some dreams call into consciousness aspects of one's self that have been denied, dissociated, or unrecognized. While the reception of these dreams is not typically comfortable, the arrival of this news from the unconscious is not always being welcomed at first view. They emphasize that "the risk is, that if the transformative dimension of such dreams is not grasped by the therapist and, on the contrary, the dreams are read as regressive, they can in fact induce regression in the patient".

Tangolo, with her colleague Anna Massi, has previously written a book on group therapy in transactional analysis, and here one of the rather unique aspects of this book is the model of dreamwork in groups:

The group therapy setting is particularly fertile for dreamwork because the group itself constitutes a dreamlike, evocative place for each participant. The group conjures up childhood experiences within the family, archetypal and primordial experiences of circles around the fire, in caves, and villages, when dream storytelling accompanied evenings and nights under the stars. Thanks to the mystery and fascination that surrounds their representations, therapy groups facilitate listening to dreams as well as dreaming together and learning from each other's dreams (Chapter 11, p. 209–224).

The dream worlds explored in this book are those associated with script and repetitive beliefs and defenses, trauma, nightmares, transformation and healing, transference, and countertransference, each of which has its own chapter of exploration and discussion. Every chapter is enhanced by case material of their dreamwork with their clients. The book concludes with a presentation of their own research on dreams in their clinical practice.

A unique and very rich element of *Dreamwork* is that some chapters, clinical in focus, are followed by a separate "suggestion" which extends the topic of that chapter to similar expressions in fiction, poetry, myth, film, and theater. Here we are reminded that our dreaming, our oneiric worlds, states of reverie, are not confined to the night, to sleep, or even to the individual.

References

Berne, E. (1947). *The mind in action*. New York: Simon and Schuster.
Berne, E. (1968). *A layman's guide to psychiatry and psychoanalysis*. New York: Simon and Schuster.
Berne, E. (1972). *What do you say after you say hello?* New York: Grove Press.
Cornell, W. F. (1988). Life Script Theory: A Critical Review from a Developmental Perspective. Transactional Analysis Journal, *18*(4), 270–282. https://doi.org/10.1177/036215378801800402
Cornell, W. F. (2008). What do you say if you don't say unconscious?: Dilemmas created for transactional analysis by Berne's shift away from the language of unconscious experience. *Transactional Analysis Journal*, *38*(2), 93–100.
Ogden, T. H. (2005). *This art of psychoanalysis*. London: Routledge.
Ogden, T. H. (2022). *Coming to life in the consulting room: Toward a new analytic sensibility*. London: Routledge.
Quinodoz, J.-M. (2002). *Dreams that turn over a page: Paradoxical dreams in psychoanalysis*. London: Brunner-Routledge.
Tangolo, A. E., & Massi, A. (2022). *Group therapy in transactional analysis: Theory through practice*. London: Routledge.

A PRESENTATION IN TWO VOICES

Anna Emanuela:
I am very excited as I am about to write this. It has long been in my desires as a psychotherapist and researcher of the psyche to write what I think about dreaming and the activity of dreaming: at least since visiting the remains of Apollo's temple at Epidaurus, when I discovered that the priests did with pilgrims in search of healing a work not unlike ours, that is, they sought in dreams the presence of the healing god, or, as we would say today, the presence of the intuition that guides our drive toward physis, toward the vital and healing force of nature that is written within us. The trip to Epidaurus and my youthful studies of philosophy the classical world certainly marked my early curiosity, but my personal experience as a child listening to and recounting dreams in my grandparents' house, by the fire on winter nights or on starry summer nights, also made a fundamental contribution. Even in that early context, dreams were considered important messages like poems and the voices of crickets in the night. These suggestions of my childhood remained within me, generating curiosity and interest in discovering in my patients' stories that hidden wisdom that could guide us toward the healing path.

Often, in the difficult work as a therapist and mind analyst, I have felt that I needed an ally to heal my patients, and I have always found this alliance in listening deeply to their will to live, to the daimon present in the slumbering child, to the parental voice that was the protection of the past, and these forces have often been recognizable in dreams even before daytime waking behaviors.

I have, therefore, always looked at dreams as revealing the forces that have guided the patient to me, but also undoubtedly as revealing the conflicts, and the anxieties, as in the case of nightmares and recurring dreams that carry scripted themes.

Psychotherapy is a journey of self-inquiry that allows us to rediscover our truest nature, and on this journey, dreams are useful companions for both patient and therapist. In this work we will give special emphasis to dreams that are had during periods of transformation and to dreams that are had during group therapy—a special "matrix" in which change and the resolution of deeper conflicts are inscribed. We also left some space for therapists' dreams and therefore, also, for mine, because often even the dreams of us therapists are a voice to be listened to that comes from our inner world and leads us to think about patients in a new and different way from the diurnal perspective of our clinical reflection.

Many fears have accompanied this project and many dreams. One of the first ones I had when I started thinking about it.

Dream of 30 December 2013

I am in Castellina (my hometown, in Tuscany), in the countryside and I have to go with someone to the old kindergarten. I arrive in the park, which appears larger than it is, full of trees. The man who is with me leads me on foot, walking ahead of me. There are cliffs and landslides along the steep, impervious terrain, among moss and scrub. At one point he plunges into a ravine, I get scared, call out to him and he tells me he is alive, he is okay, but needs help to get back up. I have to look for someone and, therefore, go on alone, in order to help him, too. I am frightened, but I tell myself that I am persistent and will slowly go on. This voice reassures me, calms me and I wake up thinking that I will make it.

When I wake up I think that the ravines and landslides represent the gaps in my knowledge and that's why I can't write the dream article I am supposed to write: the day before I felt really discouraged. The next day, when I wake up, I tell myself that I can make it through, but I realize that it is very tiring for me. I start writing fluently.

As we began writing this book, the dreams became more intense and signaled to me that we could make it only by working together.

Dream of 24 March 2020

Part 1

I am on a road trip with Franco and we are driving along a road in a desolate countryside (it looks like the road to Nisiros, which leads to the volcano). At one point we get off and continue on foot; there is a small crack to go through, like the door of a shack. Beyond is a landslide hill where the road gets smaller and smaller and slippery, you can't go on. Forced to turn back, beyond the crack we are discouraged: there are no other roads and we still have to proceed.

Three people arrive with considerably more energy. They tell us that there is another way through that we just have not seen. Under the landslide hill there is a small lake, the water is shallow and there are stones you can step on. We can cross from there and we walk with them. We make it and I think, strangely enough, we had not seen the crossing on our own.

Part 2

Again, Franco and I face a short space journey, as if it were a rehearsal, on a spacecraft. The problem, on re-entry, is to slow down to get back to Earth. We each have to do it on our own, as if we were each inside our own individual capsule. I'm terrified because there's a near-vertical ramp to go down; I'm afraid I'll get crushed. But, from the outside, those instructing me tell me to trust them: you really have to go through there. With much anxiety I jump and instead of accelerating as I feared I brake and get down to the ground safely.

These last dreams made it clear to me that the project that scared me a lot could become a reality if I collaborated with Francesca and Silvia, our editor, and Caterina, the researcher who helped us with the research process. Dreaming alone is often a gamble, dreaming in two and dreaming in a group means finding ways and crossings that alone we had not even imagined.

Francesca:
Let me make it clear right away that if it were up to me this book would never have been born, the very idea of its existence would never have seen the light of day. And this, the reader will be astonished to know, is due in part to the fact that I have never been much of a dreamer. When I woke up, I often had the vague feeling that I had dreamed something that invariably escaped me, although with the writing of the book and a more developed attention span, my ability to remember dreams has greatly improved. As for daydreams, however, I can recognize in me an alternation of light and shadow. Two souls exist in me that do not easily coexist. One creative, original, outspoken, and free, that hates formalism and sugarcoating, that loves to go beyond, to the gist of things, loves to plan adventurous journeys, to tickle the limit, to dare. Another part of me, on the other hand, is frightened, holds back, and under its hegemony I am uncertain, I stumble and become quiet, docile, ashamed, and compliant, I fear the same limit just challenged. And so, in an endless strain to find a balance in me between day and night, I keep silent and still. For such reasons, if this book exists it is thanks to Anna Emanuela. My visionary teacher is not only capable of dreaming but capable, above all, of building a world where those dreams come alive. This is the world of the PerFormat forge, a school that is above all a laboratory of thought, planning, training; where people working together exchange ideas, experiences, desires. The realization of this book for me is a dream come true. If writing a book until a few months ago was a Herculean feat for me, writing one about dreams was pure utopia. It has been an incredible adventure to open myself up to the exchange of ideas with Anna Emanuela, to her cultural and literary proposals in front of tables overflowing with books and cups of coffee. As well as that of locking myself in the intimacy of my room in the early morning hours, meeting Freud, Ferenczi, finding Berne again, making the acquaintance of McNamara. Interacting with them and exploring my

thoughts in depth was an extraordinary journey that lasted several months and that each time was interrupted, like a rude awakening, only with the light of day and the first notifications on my phone, a clear signal that the world out there had stopped dreaming and had gotten out of bed. From this whole experience I certainly take with me this simple lesson. You can learn to dream alone, but together you dream harder. Happy journey, then, to the reader who will want to go on this dream adventure that has moved us so much, in the expectation that they too, like us, may experience the thrill of discovery, the courage of possibility, the tenacity of hope that dreams inexorably continue to teach us.

Introduction

This book that found its way into the hands of the reader has had a long gestation. It was about ten years ago that we first thought about writing a book on dreamwork, a text that would fill a void in the literature on the subject of the transactional analytic field. And so, with the outstanding editor of this volume, Silvia Rosa, we began to meet monthly to build an archive that would collect our patients' dreams, those dreams celebrated in literature and history, along with our own, in which we found amazing connections with those of our patients and with our clinical work in general. Today that archive amounts to hundreds of dreams. In an attempt to bring order to such a great volume of material we wondered about categories and genres, and those considerations led us to the construction of new theoretical knowledge of dreams and the evolution of the process of dreaming within therapy. This handbook is the synthesis of that long work, which over the years has obviously been enriched by much research and the many published works on the subject.

This book aims to describe a method of dream analysis in psychotherapy that is useful for both individual psychotherapy and group work. Transactional analysis is the reference matrix of this method, also integrated with the relational psychoanalytic approach. At its core is our belief that paying attention to dreams provides access to the deepest time of psychic functioning and insight into the evolution of changing relational script patterns.

The book consists of 12 chapters that lead the reader in exploring their own dream world and the therapist in preparing to address dreamwork in the analysis and treatment of patients.

Dreams belong to everyone, and artists and thinkers help in growing our imagination and creativity. Thus, we suggest that readers, including therapists, regardless of their background, nurture their humanistic and artistic culture, even as they study neuroscience, medicine, and clinical psychology. Working on dreams requires that we educate ourselves and listen to music, read poetry, experience film, theater, and open ourselves to any cultural experience through readings and traveling. The *Suggestion* path we offer at the end of some chapters is therefore an invitation to approach the artists and thinkers who have made dreams into works and masterpieces that heal our imagination through beauty and give color and music to the soul.

Our hope is that those who will delve into these pages will experience the same exciting thrill of discovery that accompanied us throughout this journey and which is the same spirit, we are sure, with which Neo, the protagonist of *The Matrix*, ended up choosing the mythical red pill, choosing in turn to discover the reality of dreaming.

1
DREAMS IN PSYCHOLOGY AND PSYCHOTHERAPY

Introduction

Every research paper or clinical study on dreams starts off with Freud's fundamental contribution, *The Interpretation of Dreams*, which paved the way in the 20th century for the scientific and clinical interest toward this particular dimension of the functioning of the human mind.

Indeed, Freud's work is still impossible to ignore. Similar to how philosophers cannot disregard Plato's or Aristotle's works, the same can be said for psychotherapists and Freud, and so we must start our study from its origins.

To those students who wish to pursue dreamwork, we often say that to do so they must start by reading Freud's work. Everything that hereby follows is in constant dialogue with his thought and teachings.

We will then move on to Jung and analytical psychology, Perls and Gestalt theory, and finally we shall explore the evolution of psychoanalysis and cognitivist psychotherapy's recent interest in dream analysis in terms of narrations. A separate chapter will explore the relationship between dreams and the neurosciences.

We eagerly invite our readers to study and interpret the contributions of the great 20th-century clinicians and researchers, starting from the publication of the first systematic study on dream analysis provided by Sigmund Freud. To Freud goes the undisputed title of giving birth to a clinical and scientific thought which is still very much fruitful in terms of developments in clinical/psychotherapy field, as well as extraordinary for the intuitions and discoveries it yielded.

Freud (1856–1939) and dream interpretation

In the introduction to the Italian edition of *The Interpretation of Dreams* (1899/2005), Cesare Musatti clarifies that Freud's work was born out of a period of self-analysis following his father's death in 1986, when he realized the failure of his hypothesis that defined hysteria and obsessive neurosis as the result of real abuse suffered by clients during their childhoods. Musatti urges us to accept the "oddity" of this work, which seeks to be scientific and autobiographical at the same time, because in it Freud gives ample space to the analysis of his own dreams.

Freud's interest in dreams came as a consequence of his decision to abandon hypnosis in favor of free association, since during sessions his clients started spontaneously mentioning their own oneiric material. In the eight editions he published in his lifetime, the essential structure of his theory remained the same.

Dreams are the "*via regia*" to the unconscious and provide the perfect means to explore the deepest part of human personality.

It is not a coincidence that Freud mentions two of Aristotle's works in which dreams are considered for the first time as being of demonic instead of divine origin, that is to say, an autonomous psychic formation of the human mind. References to Artemidorus and in general to the ancients' interest in dreams are summarized rather briefly, in order to give ample space to a more scientific perspective on dreams and sleep, given the knowledge available at the time.

Many dreams described in the text are Freud's own, who embarks on a rigorous self-analysis.

His work on his dream about Irma's injection is well-known (Freud, 1899/2005, pp. 107–120), and Freud regards it as the beginning of a great discovery: dreams are the hallucinatory realization of desires. Irma was a client he was treating for a series of disorders connected to hysteria, but the treatment wasn't having the expected success. After a common friend brings him news of Irma, saying she is feeling better but is still not entirely well, Freud has the following dream: he imagines meeting her at a party with several common friends. He then proceeds to visit her and discovers that Irma's disease is actually connected to an infection caused by an injection given to her by their shared friend Otto. The dream thus frees him from his sense of guilt for not having cured this woman properly.

Freud's long work of self-analysis on the Irma dream brought him to many crucial discoveries. In his novel *L'interpretatore dei sogni* (2017), the famed writer Stefano Massini dedicates an entire chapter to a dramatization of Irma's dream (pp. 215–235), and ends it with the protagonist giving voice to the following consideration:

> Today, January 23rd 1896, after many long weeks of self-analysis on the Irma dream, I can finally note that dreams realize our unspoken desires. That which we wished happened, and dare not say out loud, dreams allow us to live it out. Irma's injection told me explicitly what the more adult part of me could never say out loud without feeling

arrogant: I wish to get rid of a difficult client, I wish to humiliate my jealous colleagues, I consider myself immune to error, I am the only one worthy of a tenured position in academia.

It might very well be that a human being whose desires are utterly fulfilled would not dream at all. Our dreams are that which we lack. Only in dreams we are complete.[1]

(2017, p. 235)

How to explain then the more anguished dreams? Freud introduces the concept of dream disfigurement. Those desires which we cannot accept, the id-originated impulses which need to be satisfied, are thus processed through oneiric imagery, which in turn is transformed by the impact of such violent drives on our conscience. Oneiric stories and imagery are therefore born from the conflict between the Id's drives and the censorship of the superego. Recounting dreams allows us to discharge those drives, but in a concealed form. This way we are permitted to guiltlessly dream about incest, betrayal, the death and murder of our loved ones, by attributing responsibility to an external agent. The experienced despair thus protects us and we can wake up in tears and not sadistically satisfied for the eradication of the competition.

This is how Freud introduces the idea of manifest and latent content and deems the analytical process based on free association to be the most efficient way to access the latent content and allow previously repressed drives and feelings to surface.

The interpretative work becomes necessary when certain repressed contents and certain conflicts start conditioning a person's adult life, creating symptoms, psychic distress and unhappiness. It is precisely in these occurrences that psychotherapists are sought out and the analyst embarks with the client on a journey of exploration of their deepest conflicts, which they were incapable of facing and have festered into malady and existential suffering. Dreams speak just as much as symptoms do, employing ancient, symbolic languages and imagery that recalls the functioning of a child's mind.

In the final section of the book, Freud dwells on the usefulness of dreams for everyone's mental health, and quoting Plato's Republic, states that "the virtuous man is content to *dream* what a wicked man really *does*". So "it is best [...] to acquit dreams" (Freud, 1899/2005, p. 614).

Therefore, dreaming is an essential activity for the healthy mind, and while getting to know one's own dreams may represent a resource for each individual, their analysis is a fundamental tool to understand the causes of people's suffering and find a way to solve the conflicts that paralyze them.

---

1 My translation.

Carl G. Jung (1875–1961) and the archetypes of the unconscious

Freud's most beloved pupil for many years, Carl Jung considerably diversified his metapsychology and his approach to dreamwork after parting ways with Freud in 1913. To the analytical psychology born out of this rift we owe the studies on the collective unconscious, the Shadow, and the archetypes. In particular, Jung placed great value on mental images, as well as the cultural and artistic expressions of each civilization.

Humankind's symbolic language has been an object of great interest in analytic psychology, and each therapist must be able to read the visual arts, theater, cinema, and music as recommended by Jung. Federico Fellini, one of the greatest directors of all time (for more see *Suggestion 10*), left us a significant book of dreams accompanied by illustrations which inspired many of his cinematographic masterpieces. In this book Fellini admits his lifelong debt to analysis.

Jung wrote that "the dream is a little hidden door in the innermost and most secret recesses of the soul" (2014, Vol. 10, par. 304). He agrees with Freud that dreaming is one of the main ways to access the unconscious.

It is worth keeping in mind some key ideas in Jung's work on dreams and the unconscious. First, the difference between sign and symbol. Jung reminds us that while a sign is a word or a denotative image designating a specific object, a symbol is a word or connotative image which holds multiple meanings, some not directly accessible through logical-rational thought. Symbols are born as representations of the sacred and the divine, and are reminiscent of how the unconscious mind explores the world and gains instinctual knowledge. Jung reminds us how Freud and Breuer themselves, during their studies on hysteria, came to discover the symptom's symbolic meaning:

> Neurotic symptoms are meaningful and make sense since they express a certain thought. In other words, they function in the same manner as dreams: they *symbolize*. A client, for instance, confronted with an intolerable situation, develops a spasm whenever he tries to swallow: "He can't swallow it". Under similar conditions another client develops asthma: "He can't breathe the atmosphere at home".
>
> (Vol. 18, par. 421)

Jung discards free association and invites us to embark on "a circumambulation whose center is the dream picture", always repeating to the client: "Let's get back to your dream. What does the *dream* say?" (Jung, 1964, p. 29).

Jung's unconscious is not just the place of that which has been repressed, but a fertile ground where new feelings and ideas can bloom, the home of creativity and a search for future directions. On this matter Jung mentions the creative success of Robert Louis Stevenson, where the plot to *Dr Jekyll and Mr Hyde* was revealed to him in a dream, after having contemplated for years the duplicitous nature of humanity (p. 38).

> I recall a dream of my own that baffled me for a while. In this dream, a certain Mr. X was desperately trying to get behind me and jump on my back. I knew nothing of this gentleman except that he had succeeded in twisting something I had said into a rather grotesque travesty of my meaning. This kind of thing had frequently happened to me in my professional life [...]
>
> (Jung, 2014, Vol. 18, par. 463)

This is the primitive part of us that we lost, and it is because of such loss that we cannot directly access the symbolic world full of emotionally charged imagery that once belonged to a primitive humanity and still belongs to children.

> The general function of dreams is to balance such disturbances in the mental equilibrium by producing contents of a complementary or compensatory kind.
>
> (Vol. 18, par. 471)

Here Jung is referring to the complementary and compensatory role of dreams. Symbols bring with them an instinctual and intuitive knowledge which might be a useful guide for the future, even if it is seldom easy to understand their meaning. However, no oneiric symbol can be separated from the individual, and this explains the pointlessness of symbol interpretation handbooks.

The recurrent dream is another interesting phenomenon: "Such dreams usually compensate a defect in one's conscious attitude, or they date from a traumatic moment that has left behind some specific prejudice, or they anticipate a future event of some importance" (Vol. 18, par. 478).

In the following paragraph, Jung writes about a recurrent dream of his:

> It was that I discovered a part of a wing of my house which I did not know existed. Sometimes it was the place where my parents lived—who had died long ago—where my father, to my great surprise, had a laboratory in which he studied the comparative anatomy of fishes, and where my mother ran a hostelry for ghostly visitors.
>
> (Vol. 18, par. 478)

He then adds that toward the end of this dream he finds a mysterious tome full of symbols: as a matter of fact, shortly after the dream he received an antique volume on medieval alchemy. The excitement toward this new field of study put an end to the recurrent dream. According to Jung, the house represented himself and the unknown wings were the parts he had yet to discover about himself.

He goes on to describe the conflict with Freud by recounting the analysis of a dream Jung himself told Freud. In this dream, Jung uncovers two skulls in his cellar. Working on the interpretation of it through free association, Jung finds himself lying to Freud in order to appease his master's belief that he might desire the death of some of his family members. For his part, Jung declares rather decisively that only he could have known that the skulls represented his passion for his paleontology studies and Darwin's works, as symbols of a culture that had broken free from his parent's medieval prejudices and convictions.

The whole theme of the conflict and comparison with Freud remains to this day extremely stimulating, since we can read it without feeling the need to set them up one against the other.

Fritz Perls (1893–1970) and Gestalt theory

A timid analyst from Berlin who first moves to South Africa and then to the United States, Fritz Perls starts his clinical research as a psychoanalyst after having been a student of Karen Horney, Helene Deutsch, and Wilhelm Reich. Thanks to his vivid curiosity pushing him to pay more attention to the body and to dreams' emotional expressions, Perls makes an important contribution to the discipline by founding the Esalen Institute and the Gestalt school of psychology in the United States. He writes:

> But the dream is concrete, nonverbal, sensory—"eidetic". In general, that is, the dream is not a possible experience not so much for its content but for its form.
>
> (1951, p. 437)

The conflict between the dream state and wakefulness is the same as that between a figure and its background, and it stems from the impossibility of accessing the dream without changing one's perceptual perspective: the language of dreams is untranslatable in verbal form.

The Gestalt technique of dream analysis had great success and circulation, and Perls' recorded analysis is a stunning example of psychotherapy.

This technique consists of making the dreamer identify with each of the dream's characters and objects by talking about it using the present tense and inviting them to feel the emotion stirred up by such an identification.

The underlying assumption is that each part of the dream is a part of the client, only split and projected. Understanding projections and reclaiming them might provide the key to working out a solution to an existing conflict. Thus, the therapist invites the client to re-experience the oneirical state while telling the therapist and the group a brief story about each animated and inanimate character in the dream. In the next chapter we shall take a closer look at those Gestalt techniques that have been incorporated into several different schools of transactional analysis from the second half of the 1970s onwards.

Sandor Ferenczi (1973–1933) and the dream's traumatolitic function

One of the first pupils of Freud and friend of Jung was Sandor Ferenczi, a Hungarian doctor known to many of us as the analyst and professor of Melanie Klein, and thus the forerunner of the object relations school. His contribution to the theory and practice of psychoanalysis was extraordinary and in many ways overlooked. Recently (Borgogno, 2004) he has been rediscovered and newly appreciated because of the current interest in trauma treatment. It was his idea to investigate the functioning of the mind by taking into account the splitting and fragmentation generated by traumatic experiences. Ferenczi was also recognized for his great commitment to curing his most suffering and vulnerable clients, as well as the exploration of all the ways in which the transference–countertransference matrix generates a dialogical condition that today might be called intersubjective. Ferenczi worked a lot on dreams, regarding them as an attempt to face unresolved trauma and ascribing them a fundamental function of restoration of mental health and balance. In an essay first published in 1931, he states that

> While following up the connexions, it strikes us more and more that the so-called day's (and as we may add, life's) residues are indeed repetition symptoms of traumata […] every dream, even an unpleasurable one, is an attempt at a better mastery and settling of traumatic experiences.
>
> (1955, p. 238)

During the last 20 years, we have noticed a renewed interest in Ferenczi's thought thanks to the development of the psychotraumatology field of study.

In his important essay mentioned above, Borgogno (2004) states that:

> Freud's *Traumdeutung* is for Ferenczi a sort of Traume-deutung, where what is traumatic is the amount of pain within a psychic experience which the client might have internalized without having the proper tools to metabolize it. The "traumatolitic" function of dreams is to recreate an excessively painful experience in order to give it a more creative solution: a repetition that is not purely instinctual but belongs to the Ego, in an effort to transform pain and suffering in a more economical and beneficial way.

This perspective is predominant in his later works, where Ferenczi points out that by imposing a distortion, censorship

> evaluates both the entity of the damage and the extent to which the individual can tolerate it, and allows only the perception of the dream's tolerable form and content, presenting it, when necessary, as the fulfillment of a wish.[2]
>
> (Borgogno, 2004, pp. 85–86)

Melanie Klein (1882–1960) and object relations

The Austrian psychoanalyst—who was also Ferenczi's student in Budapest and Abraham's in Berlin—is best known for her brilliant studies on object relations and for founding child psychoanalysis, which she practiced in London until her death. Klein replaced free associations with the Play Technique, which allowed her to start treating children, thus making great discoveries on developmental stages and how the functioning of the mind is structured.

She discovered an analogy between play and dreams:

> In their play children represent symbolically phantasies, wishes and experiences. Here they are employing the same language, the same archaic, phylogenetically acquired mode of expression as we are familiar with from dreams.
>
> (1948b, p. 146)

Her studies on split mechanisms, introjection, and the depressive stage—which include the differentiation between normal and pathological grief—are especially of interest here. In a 1940s paper, Klein described a client of hers, D., who had the following dream the night before his mother's death:

> He saw a bull lying in a farmyard. It was not quite dead, and looked very uncanny and dangerous. He was standing on one side of the bull, his mother on the other. He escaped into a house, feeling that he was leaving his mother behind in danger and that he should not do so; but he vaguely hoped that she would get away.
>
> (1948a, p. 332)

Commenting on Klein's analysis of this dream, Hanna Segal observes that the client feared that his mother would be destroyed by her violent sexual impulses or his father's (1979, pp. 84–85). We could add that the dangerous half-dead

---

2   My translation.

bull might also represent the client's own fear of death: he surrenders himself to the hands of his analyst, who "would get away" with the negative and heavy feelings which he, as son/client, doesn't feel himself capable of handling. Sure enough, in another dream he had after his mother's death, he dreams of an unmanned out-of-control bus, identifying himself with it (Segal, 1979, p. 85).

Her studies on *Envy and Gratitude* (1957) are the last important contribution Melanie Klein offered to the field of psychoanalysis, and provide us with great insight which will be useful in treating the theme of ambivalence in the last stages of the therapeutic journey and the dreams of healing.

Worth mentioning are also her works on manic-depressive disorder and the integration of the depressive stage of development (Klein, 1975, p. 67).

In this regard we might quote the words of a client suffering from manic-depressive disorder, who, after having reached brilliant personal success, brings the following dream to her analyst:

> In the dream she was up in the air on a magic carpet which supported her and was above the top of a tree. She was sufficiently high up to look through a window into a room where a cow was munching something which appeared to be an endless strip of blanket.
>
> (Segal, 1979, p. 145)

In her analysis of the dream, Klein associates the cow with the mother/breasts who feed her and the blanket to the words that make up the analysis itself, which the mother/therapist now has to swallow.

We might add that perhaps the client also wished to get out of the room where the analysis took place and fly away on her own, breaking her dependence on the analyst/mother, as if saying "I'll be here on top of the tree with my flying carpet, while my mother eats the blanket with which she was holding me inside her". Obviously, when we attempt such interpretations we are no longer talking about Klein or her client, choosing instead to position ourselves as active listeners and partakers of this narration and thus taking possession of the dream by talking a fair bit about ourselves. In such a case, observing that the bull is a symbol of many an ancient civilization—from the golden calf of the Bible to Crete's minotaur, from the Babylonian and Sumerian god Shamash to the Catholic symbology of Christ—we might dare to say that there is also a sacrifice that takes place during the separation, which takes the form of the mother's death.

Wilfred R. Bion (1897–1979) and the alpha function

The great psychoanalyst Wilfred Bion is especially well-known in transactional analysis for his book *Experiences in Group* (1961), from which he adopted the analytic model of basic assumptions to explain the organismic aspect of groups that evolve according to apparently irrational models, veering away from their stated objectives. Bion's studies on psychosis allowed him to understand better the madness he encountered in the course of the two World Wars and during the worst moments of 20th-century history.

However, here we will mostly refer to his studies on reveries and the alpha function, since they open new perspectives to the analysis of dreams. It is in the early mother–child relationship that the alpha function is born: a function that processes the child's primordial fears (beta elements) by projecting them on to the mother, who gathers them and transforms them into acceptable and complex thoughts (alpha elements).

Dreams continue the work of maternal reverie by bridging the gap between consciousness and unconsciousness, representing at the same time a barrier and a point of contact between such distant and perturbing worlds. We might say that within the alpha function also lives one of the functions of art, cinema, and every narration which allows us to cope with our fears and experience them as a perturbing element which however can never destroy us. Therefore, in Bion we find the Kleinian idea of projective identification applied to the need to transform the kind of content that is most distressing to the mind. His invitation to use the poetic language of art to express what would be otherwise impossible through secondary language is indeed very evocative.

He takes us in a similar direction in his last work, *A Memoir of the Future, Book 1: The Dream* (1975), where a story inspired by Alice's dream pulls the readers inside a world of narrations which is very similar to an incredibly creepy hallucination.

To clarify what the alpha function is (Bion, 1962, 1992): it refers to the human mind's ability to create images which make it possible to conceive the archaic and corporeal emotional-sensorial experiences in the form of thought (beta elements). We could say that this is a oneiric function which takes place during the night as well as the day, as the capacity to process corporeal expressions and transform them into thoughts. It is the alpha function which builds the unconscious and the dream itself. Bion's theories inspired many group analysts, and, as we will see later, all the researchers working on social dreaming.

Drawing inspiration from Bion, Ogden (2005, p. 6) declares that the goal of the analysis is to improve the client's ability to "dream his undreamt and interrupted dreams".

Donald W. Winnicott (1896–1971) and the transitional space

The transitional space is the experience generated between mother and child which allows the child's definition of the self, since it grants a relational exchange in a safe communication environment. Winnicott finds some similarities between that intersubjective space generated between mother and child during development, and the space that forms between client and analyst.

According to Winnicott, the dream's formation depends on the quality of this space and on the dreamer's ability to use it. In borderline disorders, as well as in post-traumatic situations, difficulty in accessing the transitional space is connected to the instability of the psychic structure and leads to a general difficulty in analytical work. Winnicott insists on the need to welcome the dream content without interpreting it at all costs. Sometimes interpreting means being a "bad analyst making good interpretations" (1965/1990, p. 251). He recounts a clinical case in which a client talks about her dreams at the end of each session and is very scared by regression and by being dependent on the analyst. Thus she dreams of being "a tortoise with a soft shell" (p. 251).

Eric Berne (1910–1970) and transactional analysis

Eric Berne, whom we shall deal with extensively in Chapter 2 as well as periodically throughout the entire course of this book, was a student of Paul Federn and Erik Erikson before having his request to join the American Psychoanalysis Association denied and deciding, as a consequence, to found his own school of psychotherapy by presenting it in the *American Journal of Psychotherapy* as a "new method of group therapy" (Berne, 1958). His conceptual model of the ego states, derived from Federn and Fairbairn's studies, was the foundation for the construction of a solid theory of interpersonal communication through the concepts of transactions and psychological games. His psychoanalytic-based script theory was the starting point for the development of a theory of personality and psychopathology. As far as dreamwork is concerned, Berne's approach was ambiguous, oscillating between the idea of treating dreams in groups as revelations of the deepest unconscious motivations underlying games and the idea of treating them on the couch in a more psychoanalytic setting.

Donald Meltzer (1922–2004)

A student of Klein and Bion, Donald Meltzer offered an important contribution to the psychoanalytic treatment of adolescents. On the matter of dreams he highlights the need to work on the dreamer's emotional experience, since this represents the living part of the dream, the one giving it meaning.

According to Meltzer (1983), during the analysis, the analyst takes on the mother's role and offers their clients that reverie ability which allows them to access their inner world with less fear. Dreams need to be welcomed, and the analyst dreams together with the client.

Thomas H. Ogden (1946–)

Psychoanalyst and student at the Tavistock Institute, Thomas Ogden served as Director of the Center for the Advanced Study of the Psychoses in San

Francisco, and his work focuses mainly on the treatment of psychosis. His development of Bion's thought was also a great contribution to contemporary psychoanalysis. Ogden sees therapy as an intersubjective field, in which

> client and analyst engage in an experiment within the terms of the psychoanalytic situation that is designed to generate conditions in which the analysand (with the analyst's participation) may become better able to dream his undreamt and interrupted dreams. The dreams dreamt by the client and analyst are at the same time their own dreams (and reveries) and those of a third subject who is both and neither client nor analyst.
>
> (Ogden, 2005, p. 2)

And it is precisely on the dream's function that Ogden builds his idea of analytical therapy.

Here he claims that the client needs to regain his capacity to dream because "to the extent that he is unable to dream his emotional experience, the individual is unable to change, or to grow, or to become anything other than who he has been" (p. 2).

Dreams can be interrupted or even undreamed, and it is therapy's responsibility to create that atmosphere of reverie which allows a deep knowledge of the self and the unlocking of that limit which is so necessary to grow and heal. We will return to Ogden's ideas on the analyst's participation in the client's oneirical work in Chapter 12, which will be focused on countertransference and the therapist's dreams.

Hans Kohut (1913–1981) and the psychology of the self

Thanks to his studies on narcissism, Kohut helped us understand the fundamental needs of the clients, with regards to both healthy and pathological narcissism.

As far as dreamwork goes, to the analysis of dreams expressing conflict— already treated by Freud—Kohut added the analysis of those dreams that have the function of restoring the dreamer's sense of self, especially in narcissistic pathologies, in which the psyche risks shattering because of the client's fragility and traumas. Kohut calls such dreams "self-state-dreams" and we find this perspective especially helpful to understand the function of dreams in both post-traumatic and personality disorders.

James L. Fosshage (1940–)

To Fosshage, a Kohutian psychoanalyst with a special interest in Kernberg's work and relational psychology, we owe a great debt of gratitude for his work on a dream analysis technique more closely related to our methods in transactional analysis (Kohut, 1971, 1984). In line with TA's notions, Fosshage (1997) centers the dream's function on its restorative, self-therapeutic, and creative aspects, which the dreamer expresses through their oneiric activity. His method and seven technical rules will be outlined in Chapter 4.

Relational psychology and Stephen Mitchell (1946–2000)

Studies on the client–analyst relationship and on the interpersonal level of analysis have represented and still represent today one of the most stimulating areas of study for contemporary therapists. Even if the founder of this school, Harry Stack Sullivan (1892–1949) did not give a specific contribution to dream analysis, his interpersonal perspective on therapy is fundamental in that it centers the bipersonal dimension of interpretation work.

On this matter, Irwin Hirsch, an author especially useful for his study of countertransference in therapy, writes:

> The scientist as personal researcher inevitably interacts with the data under study, and thus knowledge becomes contextual. The ideas and perceptions of the analytic researcher/observer are inextricably bound up with the observed. The application by Sullivan of this point of view to the data of psychoanalysis shifted the emphasis from observation of the client—from transference—to observation of the client and analyst in interaction—the transference–countertransference matrix.
>
> (Hirsch, 1995, p. 643).

Stephen Mitchell—whose great contribution to the relational approach of contemporary psychoanalysis can be traced back to the foundational book written with Jay Greenberg titled *Object Relations in Psychoanalytic Theory* (1983)—writes that "The boundary between conscious and unconscious mental content is actually more permeable, shifting, and indistinct" (1988, pp. 261–262) than Freud thought. And adds:

> Fromm, for example, argued that the power and incisiveness of language and metaphor in dreaming often highlight how impoverished an analysand's conscious experience can be in comparison with what he knows, perceives, constructs, outside awareness.

Toward the end of the same text, Mitchell describes a clinical case and an instance of dreamwork.

Sam, the client, who came from a family with a history of depression, lived with a strong sense of guilt whenever he experienced joy. Toward the end of treatment he has the following dream:

During a period when he had been experiencing himself and his relationships with others in a more positive way. Like all important experiences which stretch the boundaries of character, these changes made him anxious.

I am on a small island off the mainland with my parents and sister. I take a boat to the mainland to pick up some things or do some errands. There is a carnival going on. I walk around, watching the people, participating, having a great time. Then I remember that I must return to the island. I get in the boat and try to go back, but insects come and sting me. If I move back and stop rowing, they stop. I start to move toward the island and they sting again. I stop; they stop. I am very conflicted about what to do. After a long time of trying and stopping, I give up with a sense of relief and rejoin the activities on the mainland.

(Mitchell, 1988, p. 304)

Mitchell remarks that the client is becoming aware that he was using pain to hold on to his bond with his family, and that his loyalty to them did not allow him to feel the right to heal and be happy. He could do it only by moving away. Mitchell declares that changing old object relationships is not something that happens suddenly and permanently, but "constructive, creative living necessitates continual choice" (p. 306).

Philip M. Bromberg (1931–2020)

A relational psychologist and a student of Sullivan, Bromberg provides us with an interesting perspective on dreamwork and the co-creation of meaning in analytic therapy by client and analyst.

> "Awakening the Dreamer" is a metaphor for what I see as central to a clinical process informed by the phenomena of self-states and dissociation. The "dreamer" refers to a self-state with which people are most familiar during sleep when it emerges as part of the dissociative phenomena, we call dreams.
>
> A dream, in its essence, is a nonlinear reality and must be related to as such—not as a kind of story or a kind of movie, but as a real space in which the client has been.
>
> (Bromberg, 2006, pp. 31–39)

During the course of this book, we will often refer to his work, which we value a great deal and follow closely.

Wilma Bucci and multiple code theory

Wilma Bucci is especially well-known for her *multiple code theory* model, which constitutes an investigation into the Freudian differentiation between primary and secondary process. According to multiple code theory, humans have three different systems of experiencing and processing information, including emotional ones, and each system forms its own inner representations, which could be sub-symbolic non-verbal, symbolic non-verbal, and symbolic verbal. The sub-symbolic system concerns all those non-verbal stimuli (from emotions to motor and perceptive information) which are processed simultaneously: for instance, recognizing emotions in someone else's facial cues or composing a piece of music or recognizing a familiar voice in the middle of a loud party or hitting the ball at exactly the right time and height in a header, or, to keep ourselves on a more professional ground, knowing *when* to relay a particular interpretation to a patient. The non-verbal symbolic system, on the other hand, concerns all that mental imagery (a face, a song, an expression, or, as the Beatles used to say, *something in the way she moves*) which, albeit forming part of the client's conscious awareness, cannot be translated into words. Finally, the verbal symbolic system concerns that powerful tool through which the individual communicates their inner world to others, and through which knowledge and culture are passed from one person to another. According to Bucci's model, the three systems are ruled by different principles, but are also obviously connected. To go back to the Beatles' example, the particular emotion aroused by a woman is connected to the mental imagery of the way she walks, and it was put into words in the lyrics of a song. Bucci defines such a complex connection as a "referential process", one that goes from emotions to words and vice-versa, and has elaborated specific tools of referential activity assessment. The "emotion schemas" are one of the most important organizers of inner representation and determine how we build interpersonal experiences and relationships, as well as how we express our emotional states. In a way, emotion schemas are very similar to other cognitive and psychoanalytic construct such as Bowlby's *internal working models* or Luborsky's *core conflictual relationship theme*. What follows is that each internal or external stimulus we process activates mental schemas of relationship (starting with those stemming from the first exchanges with the mother figure, or its substitute) as well as non-verbal symbolic and sub-symbolic schemas of feelings, thoughts, expectations, and remembered behaviors. To this effect, as Piero Porcelli explains in his introduction to the book *Symptoms and Symbols* (Bucci, 1997), the psychological treatment is an effort to repair the splits between the three systems and alter the emotion schemas, that is, connect or re-connect the split sub-symbolic pathological experiences to the symbolic system of experiences.

According to multiple code theory, the development of emotional meaning in free association takes place in a three-stage process called the "referential cycle" (Bucci, 1993, 1997). This same process, rooted in emotional development, can be seen at work in oneiric activity, and its failures as well as its efforts of reparation are obvious in somatization. In the first stage of the cycle, clients experience the different non-verbal components of emotion schemas, including specific non-symbolic elements (feelings, smells, corporeal experiences, motor patterns) that they have trouble putting into words. In the second stage, clients retrieve a memory or a specific fantasy stemming from past experiences, which are either everyday or traumatic events, and connect the sub-symbolic content first to the imagery and then to the words. At the optimal level, in the third stage, clients reflect on the imagery and the stories they recounted and are able to make ulterior connections within the verbal system and the shared discourse. In the end, the verbalization process of the contents of emotion schemas makes it so that clients are finally able to define their emotions: i am angry, i am scared. The new connections within the verbal and non-verbal systems can thus become retroactive and open even further the emotion schemas, reprising the cycle at a deeper level.

A similar progression can also be conceived for the construction and interpretation of dreams. The latent content, primarily in a sub-symbolic form, is connected to the specific and discrete imagery of the manifest content, and then verbalized through dream narration (Bucci, 1993; Bucci et al., 1991). In dream interpretation, the latent content, including desires and other repressed emotional structures, can become known and verbalized in and of themselves.

The development of emotional meaning in free association and dreams has its roots in the basic processes of emotional development itself. Normal emotional development depends on the integration of somatic, perceptive, and motor processes within emotion schemas, and the failure to integrate may become the cause of emotional disorders (Bucci, 1997).

Social dreaming: from Lawrence to Neri

Social dreaming was born in the 1980s within the Tavistock Institute, thanks to the work of Gordon Lawrence.

Lawrence (1998) claims that dreams incorporate fundamental information on people's living situation at the time of dreaming.

As part of the group relations program of the Tavistock Institute, Gordon Lawrence developed an approach centered on the idea of "relationality": that is, how an individual's experience and behavior reflect the existence of informed or uninformed contents connected to the group or the home institution (Rotondo e Bertolini, 2008).

Lawrence believes dreams to be the key to all those past experiences and inner constructs useful to comprehend the social or institutional reality in which the dreamers live. Far from challenging the great value of the classic psychoanalytic approach to dreamwork, the goal of social dreaming is instead to highlight the social dimension of the dream (Neri, 2002).

During his research, Gordon Lawrence gathers information about the dreaming habits and narrations of several indigenous peoples. In such communities, one individual's dream goes beyond the dreamer's personal life, and indeed speaks about the life of the group, and therefore it is narrated and lived in the group. For the Senoi people, for instance, the act of interpreting a dream and sharing it with the community is reserved for a specific moment in the tribe's everyday life (Rotondo e Bertolini, 2008).

Lawrence's considerations induced him to speculate that it might be possible to have dreams about unconscious fears and anxieties related to the society we live in. The individual dreams about a few essential themes, such as family, work, the relationship with their parents, and other significant relations. "Society", however, exists only in the individual's mind as a construction based on the experiences we have of our relationships with others (Lawrence, 1998).

According to social dreaming, the dreams of people belonging to any one organization might be key to the deepest, most unconscious levels—which are usually the least accessible—of a social reality. Claudio Neri (2002, p. 95) writes that:

> It's as if dreamers [...] are able to see details that those who are awake cannot or do not want to see. Perhaps the eyes of the dreamer exist outside the constrictions of the individual's social group and can thus see facts, forces and tensions which go unnoticed by the eyes of those who are awake.[3]

Dreamwork in cognitive psychotherapy

Although cognitivist psychology has always shown skepticism and little interest in dream analysis, since it considered oneiric activity as nothing more than the background noise of the mind, it has nonetheless produced several considerations on the use of dreams in psychoanalysis (Beck, 1979): Beck speculated that dreams might help to signal clients' emotional changes during a depressive episode, going back to the idea that dreams could reflect the idea that clients' have of themselves, the world, and their future.

During the last ten years the constructivist approach developed an interest in dreamwork in terms of re-narration in a therapeutic setting, that is, in the co-construction of the dream narration aimed at assigning meaning to the client's emotional experiences.

---

3   My translation.

Therefore, in cognitive-behavioral psychotherapy, dreamwork is possible within specific guided activities, which are aimed at helping the client recognize their own mode of functioning through different materials. Such activities might aid the therapist in the process of recognizing cognitive distortions and thus help them in the stage of cognitive restructuring.

On this topic, as far as Italy goes, we recommend the contributions of Bruno Bara:

> During the last few decades, cognitive psychotherapy has started getting earnestly but carefully closer to the world of dreams, previously considered taboo, a strict psychodynamic legacy, or simply of little importance from a clinical point of view. In the first thirty years of cognitivism, dreams didn't play much of a role (if they played one at all), with regards to theory as well as clinical practice and experimentation. Only from the 90s onwards, thanks to the growingly integrated atmosphere prevailing in the field, some cognitivist therapists, especially those working in-between cognitive psychotherapy and others therapeutic schools, renewed their interest for the oneiric experience.
>
> (Bara, 2012, p. 44)[4]

Paolo Migone and the ongoing debate on dreamwork in psychoanalysis

In his thoughtful analysis of the historical evolution of psychoanalysis and the scientific debate, Paolo Migone pointed out how Wilma Bucci's studies (1993, 1997) on the different functionings of primary (visual thinking) and secondary processes (rational, logical, and verbal thinking) and language lead us to support the hypothesis of the autonomous nature of the two systems, which are not directly translatable into each other. This confirms the need to go beyond the idea of the latent content of the oneiric process.

> It is roughly from the 1960s that dreams have lost the central role they previously played in the psychoanalyst's clinical practice. General interest shifted progressively from the interpretation of dreams to the interpretation of a client's behavior during their waking hours, a material that is therefore closer to the ego and to the conscious side of the client: symptoms, bungled actions, fantasies, relational styles, etc. Thanks to analysts' evergrowing experience and attention, such material is already rich and interesting in and of itself for the comprehension of the conscious and unconscious functioning of the client, and

---

4   My translation.

it is in no way inferior to the material uncovered in what Freud called the "via regia" to the unconscious, that is to say, dreams.

(Migone, 2005, p. 250)[5]

Migone also adds:

> The manifested imagery of dreams might not conceal any additional meaning, but have value in and of themselves, simply representing a way of actively processing information during sleep, as well as a specific cerebral activity.
>
> (Migone, 2005, p. 17)[6]

In a series of interviews conducted with the Italian magazine of psychoanalysis *Psicoterapia e scienze umane* for the 50th anniversary of the magazine's foundation, Migone asked several of his psychoanalyst colleagues what remains of Freud's theory and what is the role of dreams in the therapeutic process. Some did not answer, others merely claimed that the theory is still valid. Kernberg declared that:

> Dream analysis cannot be conceived anymore as the "via regia to the unconscious" because we have equally important ways to access the unconscious: the analysis of personality, primitive defense mechanisms, enactments and unconscious fantasies.
>
> (Comitato di Redazione, 2016, p. 497)[7]

In a recent exchange with Peter Fonagy, published in the magazine *Percorsi di Analisi Transazionale*, Migone states that:

> All verbal therapies find themselves almost backed into a corner before the recognized importance of implicit memory, especially the type of psychoanalysis that always relied on the verbal communication of interpretation as healing factor.[8]
>
> (Migone, 2021, p. 18)

As for Peter Fonagy and his work on mentalization, we find very little mention of dreamwork in it, since dream narration is not especially encouraged during

---

5   My translation.
6   My translation.
7   My translation.
8   My translation.

treatment, and dreams are considered in a similar fashion to fantasies and simply taken as any other of the client's narratives.

> The ability to work with unconscious communication underpins the next two areas of competence, namely facilitating the exploration of unconscious feelings and of the unconscious dynamics influencing relationships [...] The primary means of unconscious communication are the client's narratives, dreams and their free associations.
> (Fonagy, 2011, p. 29)

Thanks to the work of Daniel Stern and the Boston Study Group, the research on going beyond the classic interpretation has received an important validation. We consider it especially useful to dreamwork the approach that takes into account the most recent discoveries on implicit memory and the preverbal aspects of the script. Migone suggested we connect these themes to the body, the therapeutic relationship, and the subtle dimensions in the exchange between client and therapist, which today are so essential to dreamwork.

The Boston Group (BCPSG) on change in psychotherapy: *the something more than interpretation*

In this section we will see a brief overview of the more extensive work taken on during the first years of this century by the Boston Study Group (which includes Sander and Stern and many other brilliant psychoanalysts and researchers) on what principle lies at the basis of change, and, in general, the efficacy of psychoanalytic therapy. Especially useful is their work on memory and implicit learning, as well as on the relational moves, observed during the video recording of therapeutic sessions by focusing on what happens in the here and now of the session. This approach is in line with the way we work on dreams and we will take a closer look at it in Chapter 4, where we shall outline our methodology, making specific reference to three of the group's most important concepts: implicit knowing, relational moves and sloppiness.

According to BCPSG scholars, implicit relational knowing is an experience that is reinforced with each relational encounter by building up such a memory that we know what to expect from the encounter even without explicitly telling ourselves. For example, we would approach an encounter with either fear or confidence based on our relational memory (BCPSG, 2010).

The concept of "relational move" replaces the one of insight. What is recorded in the client's mind as a central element of the session is a relational move of the therapist which lasts no more than a breath (from one to ten seconds) and works as a moment of syntonization and deep emotional understanding felt by both members of the session.

The third concept we need to work on in dreams is that of "co-creative sloppiness". Paying attention to what happens during a session, the Boston researchers try to explain that particular kind of indeterminateness which exists in the client–therapist dynamic. Scholars understand that exchanges between client and therapist can be comprehended only within their specific relationship, and dreamwork is clear only within this specific language that is being co-constructed by the two subjects involved in therapy (BCPSG, 2010). Chapter 4 focuses on an in-depth analysis of a session in which a client talks about two of her dreams to the therapist. The way in which that oneiric material is treated demonstrates the specificity of the analyst's approach.

In the following chapters we shall illustrate our perspective on relational moves, interpretation, insight, emotional and corporeal dreamwork, and all the reasons why we believe the exploration of dreams to be extremely useful and therapeutic.

References

Bara, B. G. (2012). *Dimmi come sogni: Interpretazione emotiva dell'esperienza onirica [Tell me how you dream: Emotional interpretation of the dream experience]*. Milano: Oscar Mondadori.

Beck, A. T., Rush, A. J., Shaw, B. F., & Emery, G. (1979). *Cognitive therapy of depression*. New York: Guilford Press.

Berne, E. (1958). Transactional analysis: A new and effective method of group therapy. *American Journal of Psychotherapy*, *12*(4), 735–743. https://doi.org/10.1176/appi.psychotherapy.1958.12.4.735

Bion, W. R. (1961). *Experiences in groups: And other papers*. New York: Routledge.

Bion, W. R. (1962). *Learning from experience*. London: Karnac.

Bion, W. R. (1975). *A memoir of the future, Book 1: The dream*. Rio de Janeiro: Imago.

Bion, W. R. (1992). *Cogitations*. London: Karnac Books.

Borgogno, F. (2004). *Ferenczi oggi [Ferenczi today]*. Torino: Bollati Boringhieri.

Boston Change Process Study Group. (Ed.). (2010). *Change in psychotherapy: A unifying paradigm*. New York: W.W. Norton & Co.

Bromberg, P. M. (2006). *Awakening the dreamer: Clinical journeys*. New York: Routledge.

Bucci, W. (1993). The development of emotional meaning in free association: A multiple code theory. In Wilson, A., & Gedo, J. E. (Eds.), *Hierarchical concepts in psychoanalysis: Theory, research, and clinical practice* (pp. 3–47). New York: Guilford Press.

Bucci, W. (1997). Symptoms and symbols: A multiple code theory of somatization. *Psychoanalytic Inquiry*, *17*(2), 151–172. https://doi.org/10.1080/07351699709534117

Bucci, W., Creelman, M. L., & Severino, S. K. (1991). The effects of menstrual cycle hormones on dreams. *Dreaming*, *1*(4), 263–276. https://doi.org/10.1037/h0094338

Editorial Board. (2016). Cosa resta della psicoanalisi. Domande e risposte [What's left of psychoanalysis. Questions and answers]. *Psicoterapia e Scienze Umane*, *3*(3), 357–358. https://doi.org/10.3280/PU2016-003001

Ferenczi, S. (1955). *Final contributions to the problems and methods of psychoanalysis.* Oxford: Basic Books.

Fonagy, P., Lemma, A., & Target, M. (2011). *Brief dynamic interpersonal therapy: A clinician's guide.* New York: Oxford University Press.

Fosshage, J. L. (1997). The organizing functions of dream mentation. *Contemporary Psychoanalysis, 33*(3), 429–458. https://doi.org/10.1080/00107530.1997.10746997

Freud, S. (2005). *The interpretation of dreams* (D. T. O'Hara & G. M. MacKenzie, Eds.; A. A. Brill, Trans.). New York: Barnes & Noble Classics (Originally published in 1899).

Hirsch, I. (1995). Therapeutic uses of countertransference. In M. Lionells, J. Fiscalini, C. H. Mann, & D. B. Stern (Eds.), *Handbook of interpersonal psychoanalysis.* New York: Analytic Press, pp. 301—318.

Jung, C. G. (1964). *Man and his symbols* (M. L. von Franz, J. L. Henderson, A. Jaffé, & J. Jacobi, Eds.). New York: Doubleday.

Jung, C. G. (2014). *The collected works of C.G. Jung: Complete digital edition* (G. Adler, M. Fordham, H. Read, & W. McGuire, Eds.; R. F. C. Hull, Trans.). Princeton: Princeton University.

Klein, M. (1948a). Mourning and its relation to manic-depressive states. In *International psycho-analytical library: Contributions to psycho-analysis, 1921–1945.* London: Hogarth Press.

Klein, M. (1948b). The psychological principles of infant analysis. In *International psycho-analytical library: Contributions to psycho-analysis, 1921–1945.* London: Hogarth Press.

Klein, M. (1975). *Envy and gratitude, and other works, 1946–1963.* London: Hogarth Press and the Institute of Psycho-Analysis.

Kohut, H. (1971). *The analysis of the self: A systematic approach to the psychoanalytic treatment of narcissistic personality disorders.* Chicago: University of Chicago Press.

Kohut, H. (1984). *How does analysis cure?* (A. Goldberg, Ed.). Chicago: University of Chicago Press. https://doi.org/10.7208/chicago/9780226006147.001.0001

Lawrence, W. G. (1998). Social dreaming as a tool of consultancy and action research. In W. G. Lawrence (Ed.), *Social Dreaming @ Work.* Routledge. https://doi.org/10.4324/9780429480317

Massini, S. (2017). *L'interpretatore dei sogni [The dream interpreter].* Milano: Mondadori.

Meltzer, D. (1983). *Dream life: A re-examination of the psychoanalytical theory and technique.* Perthshire: Clunie Press.

Migone, P. (2005). Introduzione all'articolo di James Fosshage "Le funzioni organizzative del sogno" [Introduction to James Fosshage's article "The organizational functions of dreaming"]. *Quaderni Di Psicologia, Analisi Transazionale e Scienze Umane, 43,* 12–16.

Migone, P. (2021). Il recupero dei ricordi e l'azione terapeutica. Uno scambio con Peter Fonagy [Memory retrieval and therapeutic action. An exchange with Peter Fonagy]. *Percorsi Di Analisi Transazionale, VIII*(4), 16–23.

Mitchell, S. A. (1988). *Relational concepts in psychoanalysis: An integration.* Cambridge: Harvard University Press.

Mitchell, S. A., & Greenberg, J. R. (1983). *Object relations in psychoanalytic theory*. Cambridge: Harvard University Press. https://doi.org/10.2307/j.ctvjk2xv6

Neri, C. (2002). Introduzione al Social Dreaming. Relazione sui workshop tenuti a Mauriburg, Raissa e Clarice Town [Introduction to Social Dreaming. Report on workshops held in Mauriburg, Raissa and Clarice Town]. *Rivista Di Psicoanalisi*, *XLVIII*(1), 93–114.

Ogden, T. H. (2005). *This art of psychoanalysis: Dreaming undreamt dreams and interrupted cries*. New York: Routledge.

Perls, F., Hefferline, R., & Goodman, P. (1951). *Gestalt therapy: Excitement and growth in the human personality*. Julian Press.

Rotondo, A., & Bertolini, G. (2008). Il social dreaming a Terrenuove [Social dreaming at Terrenuove]. *Quaderni Di Psicologia, Analisi Transazionale e Scienze Umane*, *50*.

Segal, H. (1979). *Klein*. London: Routledge. https://doi.org/10.4324/9780429476440

Winnicott, D. W. (1990). *The maturational processes and the facilitating environment: Studies in the theory of emotional development*. London: Karnac Books (Originally published in 1965).

2
NEUROSCIENCES AND DREAMS

The dawn of dreams

Ever since the 1950s, with the development of neuropsychology, neuroscience's interest in dreams has been significant. There have been several theories behind the research, and the gathered data has been varied and—thanks to the development of neuroimaging—ever more detailed. Beyond established knowledge and gathered facts, the most important question underlying all questions still unanswered about the oneirical process is: Why do we dream? However, asking these questions is already an answer to another, deeper question. Does it make sense to ask ourselves why we dream? Is oneirical activity merely a mental phenomenon? Is it *also* a mental phenomenon? Or are dreams only a product of the chemical and electric activity of the brain, and thus fundamentally lacking any psychological meaning? We will see where on this hypothetical continuum the answers from several popular areas of research are situated, and we will pose the further question of whether it makes sense to juxtapose the two dimensions—mind and brain—rather than integrate them. But let's start from the beginning.

The first studies

Neuroscience's interest in dreams developed for the first time in the 1950s when Aserinsky and Kleitman (1953) found themselves studying a particular psychological state which occurs at regular intervals during sleep, characterized by intense cerebral activity with low-voltage fast waves, desynchronization of EEG rhythms very similar to the waking state (hence the name "paradoxical sleep") increased breathing and cardiac frequency, paralysis of bodily movement and rapid eye movement, hence the well-known name of REM (Rapid Eye Movement) sleep. In adults, the first episode of REM sleep occurs roughly 90 minutes after falling asleep and the duration of each episode—four or five during a night's sleep—increases in later stages, until the longest one which is the one right before waking (Mancia, 1996). A few years after the Aserinsky and Kleitman study, the same Kleitman, together with then-PhD-student Dement, observed that 79% of volunteers who were woken up during REM sleep reported they had dreamed. On the contrary, when they were woken during NREM sleep the subjects reported the presence of dreams only 7% of the time (Dement & Kleitman, 1957). This data, backed up by further research, was considered proof that REM and NREM sleep are each the product of different mental activities, and, most of all, that REM sleep is at the neurobiological basis of dreams. The close association between REM sleep and dreams led researchers to think that the former might represent the neurophysiological substrate of the dream event. It is precisely in this epistemological framework that is situated Hobson and McCarley's (1977) theory of the inner primitive generator. According to this theory, REM sleep acts as a veritable generator of the dream state. Through their experiments, Hobson and colleagues found that cholinergic neurons situated in the brainstem area of the pons were responsible for the activation of desynchronized sleep. This neurotransmitter, in the absence of external sensory stimuli, activates higher brain structures such as the visual cortex, which, flooded by PGO (ponto-geniculo-occipital) waves, produces the classic eye movements and visual hallucinations so typical of dreams. After a few minutes, the activity driven by cholinergic neurotransmitters is opposed by another kind of neurotransmitter, also secreted by pons neurons. These are norepinephrine and serotonin, two aminergic systems which support wakefulness and whose secretion inhibits REM sleep. As such, the interplay between these transmitters automatically and rhythmically generates REM sleep and the dream state, alternating them with NREM sleep and wakefulness. According to this model, the prefrontal cortex—the more developed part of the brain which represents the physiological substrate of consciousness—is thus activated by the brainstem. The fact that dream production depends on the stimulation of the limbic system and other cortex structures by the pons structures is viewed by Hobson and McCarley as definitive proof that dreams lack any symbolic meaning whatsoever. Dreams are instead considered merely a side effect of REM sleep, a product of the cortex's efforts to give coherence and organic unity to the disorganized impulses coming from the brainstem. Hobson and McCarley's mutual interaction and activation-synthesis models (1977) have long dominated the field of neuroscience, and have greatly influenced the clinical work on dreams. As we shall see in the next chapters, the idea that since all the distinctive cognitive features of dreams are electrically and chemically determined then the subjective motivational dimension that accompanies the dream experience must be totally irrelevant—an idea which today appears naïve and only pseudo-scientific—has for years discouraged clinicians from doing research on dreams, from writing about dreams, and especially from learning how to use this very rich reservoir of information to explore their clients' inner worlds. When Hobson, in 1976, presented his activation-synthesis theory to the American Psychiatric Association, the association members put the scientific validity of the Freudian dream theory to a vote, and the response was negative in most cases (Zanasi, n.d.): the relationship between psychotherapy and dreams seemed to have reached its permanent end.

The mind has reasons of which the brain knows nothing: Solms' studies and further contributions

Not everyone in the field of neuroscience agrees with the idea of a strict causal relation between physiological and mental events, and some fully reject the mind–brain isomorphism according to which mental events—the subjective oneiric experience—and neurophysiological events—universal and objective data—should be considered on equal footing (Mancia, 1996). The research carried out by such dissenting scholars has refuted Hobson's axioms and produced interesting new findings about the dream process. Let's see which ones.

Foulkes and Vogel (1965) found that about 50–70% of dreams occur immediately after falling asleep, that is, even before the REM and NREM sleep cycles begin. These data disconfirm the total overlap between REM sleep and dreams and refute the idea that dreaming is an exclusive product of REM sleep. Although REM sleep is still considered the preferred biological substrate of dreaming, it is nevertheless not the only one (Foulkes, 1962). It is in fact possible to dream even during NREM sleep, although dreams occurring during this stage are characterized by less vivid images and are composed of narratively unorganized fragments of thoughts and reality. Additionally, hallucinations are scarce, and the dreamer's emotional involvement is almost non-existent (Bosinelli, 1991; McNamara, 2019). Further research on the neurophysiological mechanisms of sleep has shown that there are other structures besides the pons that are responsible for REM sleep. These include the posterior hypothalamus, some intralaminar thalamic nuclei and the amygdala, whose same neuroanatomical structures are activated during the cognitive activities of wakefulness in which memories and emotions converge (Mancia, 1996).

Some research conducted at the dawn of the new millennium definitively refutes the hypothesis that REM sleep and dreaming are produced by the same brain mechanisms. A 2012 study by Oudiette and colleagues (2012) demonstrated the persistence of the ability to dream in subjects whose REM sleep is pharmacologically suppressed. Even before this study, Solms (2000) analyzed a sample of 361 brain-injured subjects and observed that subjects with pontine lesions continued to dream even though they no longer entered REM sleep. In contrast, many patients with diffuse brain damage but with the pons intact had lost the ability to dream but not the ability to enter REM sleep. In particular, if the brain is damaged in the parietal areas of both hemispheres or in the deep ventromedial frontal area, dream activity ceases completely. With respect to this, Kaplan-Solms and Solms (2000) write:

This does not mean that the function of dreaming can be narrowly localized within these three parts of the brain. Rather, it tells us that the component functions localized in these three parts of the brain are fundamental to the whole process of dreaming, for when any one of them is damaged, the conscious experience of dreams becomes impossible.

(2000, p. 45)

Contrary to Hobson's statement, it is not the role of brainstem structures to regulate dream mechanisms. The results show that it is the parts of the brain involved in symbolic operations, spatial thinking, and drive control, such as the parietal and frontal areas, that are crucial to the dream process. In particular, the frontal ventromedial area of the brain transmits dopamine to the higher cortical areas. Dopamine-stimulating agents (L-DOPA) significantly increase the frequency and vividness of dreams (Sacks, 1973 1990). In contrast, antipsychotic drugs, which block dopamine release, decrease dream activity while keeping the REM sleep cycle unaffected. The dopaminergic circuitry is linked to motivation. Indeed bilateral lesions to the ventromedial frontal region's white matter produce adynamia, as well as cessation of dream activity, that is, the loss of spontaneous motivational drive. Hence the idea that the function of dreams may be to maintain and implement an effective connection with the external world to satisfy the organism's internal needs. Solms draws on Panksepp (1998), according to whom the production of dreams can be attributed to the activation of an ancestral emotional vigilance system linked to pre-programmed motivational routines that regulate animal behavior. Panksepp named this neural system: the *"curiosity/interest/foraging/anticipation/craving/expectancy system"* and observed that when stimulated in mice it caused an increase in movement and search behavior (Panksepp, 1998; Panksepp & Biven, 2012). This circuitry is activated in the brain areas in operation during REM sleep, therefore, according to Solms', Panksepp's discovery confirms the Freudian hypothesis that at the origin of dreaming is the drive or hunger, as Panksepp calls it (Freud, 1899/2005). However, in Panksepp's view, contrary to the Freudian hypothesis, dreaming would be related to the individual's search for satisfaction of different needs and not only those of a sexual nature. The other brain area that plays a key role in dream production is a portion of gray cortex located at the back of the brain, immediately above and behind the ears, called the parietal-temporal-occipital (PTO) area. Connecting bundles link the posterior portions of the encephalon to the anterior—frontal—portions of the brain, enabling the processing of information into abstract thought, as well as its storage in internal patterns (Luria, 1976).

These findings identify motivation, linked to the dopaminergic circuitry of the ventromedial frontal area, and memory, linked to the PTO area, as the main functions involved in dreaming. Modern neuroradiological methods that make it possible to verify the metabolic activity of the brain during dreaming confirm that the brain structures involved in the dream process are the frontal and limbic areas, implicated in the activation and functioning of emotions, motivation and memory, as well as the occipital area, associated with abstract thought and visual perception. In his theory of motivational reward, Solms emphasizes the involvement of limbic and cortical dopaminergic circuitry, thereby shifting the focus to affections and memory, two dimensions that are closer to the psyche than the areas identified by Hobson. His studies identified the neural circuitry of the dream process. However, while such circuitry is able to explain dream characteristics—vivid imagery, the dreamer's intense emotional involvement, narrative inconsistencies and lack of self-reflection—it is still not enough to explain the contents of dreams.

The contents of dreams

A great deal of what we know about the content of dreams has been obtained through the content categories of Hall-Van de Castle's (1966) classification system, the most widely used method of dream content analysis in the world. A first finding that deserves attention is that dream contents are not easily influenced by pre-sleep manipulation (Foulkes, 1996) and are, instead, predominantly autonomous and self-generated experiences. An exception to this are some types of external sensory stimulation, which *have* the ability to influence dreams, as demonstrated by laboratory experiments conducted by Schredl (2010). From his analysis of dream content, Foulkes (1985) observed that dreams often "simulate" real life, emphasizing a parallelism between oneiric and conscious activity. Consistent with these observations, many researchers, including Schredl (2015), have confirmed the theory of the continuity of dreams (Hall & Nordby, 1972) according to which, in their dreams, the dreamer continues to attend to affectively significant persons and matters that are meaningful to their waking life. An interesting study by Schredl and Engelhardt (2001) found continuity between dreams and conscious thought in psychiatric patients whose issues that are meaningful during wakefulness continue to be so during dreams. Once the dream has been activated, it draws on episodic and declarative mnemonic patterns, general knowledge, and personal conceptions to "build" and represent a pseudo-reality. Such research shifts the focus from dreams with bizarre and hallucinatory content to the far more numerous kind which concerns itself with the trivial interactions between the dreamer and people in their social and emotional circles (Schredl, 2015). About 80% of people report having dreams with recurrent and repetitive themes, that begin during adolescence and sometimes continue throughout life (Cartwright & Romanek, 1978). Domhoff (2011) refers to this as the repetition principle. In substantial agreement with other dream scholars (including Solms) with regard to the extensive neural networks responsible for dreaming, he adds that dream content depends on the activation of conceptual systems of schemas and scripts located in the cognitive system. Confirmation that the content of dreams is personal comes from longitudinal and cross-cultural studies that highlight the existence of typical dreams, such as losing one's teeth, arriving late, and finding oneself naked among people: dreams that are common in all cultures and remain the same over time even if the culture and society to which they belong changes significantly over decades (Malinowski, 2020) or even millennia. Even though social interactions are always at the center of dream events, dreams do however change according to the life stage of the dreamer. Children's dreams feature the presence of animals in significantly greater numbers than adults' dreams, while dreaming of reuniting with deceased loved ones is a cross-cutting theme in people on the verge of death from all parts of the world (McNamara, 2019).

Taking into consideration Hall-Van de Castle's (1966) categories of content analysis, McNamara (2019) identified specific narrative threads within the dreams themselves, common plots that can be recognized not unlike in literary texts. These correspond to the seven basic plots described by Christopher Booker (2004/2019) and are as follows:

1. overcoming the monster
2. rags to riches
3. the quest
4. voyage and return
5. comedy
6. tragedy
7. rebirth

These themes can be found in the vast majority of dreams, just as their opposites can occur in bad dreams or nightmares: in the case of "rebirth," the hero learns from experience and becomes stronger after a fall, but its opposite, the "man in the hole," is where the hero fails to get back up and thus succumbs. According to the author, the fact that these archetypal themes—and their opposites—can be identified in almost all dreams is evidence that the dreaming mind is not confabulatory nor weakened compared to the waking mind. In general, the evidence collected so far on the consistency and repetitiveness of dream plots would substantiate the hypothesis that dreams cannot be regarded as a collection of random and chaotic images and emotions produced by a mind incapable of self-reflective thought. They contain personal themes that are emotionally relevant to the dreamer, expressed in a typical, common and universal form. Dreams are *visual* experiences, exhibiting characteristics that Malinowski associates with terms such as *world simulation, narrative, sudden change, real, social, emotion, fortunes* (Malinowski, 2020, p. 7): happenings happen independently of the dreamer's will. However, in addition to these common features, there are several differences in dreams produced during REM sleep compared to those in NREM sleep. Let us take a closer look.

Functional differences between REM sleep and NREM sleep can help us understand dreams

By now the peculiar neurophysiological characteristics of REM and NREM sleep are well-known to neuroscientists, as is the circadian rhythm mechanism. Some functional aspects of either sleep state have also been clarified by research. However, there are still many questions that remain unanswered.

> Although humans spend almost a third of their lives sleeping, we are still unable to give a satisfactory definition of the functional significance that this physiological state has for the individual.
> (Mancia, 1996, p. 104)

Such considerations expressed by Mauro Mancia at the end of the last century (1996) still hold true 30 years later. Investigating these aspects is of considerable importance to dream scholars because there is no dream without sleep, and understanding the function of sleep can help us understand the function of dreaming as well. What do we know about this physiological state of the animal brain? On this matter, Vedfelt writes:

> NREM and REM sleep arose as our species evolved and faced more and more complex tasks. It would indeed be an odd whim of Mother Nature if this extensive biological and psychological phenomenon in such a successful species as human beings did not have a function for the organism as a whole.
> (2017, p. 35)

We know for a fact that its absence is incompatible with life, so it is obvious that sleep meets adaptive and survival needs. Sleep deprivation indeed causes severe stress to the body and organic deterioration up to a lethal extent, as demonstrated by the dramatic outcome of Fatal Familial Insomnia (FFI), a degenerative disease that causes in those affected a complete inability to sleep to the point of inducing death in the span of a few months. The health risks related to sleep deprivation are well-known to psychotherapists since psychiatric disorders are often accompanied by disturbed or deficient sleep. When such elements emerge while collecting anamnestic data, a timely referral to a psychiatrist should be made in order for the client to undertake a pharmacological treatment with the primary goal of restoring sleep. Another known aspect is that during sleep, due to the inactivity of waking neurons, the cortex is unable to process information properly, so the brain is isolated from the outside world, even while remaining capable of generating mental events such as dreams (Strata, 2017).

However, REM and NREM sleep seem to have distinctive meanings and functions, as evidenced by numerous research studies conducted at the beginning of the XXI century. The functions of NREM sleep are more obvious and better known: NREM sleep is essential for maintaining a good level of efficiency throughout the body, particularly the immune system. In addition, research has shown that after a prolonged waking state, the amount of NREM sleep increases. It is also associated with the release of growth hormones and the activation of homeostatic, metabolic and thermoregulatory processes (Mancia, 1996; Strata, 2017).

As is commonly known, NREM sleep consists of three phases that follow one another throughout the night, to which a fourth phase of REM sleep is added for each sleep cycle. While, on the one hand, we have theories based on the evidence of the potential functions of N1 and N2 phases, on the other hand, the slow waves, released especially in the N3 phase of sleep—indeed defined as slow-wave sleep—seem to be crucial for the acquisition and consolidation of new memories (Walker & Stickgold, 2004). Although no such strong data exist on the functions of REM sleep, a significant amount of research nevertheless proposes the hypothesis that REM sleep also facilitates information processing and storage. For instance, it increases after intense learning sessions. Indeed, the storage of information acquired during wakefulness depends on hippocampus-cortical interactions that are active during both slow-wave sleep and REM sleep, yet the two sleep states, equally engaged in this function, have different roles: slow-wave sleep is reportedly essential for the consolidation of episodic and spatial memories, while REM sleep seems more crucial for the consolidation of emotional and procedural memories. Alternating REM and NREM would allow for different cycles of memory stabilization and integration (McNamara, 2019).

What is certain is that REM sleep dominates in intrauterine and early life and tends to decline with age. This finding suggests that REM sleep has a role in brain development that may be specifically related to the processing of emotions (McNamara, 2019; Strata, 2017). Moreover, one function that seems to be central to REM sleep is precisely dreaming. As mentioned above, the two sleep states produce qualitatively different dreams. In REM sleep dreams, the dreamer is the protagonist of the scene. In them, there is also a greater emotional connotation, greater levels of aggression, and more social interactions. They are narratively longer and more cohesive dreams—more words are used in their narration—than NREM sleep dreams. Dreams in the N1 phase of NREM sleep, the transitional state of consciousness between wakefulness and sleep, are called "hypnagogia" (Malinowski, 2020). Think, for example, about the almost universal experience of feeling like falling at the onset of sleep. Typical phenomena of this state of sleep consciousness are lucid dreams and hypnagogic hallucinations, accurately described by Sacks in his book *Hallucinations* (2013). As a rule of thumb, NREM sleep dreams can be considered "short films," as Dr. Atsuko Chiba, protagonist of the animated film *Paprika*, calls them.

An interesting study published in 2005 and replicated in 2010 (McNamara, 2019) found a considerable lack of aggression in REM sleep dreams with respect to NREM dreams. However, while in REM dreams it is predominantly the dreamer who is the aggressor, in NREM dreams the dreamer's aggression is completely absent. The researchers' hypothesis is that during this sleep state are activated certain processes that inhibit unpleasant or aggressive social impulses in favor of positive and cooperative social processes. Although with some differences, in both sleep stages, when the dreamer is attacked, they respond adaptively either by fleeing, and sometimes awakening, as in NREM dreams, or by attacking in turn, as in REM dreams. These data give value to Revonsuo's (2000) theory of threat simulation, according to which we prepare ourselves to respond functionally to diurnal threats by simulating them in dreams. What remains to be understood is why on earth this difference exists in the two types of dream states. Researchers observed that during REM sleep dreams the default mode network (DMN)—the neural network that characterizes the so-called dreaming brain because it is also active during wakefulness when the mind is at rest and free to roam—is activated. So far, nothing unusual. What is more interesting is that this network, which includes hypothalamic subcortical, amygdala, and limbic sites as well as prefrontal and ventromedial sites, matches the network of the so-called social brain. So, the dreaming brain is also the social brain (McNamara, 2019). And indeed, the main object of people's dreams, whether they be daydreams or closed dreams, are social interactions. Social life is a recurring protagonist in people's dreams throughout their lives. In children, dreams involve affectively significant people and seem to have the specific function of enhancing attachment. In this regard, it is worth mentioning the pioneering work of Colace, who collected 650 dream narratives from over 900 children between the ages of 3 and 8 (2015) and recently published a systematic longitudinal study of a single case, his son Marco, whose dreams were collected from the time he was 4 years old until he was 10 (2022). Related to the characteristics and function of dreams in children, the author writes:

> Wishes fulfilled in infantile dreams were experienced by the children during their daytime life, where they were associated with an intense emotional state (cheerful, surprised/excited, displeased, nostalgic, regretful, impatient) that was not fully processed and elaborated psychologically and therefore resulted as somewhat "perturbing." Through the fulfilment of the wish, the dream resolves the associated affective state and, in turn, allows the child to obtain emotional

discharge and "affective reestablishment." I call this process the hypothesis of the *affective-reestablishment (AR) function of dreams*.

(Colace, 2022, p. 171)

The discovery that dreams are made of the same stuff as our social and emotional relationships is extraordinary for psychotherapists of psychodynamic orientation who treat their clients through therapeutic relationships. Another research study opens up very interesting working perspectives for clinicians and particularly those working on trauma: in 2011, Van der Helm and Walker demonstrated that in REM sleep dreams negative emotions are much more present and significantly more intense than positive ones. This occurs because of an increase of connectivity, typical of this state, between the amygdala—an area responsible for processing certain emotions such as fear or anxiety—and the hippocampus. However, the reactivity of the amygdala is very low because of the suppression of noradrenergic activity. This could prove that REM sleep and its cognitive products, including dreaming, encourage the processing of emotions by depriving them, thanks to the unresponsive amygdala, of potentially too much stressful intensity before they are stored long-term. Thus, sleeping and dreaming could facilitate the processing of negative emotional experiences by preventing the risk of creating traumatic memories. But let's take a closer look at the relationship between dreaming and trauma.

Dreams and trauma

To discuss dreams and trauma is to discuss the work of Ernst Hartmann (1996, 1998), whose father, moreover, was the psychoanalyst Heinz Hartmann, considered the most important theorist of psychoanalysis after Freud (he was Freud's pupil and later close collaborator, and founded ego psychology, the important psychoanalytic school prosecutor of Freudian thought). His research findings are in line with the above hypothesis that nightmare imagery produced as a result of traumatic experiences facilitates the encoding of intense negative emotions in long-term memory. Through his studies, Hartmann was able to observe in particular that during dream activity the brain implements neuronal connectivity. It is evident to all, Hartmann explains, that dreams combine recent life events—the daytime residue—with past life events, just as they combine people, places, and experiences following the mechanism Freud called *condensation*. This is because, during wakefulness, the connections are specific and focused on solving a problem or achieving a goal, but, while dreaming, the connections that are activated are broader and more peripheral and therefore give rise to more global "associated" images. According to this hypothesis, the connections that are activated during dreaming are not random but driven by the dreamer's emotions. However, while meaningful emotions in individuals are usually quite varied (hence the confusion that characterizes their dreams), in the case of people who have experienced trauma the dominant emotions are obvious and usually common—terror, fear, guilt—and the dreams' meaning is clearer. Dreams in traumatized patients follow one another as if in series. Their content may change but what remains constant in each one is the dominant emotional experience: it is the emotional concerns of the dreamer that drive the entire dream process. In dreams or, more often, nightmares, such aspects related to trauma are mixed with other images and memories. Over time, as the experience of trauma is integrated into the dreamer's life, their dreams see an increase of connections and entanglements with emotionally significant prior experiences, including reenactments of previous trauma, until dreams that are typical of pre-trauma life are restored (Hartmann, 1996, 1998; Ribeiro, 2021). From a brain perspective, trauma causes huge storms in neural connections, some of which are excited while others are inhibited based on a number of factors, the main ones being related to the nature of the trauma but also to the subject's personality, daytime residue or the possible presence of previous traumatic experiences. Based on these hypotheses, dreams could represent an attempt by our brain to restore a state of greater stability after the emotional storm suffered. Nightmares would represent, in this sense, an attempt by the brain to encode intense negative emotions in long-term memory. In case the patient does not recover from trauma and develops a post-traumatic stress disorder, the bad dreams do not evolve and the dreamer experiences frequent and repetitive nightmares. According to these studies, the presence of dreams and, especially, repetitive and recurrent nightmares—as in the frequent case of trauma victims—is considered to be evidence against Crick and Mitchison's (1983) theory that dreams are determined by random activations of neural patterns with the aim of clearing the brain of irrelevant memories. Given the large number of neurons and synaptic connections, it is highly unlikely that it is only by sheer chance that the same circuits in our cerebral cortex are activated to give rise to recurrent dreams (Hartmann, 1996, 1998; Ribeiro, 2021). Chapter 7, which will be devoted to traumatic dreams, will delve into how to help patients process trauma by working on recurrent dreams and nightmares. From what has been said so far, it is clear that we cannot have unambiguous answers as to why the brain dreams. However, let's see what theories to date are most credited with explaining the fascinating world of dreams.

Recent theories on the function of dreams

After this foray into the world of neuroscience, we may know a little more about dreams. However, the question of questions has not yet been answered. What, then, is the function of dreams? As pointed out by Barrett (2015)—editor of *Dreaming* (founded by Ernst Hartmann, who was also its first editor-in-chief), the multidisciplinary journal devoted entirely to the study of dreams—there is already a problem with the question. We would never ask what is the function of waking thought. Because the answer would be simple: it is necessary for everything! Therefore, the answer would be the same for dreaming, at least according to Barrett, who points out that the only difference between dreaming and daytime thinking is the biochemical and electrophysiological state of our brain. As a matter of fact, the brain uses the same neuroanatomical structures for dreaming that it uses in wakefulness for learning, reasoning, predicting, deciding, choosing, and getting excited. It is thus evident that our brain harnesses dreams to work on our past experiences, by constructing a relative and subjective plane of reality with its own nexuses and logic. In agreement with this conclusion, Vedfelt declares:

> Dream research has made many attempts to determine, in clear specific functions, the reasons for our dreaming life. My answer to the question, "Why do we dream?" is that our dreams help us solve many and varied tasks. We dream because we are complex beings who need to shift between states of being that process information in different ways to provide us with differing perspectives on the lives we are living.
>
> (2017, p. 35)

Despite this, neuroscientists have been speculating about the specific function, or rather, functions of dreaming since the second half of the last century, although the validity of such theories has yet to be confirmed. We know that each of us dreams four to six times per night and that dreams remembered upon waking are only 1% (Zanasi, n.d.). Even those claiming not to dream actually dream, as shown in a study that looked at subjects with Parkinson's disease (Herlin et al., 2015). These patients suffered from REM Sleep Behavior Disorder, a degenerative process that destroys the cells activating motor paralysis in sleep, causing them to "act out" their dreams, mimicking them with involuntary movements during sleep. The study observed that patients dream even if upon waking they claim they did not. As McNamara writes: "Dreams accompany us and our loved ones literally from the cradle to the grave" (2019, p. 152). Dreaming is thus an activity that always involves the brain. But for what purpose? Collateral function of sleep, problem-solving, thought processing: these are just some of the hypotheses that try to explain why the brain dreams. Following a fruitful line of thought that sees the functions of dreaming in line with the functions of sleep, dreaming would have the purpose of transforming new memories into long-term memory (Cartwright, 2004; Cipolli et al., 2003; Paller & Voss, 2004). In this storage process, the hippocampus plays a key role. In fact, the various aspects of a memory are broken down and processed by different brain areas. The hippocampus, through a cortical cross-correlation process, integrates during dreaming the fragments of memory linked together at the neural level. Memories that are meaningful and useful to the dreamer's problem-solving take precedence. Once integration is achieved, it is enough to activate a single cortical fragment corresponding to a specific aspect of the incident to activate all the other links and thus recall the experience in its entirety. An adaptive function exhibited during sleep would be to merge recent individual experiences with the individual's problems, expectations and goals (Zanasi, n. d.). Connections between fragments related to different episodes may also increase during sleep, so that the level of experience processing would in turn increase in our brain, and experiences might gradually take on new meanings by virtue of a progressively effective adaptation to the environment. This theory is in line with dream accounts that do not deal with single past experiences, but rather with excerpts of memories related to various aspects of different experiences, located in different cortical areas and assembled by the hippocampus. However, dreams are composed of narratives that are not just the result of the aggregation of memories, and often the dreamer finds themselves experiencing events in dreams that they have never encountered before. As McNamara argues:

> Dreams in short are creative, productive, generative, and fecund. They are not mere reflections of waking consciousness, nor are they mere catalogs of floating memory fragments.
>
> (2019, p. 128)

As we have seen by analyzing the differences between REM and NREM sleep, Van der Helm and Walker (2011) seem to have demonstrated the emotional regulation function for REM sleep dreams.

During such dreams, the activity of the amygdala—a central area in the fear circuit identified by Le Doux (2015)—is diminished due to the suppression of norepinephrine. In addition, emotional memories are reactivated in the amygdala–hippocampus networks. These two processes lead to emotional memories being processed without norepinephrine—and thus without the stress-related excitatory activity—to be stored long-term.

But as McNamara explains:

> The fundamental theoretical importance of dream variation is that it suggests that dream function is probably multiple. Dreams do not have only one function […] the evident fact that there are multiple dream types is also consistent with the idea that dreams are products of the social brain, and function, at least in part, to shape, alter, influence, or manipulate social relationships.
>
> (2019, p. 172)

A recent theory of dreams has been developed by Tore Nielsen and Ross Levin (Nielsen & Levin, 2007). For Nielsen and Levin, the purpose of dreams is to promote the storage of emotional memories by depriving them of contextual information. Recurrent dreams are explained as a jam in this process of memory consolidation, whereby the event remains in short-term memory and is repeatedly reactivated by some form of association with it.

At the beginning of the new century, Hobson and Friston (Hobson & Friston, 2012) proposed a new theory of dreaming based on his earlier work, suggesting that dreams are virtual simulations of wakefulness and predictors of reality. According to this theory, the brain simulates reality during REM sleep in order to improve adaptation. During the day a collection of sensory information takes place that leads to the construction of a model of external reality aimed at gathering knowledge and reducing errors and surprises; during sleep, in the "offline" mode, this model is optimized and simplified. However, the authors do not explain why this process of optimization has to be carried out "offline" (that is, during sleep), increasing, for example, the risks of predation. To this Hobson responds that this pruning process really is necessary, otherwise the model would become too complex and dysfunctional. In this way, the theory ends up resembling that of Crick and Mitchison (1983) described above. According to Llinás (Llinás & Paré, 1991), the brain is a "simulator of reality," a closed system, which means that neural networks can be activated even in the absence of input coming from the outside world, and external reality is not simply perceived but reproduced in our brain, which represents it. Neural activity, already predisposed at birth, is modified through brain plasticity during ontogeny by the contribution of sensory input from outside and inside (Pally, 2003). Dreams that occur during REM sleep are an example of brain activity that is not modified by external sensory input but rather powered by the same circuits that maintain memories. Some researchers (Pace-Schott & Picchioni, 2017) have pointed out that during REM dreams a number of these key points are active, which also roughly overlap with the DMN, the brain network that is activated when the mind is relaxed and free to roam. So, the social brain is also the dreaming brain. It is therefore not surprising that daydreams, as well as night dreams, focus on social interactions. Social competence and the ability to establish stable attachment bonds are critical to a child's survival and development. Children's dreams would promote the development of this ability. Such research suggests that people use dreams to process emotional and social information at a cognitive level (McNamara, 2019). Emotions inhabit all dreams (Merritt et al., 1994). Specifically, using the Hall/Val de Castle scoring scale, we find that negative emotions account for 80% of all emotions experienced during dreams (McNamara, 2019). As we can see, Van der Helm and Walker's (2011) theory that dreams have the function of modulating, processing, and elaborating emotions is perfectly in line with these findings.

We know that, in 95% of dreams, human interactions are represented as being at times friendly, but more often than not conflictual. The most accepted hypothesis to date is that dreams are a strategic social act aimed at facilitating negotiations in alliances between people. This theory goes by the name of Social Simulation

Theory (SST). Moreover, in 80% of dreams there is an attempt by the dreamer to infer the mental states of other dream characters (McNamara, 2019). Once again, recent dream theory proves itself to be of extreme interest to us clinicians, since every day, when we meet our patients, we come across their difficulty in mentalizing their own and others' mental states: a deficiency that, according to psychoanalyst Peter Fonagy often leads to psychopathology (Fonagy & Bateman, 2004).

Between the study and the laboratory: the troubled mind–brain relationship

As seen in this brief excursus devoted to dream studies, dreams reflect the dilemma concerning the relationship between mind and brain. Among the dream scholars we met in these pages, we found, on one hand, those who explain the phenomenon of dreaming by analyzing its biological and physiological components, the study of which is highly associated with that of sleep, and on the other hand those who consider dreaming a complex mental activity whose function for humans can only be inferred from neurobiological investigations of the brain. As Mancia (1996) argues, while sleep is a nonspecific process, the same across all individuals of the same species, oneiric activity is an emotional and cognitive experience specific and unique to each individual. Then again, the hypothesis that mental activity can be traced back to biological and organic components is fascinating to humans because it is reassuring. In this regard, Paolo Legrenzi and Carlo Umiltà mention the famous experiment carried out by Yale University researchers on the "dangerous appeal of neuroscientific explanations" (2009, p. 64). Research has shown that any explanation of human behavior, no matter how superficial and false, becomes significantly more credible when preceded by a pseudo-neurobiological explanation (Skolnick et al., 2008). As we saw above, such a mistake was made when Hobson's dream theory was set against Freud's. It is wrong, therefore, to compare neuroscience and psychoanalysis, two disciplines which do have several objects of study in common, such as dreams, but that cannot be seen as two antithetical meta-theories from which to choose in our attempt to explain reality. Using neurophysiological data for the purpose of confirming or refuting Freudian theory and replacing it with another theory among many possible ones seems like a missed opportunity. As Legrenzi and Umiltà (2009) remind us, it is the data that is objective, not the theories that explain them. While both disciplines are interested in the study of dreams, their fields of inquiry are different. Neuroscience is interested in learning about the dream process in general, the brain structures involved in the process of symbolization, memorization, and semantic encoding, as well as the relationships existing between dreaming and memory. Psychoanalysis is interested in investigating the meaning of dreams, how it may be related to the dreamer's affective history and the connection with their internal objects. Legrenzi and Umiltà (2009) provide a very evocative example to understand the risk we run by confusing such different levels of knowledge: How can a detailed knowledge of all the technical components of a cell phone teach us how to make a phone call?

Mauro Mancia, a neuroscientist and psychoanalyst who has written extensively on the relationship between the two disciplines, argues that:

> While being a product of the brain, [dreams] transcend from it and are on a different level than brain functions. Neuroscience is concerned with the brain functions of sleep and dreaming. It is rather naive to think that knowing the neurophysiological substrate of such mental activities explains why the brain dreams. After all [neuroscience] cannot say anything interesting on the dream experience that is deeply linked to the subject's affective history.[1]
>
> (Mancia, 2019, para. 23)

However, it is undeniable that psychotherapy needs to be comforted by neuroscientific findings that explain why it works and how it can work better. Think, for example, of the importance, of working with trauma patients, and of knowing the brain's mechanisms for storing and retrieving memories (for a thorough examination of this topic, see Le Doux, 2015). French psychoanalyst Jacques André, for the special 50th-anniversary issue of the journal *Psicoterapia e Scienze Umane*, when questioned about the relationship between psychoanalysis and neuroscience, declares:

> It is perfectly natural that neuroscience be of interest to psychoanalysis, as long as no epistemological confusion arises. The problem of psychoanalysis is that of meaning, and meaning will never result from the MRI image of the brain.
>
> (André, 2016, p. 365)

Neuroscience, however, also needs clinical experience, since it could give way to theories of the mind that might lead us toward the pursuit of useful data. As McNamara argues:

> Although the neuroscience of sleep and dreams has made tremendous progress in the past few decades it still has not matured to the point where research is theory-guided.
>
> (2019, p. 206)

And regarding the process of validating recent hypotheses about the function of dreams that are currently engaging researchers, continues:

---

1 My translation.

> At least [the social hypothesis] provides a heuristic theoretical framework of REM sleep and dreams that can be tested and falsified experimentally in the lab in the years to come. If it is falsified the field can move beyond the heuristic framework to investigate other potential frameworks, and if it is supported then it will provide the field with theory-guided research questions, instead of blind data-driven research programs for years to come.
>
> (p. 206)

In the words of Legrenzi and Umiltà:

> The mysteries turn into problems when one reflects on what now appear to be seductions resulting from putting the brain and body [over the mind and psyche] in the foreground. Only by reflecting more deeply on this will man—who is not mere body, mere naked life—successfully avoid getting lost in the mazes that technology has opened before him.[2]
>
> (2009, p. 113)

An integration of the contributions of the two disciplines is what is needed to have an increasingly refined understanding of the dream process in its entirety. McNamara further argues:

> Needless to say, it is not at all clear why Mother Nature would, every ninety minutes or so during sleep, intensely activate your brain and your sexual system, paralyze your body, and force you to watch these things we call dreams!
>
> (2019, p. 71)

Although all dream scholars agree that dreaming is a way of processing experience, to date we can say that we have only scratched the surface of the dreaming brain and that the possibilities for future scientific advances in this field of study are truly endless.

References

André, J. (2016). Cosa resta della psicoanalisi [What's left of psychoanalysis]. *Psicoterapia e Scienze Umane*, *L(3)*, 362–365.

Aserinsky, E., & Kleitman, N. (1953). Regularly occurring periods of eye motility and concomitant phenomena, during sleep. *Science*, *118*(3062), 273–274.

---

[2] My translation.

Barrett, D. (2015). Dreams: Thinking in a different biochemical state. In M. Kramer & M. Glucksman (Eds.), *Dream research. Contributions to clinical practice* (pp. 80–93). New York: Routledge.

Bateman A. & Fonagy P. (2004). *Psychotherapy for borderline personality disorder: Mmentalization-based treatment*. Oxford: Oxford University Press.

Booker, C. (2019). *The seven basic plots: Why we tell stories*. London: Continuum (Originally published in 2004).

Bosinelli, M. (1991). Il processo di addormentamento [The falling asleep process]. In M. Bosinelli & P. Cicogna (Eds.), *Sogni: figli di un cervello ozioso* (pp. 249–270). Torino: Bollati Boringhieri.

Cartwright, R. (2004). The role of sleep in changing our minds: A psychologist's discussion of papers on memory reactivation and consolidation in sleep. *Learning and Memory*, *11*(6), 660–663.

Cartwright, R., & Romanek, L. (1978). Repetitive dreams of normal subjects. *Sleep Research*, *7*, 174.

Cipolli, C., Cicogna, P. C., Mattarozzi, K., Mazzetti, M., Natale, V., & Occhionero, M. (2003). Continuity of the processing of declarative knowledge during human sleep: Evidence from interrelated contents of mental sleep experiences. *Neuroscience Letters*, *342*(3), 147–150.

Colace, C. (2015). *Sogni dei bambini*. Roma: Edizioni Mediterranee.

Colace, C. (2022). *The dreams of a child. A case study in early forms of dreaming*. London: Routledge.

Crick, F., & Mitchison, G. (1983). The function of dream sleep. *Nature*, *304*(5922), 111–114.

Dement, W. C., & Kleitman, N. (1957). The Relation of the eye movements during sleep to dream activity: An objective method for the study of dreaming. *Journal of Experimental Psychology*, *53*(5), 339–346. https://doi.org/10.1037/h0048189

Domhoff, G. W. (2011). The neural substrate for dreaming: Is it a subsystem of the default network? *Consciousness and Cognition*, *20*(4), 1163–1174.

Foulkes, D. (1962). Dream reports from different stages of sleep. *The Journal of Abnormal and Social Psychology*, *65*, 14–25.

Foulkes, D. (1985). *Dreaming: A cognitive-psychological analysis*. Hillsdale: Lawrence Erlbaum.

Foulkes, D. (1996). Dream research: 1953–1993. *Sleep*, *19*(8), 609–624.

Foulkes, D., & Vogel, G. (1965). Mental activity at sleep onset. *The Journal of Abnormal Psychology*, *70*(4), 231.

Freud, S. (2005). The interpretation of dreams D. T. O'Hara & G. M. MacKenzie, Eds.; A. A. Brill, Trans.). New York: Barnes & Noble Classics (Originally published in 1899).

Hall, C. S., & Nordby, V. J. (1972). *The individual and his dreams*. New York: New American Library.

Hall, C., & Van de Castle, R. (1966). *The content analysis of dreams*. New York: Appleton-Century-Crofts.

Hartmann, E. (1996). Outline for a theory on the nature and functions of dreaming. *Dreaming*, *6*(2), 147–169.

Hartmann, E. (1998). *Dreams and nightmares: The new theory on the origin and meaning of dreams*. New York: Plenum Trade.

Herlin, B., Leu-Semenescu, S., Chaumereuil, C., & Arnulf, I. (2015). Evidence that non-dreamers do dream: A REM sleep behaviour disorder model. *Journal of Sleep Research, 24*(6), 602–609. https://doi.org/10.1111/jsr.12323

Hobson, J. A., & Friston, K. J. (2012). Waking and dreaming consciousness: Neurobiological and functional considerations. *Progress in Neurobiology, 98*(1), 82–98.

Hobson, J. A., & McCarley, R. (1977). The brain as a dream state generator: An activation-synthesis hypothesis of the dream process. *American Journal of Psychiatry, 134*(12), 1335–1348.

Kaplan-Solms, K.,& Solms, M. (2000). *Clinical studies in neuro-psychoanalysis: Introduction to a depth neuropsychology*. London: Routledge.

Le Doux, J. (2015). *Anxious: Using the brain to understand and treat fear and anxiety*. New York: Penguin Random House.

Legrenzi, P., & Umiltà, C. (2009). *Neuro-mania. Il cervello non spiega chi siamo*. Bologna: Il Mulino.

Llinás, R. R., & Paré, D. (1991). Of dreaming and wakefulness. *Neuroscience, 44*(3), 521–535. https://doi.org/10.1016/0306-4522(91)90075-Y

Luria, A. R. (1976). *The working brain: An introduction to neuropsychology*. New York: Basic Books.

Malinowski, J. (2020). *The psychology of dreaming*. London: Routledge.

Mancia, M. (1996). *Sonno e sogno [Sleep and dreams]*. Roma-Bari: Laterza.

Mancia, M. (2019). *Psicoanalisi e neuroscienze: un dibattito attuale sul sogno [Psychoanalysis and neuroscience: A current debate on dreaming]*. Psychiatry Online Italia. http://www.psychiatryonline.it/node/2461

McNamara, P. (2019). *The neuroscience of sleep and dreams*. Cambridge: Cambridge University Press.

Merritt, J. M., Stickgold, R., Pace-Schott, E., Williams, J., & Hobson, J. A. (1994). Emotion profiles in the dreams of men and women. *Consciousness and Cognition, 3*(1), 46–60. https://doi.org/10.1006/ccog.1994.1004

Nielsen, T. A., & Levin, R. (2007). Nightmares: A new neurocognitive model. *Sleep Medicine Reviews, 11*(4), 295–310.

Oudiette, D., Dealberto, M. J., Uguccioni, G., Golmard, J. L., Merino-Andreu, M., Tafti, M., Garma, L., Schwartz, S., & Arnulf, I. (2012). Dreaming without REM sleep. *Consciousness and Cognition, 21*(3), 1129–1140.

Pace-Schott, E. F., & Picchioni, D. (2017). Neurobiology of dreaming. In M. H. Kryger, T. Roth & W. C. Dement (Eds.), *Principles and practice of sleep medicine* (pp. 529–538). Philadelphia: Elsevier.

Paller, K., & Voss, J. (2004). Memory and reactivation and consolidation during sleep. *Learning and Memory, 11*(6), 664–670.

Pally, R. (2003). *Il Rapporto tra mente e cervello [The relationship between mind and brain]*. Roma: Giovanni Fioriti Editore.

Panksepp, J. (1998). *Affective neuroscience – The foundations of human and animal emotions*. Oxford: Oxford University Press.

Panksepp, J., & Biven, L. (2012). *The archaeology of mind: Neuroevolutionary origins of human emotions*. New York: W. W. Norton & Co.

Revonsuo, A. (2000). The reinterpretation of dreams: An evolutionary hypothesis of the function of dreaming. *Behavioral and Brain Sciences, 23*(6), 877–901.

Ribeiro, S. (2021). *The oracle of night: The history and science of dreams* (D. Hahn, Trans.). New York: Pantheon Books.

Sacks, O. (1973). *Awakenings*. New York: Harper Perennial.

Schredl, M. (2010). Characteristics and contents of dreams. *International Review of Neuro-Biology, 92*, 135–154.

Schredl, M. (2015). The continuity between waking and dreaming: Empirical research and clinical implications. In M. Kramer & M. Glucksman (Eds.), *Dream research. Contributions to clinical practice* (pp. 27–37). New York: Routledge.

Schredl, M., & Engelhardt, H. (2001). Dreaming and psychopathology: Dream recall and dream content of psychiatric inpatients. *Sleep and Hypnosis, 3*(1), 44–54.

Skolnick Weisberg, D., Keil, F., Goodstein, J., Rawson, E., & Gray, J. R. (2008). The Seductive allure of neuroscience explanation. *Journal of Cognitive Neuroscience, 20*(3), 470–477.

Solms, M. (2000). Dreaming and REM sleep are controlled by different brain mechanisms. *Behavioral and Brain Sciences, 23*(6), 843–850.

Strata, P. (2017). *Dormire, forse sognare. Sonno e sogno nelle neuroscienze [To sleep, perchance to dream: Sleep and dreams in neuroscience]*. Roma: Carocci.

Van der Helm, E., & Walker, M. P. (2011). Sleep and emotional memory processing. *Sleep Medicine Clinics, 6*(1), 31–43.

Vedfelt, O. (2017). *A guide to the world of dreams. An integrative approach to dreamwork*. London: Routledge.

Walker, M., & Stickgold, R. (2004). Sleep-dependent learning and memory consolidation. *Neuron, 44*(1), 121–133.

Zanasi, M. (n.d.). *Il sogno tra la neurofisiologia e la psicologia [The dream between neurophysiology and psychology]*. https://xdocs.net/preview/zanasineurofisiologia-del-sogno-5cf187fe31a6f

3
TRANSACTIONAL ANALYSIS OF DREAMS

Introduction

Transactional analysis is an orientation of psycodynamic-based psychotherapy, whose history, however, was marked by a break with orthodox psychoanalysis that occurred in 1957, when Eric Berne presented transactional analysis to the American scientific and clinical community as a new method of group therapy. The commitment to distinguish transactional analysis from psychoanalysis, as well as the contentious attitude Berne and his early collaborators exhibited toward the scholarly knowledge and initiatory language of certain psychoanalysts, also entailed a departure from themes and content dear to classical analysis, such as the investigation of the unconscious and the interpretation of dreams, in favor of the exploration of interpersonal dynamics through game analysis, which culminated with the successful publication in 1964 of *Games People Play*. The connection with humanistic psychotherapies, which were primarily interested in the analysis of communication and the values of non-directive therapy, shifted the interests of Berne's students toward experiments with group therapy and Gestalt techniques, which, in the 1970s, had wide dissemination and clinical application with marathon groups focused on redecision therapy. The history of this evolution of transactional analysis is brilliantly described by William F. Cornell in the article published on the 50th anniversary of Berne's death (2020), in which he retraces the milestones leading to its present state, helping us to understand the reason why the recovery of the psychodynamic matrix at the basis of our approach occurred only a few decades after Berne's death.

Eric Berne and the birth of transactional analysis

The founder of transactional analysis, Eric Bern trained as a psychoanalyst first in 1941 under Paul Federn in New York and later—after enlisting during World War II as a military psychiatrist—in 1946 in California under Erik Erikson. In his 1947 book, *The Mind in Action* (successfully reprinted after the founding of transactional analysis in 1957 under the title *A Layman's Guide to Psychiatry and Psychoanalysis*) he addresses for the first time the subject of dreams.

In its Chapter 4, which is dedicated precisely to dreams and the unconscious, Berne states that:

> The images in the unconscious look different and work differently from their product, which is conscious or thought images. This can be seen by thinking about dreams, which are halfway between conscious and unconscious images in form, and are a little like both and a little different from both.
>
> (Berne, 1957, p. 123)

Dreams are defined as "glimpse of the unconscious" and the unconscious as "a source of energy and a part of the mind where thoughts are 'manufactured,'"

and "a region where feelings are stored" (p. 123). Berne uses a brilliant metaphor to describe the difference between the unconscious and the conscious function of the mind and states that the unconscious is like an automobile factory that puts all the parts together, which has machinery that prepares the product but does not coincide with the final product, which is the automobile.

> The unconscious, then, is the source of Id energy, a "thought factory," and a storage place. It cannot think, any more than an automobile factory can go on a trip. It can only feel and wish, and it pays no attention to time, place, and the laws of the physical universe, as is often seen in dreams, where the dead may be resurrected, the separated reunited, and the laws of gravity may not work normally.
>
> (p. 127)

The second metaphor Berne uses to distinguish the functioning of the two levels of the mind is the difference between kicking and having an involuntary knee jerk caused by the spinal cord reflex, and so he concludes by saying that "a dream scene of a market place is as different from a real market place as a knee jerk is from a kick" (p. 127).

So what is a dream, according to Berne? "It is an attempt to gain satisfaction of an Id tension by hallucinating a wish fulfillment" but since the Superego "does not relax much during sleep," the Id must "still conceal the true nature of its strivings for fear of offending the Superego" (p. 129).

Berne then adds that "a dream is an attempt to keep the sleeper from being awakened by the shameful-ness or terrifying nature of his own Id wishes. The dream is the preserver of sleep" (p. 130) while "a nightmare is a dream which has failed in its attempt to preserve sleep" (p. 131).

To the already familiar considerations of the classic authors of psychoanalysis Berne then juxtaposes his own view, arguing that it is also likely that dreams have another function; that is, they help the mind heal from emotional wounds and painful experiences.

> Even ordinary emotional experiences have to be "digested" in some way through dreaming in order for the individual to feel well. A person deprived of the opportunity to dream may become quite confused; many psychoses are preceded by a period of prolonged lack of sleep, and hence lack of opportunity to dream.
>
> (p. 136)

On the technical aspects of interpretation, for which he encourages the use of free association, Berne then notes that

> It is a common error to suppose that *finding out* the meaning of the dream is the important thing. This is not so. The meanings must be felt, and these feelings must be put into proper perspective with other past and present feelings of that particular person, for the interpretation to have any effect in changing the underlying Id tensions, which is the purpose of the procedure.
>
> (pp. 136–137)

Another observation worth noting is that "Above all, the interpreter bears in mind that the dreamer writes his own scenario" (p. 138).

We would also like to add, linking these early works of Berne's to his great text on human destiny—*What Do You Say After You Say Hello?*, which came out posthumously in 1972—that the dream script has a connection with the life script that the child writes, in which they decide what their role in life will be and what they can expect from others and the world.

In this work we find the theme of dream analysis again in the chapter on adolescence, when Berne describes the case of Wanda. It is in fact a dream that allows the therapist in the group to understand the script scenario of a client who had been complaining about the same things over and over for years. Berne declares that

> for about two years, the therapist was unable to construct a coherent picture in his own mind of what was going on, until one night she had a "script dream." She was "living in a concentration camp which was run by some rich people who lived up on the hill". The only way to get enough food was either to please these rich people or trick them.
>
> (1972, p. 173)

Wanda complained that her husband kept getting into financial trouble for which she then had to ask her rich parents for help. It was clear to Berne and the group that up until that point she had been using therapy as a way to learn how to survive in the concentration camp, but that she could heal only if she decided to get out of the concentration camp and into the real world, where she could take adult responsibility for her life and decide what she wanted to do with her relationship with her husband.

> The script set is usually so far removed from the reality of the patient's life that there is no way to reconstruct it by mere observation or interpretation. The best hope of getting a clear picture of it is through a dream. The "script-set dream" is recognizable because as soon as the patient tells it, many things fall into place. Pictorially, it bears no resemblance to the patient's actual way of life, but transactionally, it is an exact replica.
> (1972, p. 174)

Despite the great importance Berne attaches here to dreams related to the script scenario, no adequate development of this theme can be found in his work, and he only explores it for a few more pages, which we will take up in the chapter dedicated to script dreams.

From the Gouldings to Margaret Bowater, the "dream lady"

For many years interest in dream analysis remained peripheral in transactional analysis texts. In the 1970s, Bob and Mary Goulding developed an important integration of TA and Gestalt theory that they called redecision therapy. In the 1979 text that described their clinical work in groups they also discussed dreams, stating that "like fantasies, they are excellent tools for redecision" (1979, p. 196). They chronicled a number of clinical cases, maintaining the focus on the possibility for the client to identify with the various characters and objects within the dream in order to understand the impasse and regain the ability to make new decisions. They themselves cite the work of George Thomson, who became famous for an article he wrote in the *Transactional Analysis Journal* in the 1980s. Thomson's 1987 article was credited with raising awareness of the technique of dreamwork from the perspective of redecision therapy, in the belief that

> The body of the dream represents the past, the emotions on awakening represent the present racket, and the redecision is made most easily in the creating of a new ending to a dream.
> (Thomson in Goulding, 1979, p. 197)

Margaret Bowater, based in New Zealand, has provided us with an extensive and interesting clinical literature on Gestalt dream analysis. Her work has been important in emphasizing the ethical approach to analysis, according to which therapist and client are valued on equal terms, and therapists are urged to be very respectful of the client's inner world, while dreams are used to raise awareness and provide options for change. Knowledge of Aboriginal culture and its focus on "dream time" further enriches Bowater's approach, who, for more than 30 years, has been holding dream workshops to help people heal from nightmares—which are considered particularly problematic for people under the most distressing conditions "in that they are unfinished, leaving us in a state of high anxiety or helplessness" (2016, p. 60)—and encourages clients to make up their own ending to nightmares, so that they can face their fears.

In Italy, Pio Scilligo's contribution to dreamwork basically follows Perls' approach and thus that of the Gestalt school.

Scilligo encourages the dramatization of dreams, that is, the act of re-experiencing a dream with the therapist, in order to impersonate the different parts of the dream and become conscious of the associations that may arise. Scilligo's book contains an interesting invitation to take into account the narrative structure of the dream: beginning, drama and crisis, favorable or unfavorable outcome. Dreams have their own completeness, and it is thus important to keep in mind the systemic and global aspects of the story.

Some imageries are understood only by taking into account both the personal experience of the dreamer and the cultural environment to which the dreamer belongs, because some symbols depend heavily on context.

> An uncle tells his niece G. that one of her friends has a loaded gun. The niece, who is dreaming, gets scared both in the dream and in real life, where she looks pale and frightened. She interpreted the dreams according to a theoretical structure that pointed toward self-destruction. While recounting the dream, every time she talked about the gun and her friend, G. would smile unconsciously. The therapist encouraged her to let herself lean into that smile and be the gun. Through this, they found that the gun was needed for a party and her friend was not worried at all but in fact she quite liked the whole party.[1]
>
> (Scilligo, 1990, p. 41)

The psychodynamic approach to dreamwork in TA

In Italy, in 1989, a scientific seminar addressing the psychodynamic approach to dreaming in TA reopened some strands of clinical research on which Anna Rotondo and Susanna Ligabue in Milan and Michele Novellino in Rome later worked.

---

[1] My translation.

In an interesting paper titled *Sogni e stati dell'Io* (1989), Rotondo goes back to Berne's cultural matrix, placing it within the framework of Paul Federn and Edward Weiss's ego psychology and calling for an approach to the analysis of dreams in terms of a reactivation of split ego states that need to express themselves and be reintegrated into the conscious psyche.

> The dream is thus a kind of contamination that draws directly on the archaic world of emotions, symbols, and the language peculiar to childhood […] To work on dreams is to get in touch directly with the most archaic part of the individual's script and its deepest contents.[2]
> (Rotondo, 1989, p. 60)

If we are to deal with script analysis and deconfusion, it is therefore essential to work with dreams. In light of this we can then better understand the urge to integrate TA with the work of psychoanalysts such as Paolo Migone and James Fosshage, which Susanna Ligabue includes in a significant and useful review comparing Gestaltic and psychodynamic TA (Ligabue, 2005).

Carlo Moiso (1989), being the brilliant innovator that he was, was the first to address the issue of comparing TA and neuroscience in the 1990s. His references are somewhat dated, but some insights remain to be noted, as, for example, when he hypothesizes that dreams that contain games referring to the dreamer's future may also be a worthy object of analysis.

> This is the kind of imagery that translates into affective experiences what is effectively the personal destiny envisioned in the script, which is often achieved by carrying out games or archaic experiences of reinforcement within the dream. It is obvious that such dreams are not prophetic in nature, but rather valid tools to make the client aware of the ultimate consequences of the life-plan they are living out.[3]
> (Moiso, 1989, p. 66)

Moiso and Novellino, recipients of the Berne Prize (in 1987 and 2003, respectively) for the epistemological aspects of psychodynamic TA, published an interesting contribution in 2000 that is still considered seminal for the return of TA to its natural neo-psychoanalytic affiliation.

In the article they write:

> The analysis of scripts is not confined to an induced emotional re-experiencing of protocol scenes; rather, scripts are seen as lived out

---

2   My translation.
3   My translation.

stories that are cocreated in an ongoing process. The trend in psychoanalysis today (often referred to as interpersonal or intersubjective) is clearly Bernean in that interpretation consists of supplying the patient with a decoded, detoxified narration about the coded narration offered by the patient through the use of ulterior transactions or games. Note that "narration" is the only word added here to how Berne (1966) presented interpretation in *Principles of Group Treatment*. When people think of a psychoanalytic approach to transactional analysis, they often remember how Berne made frequent links to classical Freudian theory. We should instead consider the most recent evolution of psychoanalysis, such as (but not limited to) object relations theory. We consider that therapy is a cocreated conversation between people, and we think that the new conversationalist approach to psychoanalysis shows how Berne was a great innovator of psychoanalysis and how Bernean (and, if we might be allowed, neo-Bernean) transactional analysis is perhaps the most promising form of a neo-psychoanalytic psychotherapy.

(Moiso & Novellino, 2000, p. 186)

Michele Novellino

His studies on unconscious communication (1990) provide a foundation for the interpretive work we use in dream analysis. Novellino encourages therapists to use their intuition to listen and understand when a client's narrative functions as a metaphor that allows them to shed light on the transference process by bringing into the session certain themes otherwise unacceptable to their consciousness, such as perhaps an envy or jealousy of protocol. Novellino calls these transactions bilogic, since they correspond to a second level of further communication that he calls monologic.

He writes in this regard:

> Bilogic transactions have a manifest meaning (social level) produced by the secondary process and an unconscious latent meaning that expresses the primary process (psychological level). They are like coded messages in which the manifest content conveys simultaneously a form of latent communication; they correspond, approximately, to ulterior transactions. This type of transaction expresses unconscious communication that, when analyzed, can provide access to the protocol. The protocol suggests in fantasy thoughts and feelings that are unacceptable to the patient's conscious mind. This content tends to come out in emotional situations that resemble the dramatic situation surrounding the protocol. A compromise is represented by their codification in biological messages, which the therapist must then decode. Because true free association is not used in transactional analysis, the

therapist must instead attend to his or her own internal associations as well as to the patient's behavior.

(1990, p. 171)

We may speculate that the transference dream is an unconscious communication of the type described above. As such, the client's narrative that conjures and suggests conflicting or disturbing aspects of the therapeutic relationship can also be explored with the help of the therapist's intuition.

Michele Novellino devoted important pages to the topic of dreams and to the psychodynamic understanding of nightmares both in the Italian-speaking field (2010) and in the *Transactional Analysis Journal*, with his 2012 contribution. This interest in nightmares and, overall, in dreams of distress is related to the view of therapy as an analysis of the depth-oriented to deal with the script, and therefore interested in listening to the most terrible symptoms and imagery that reveal the themes of their deepest conflicts. On the contrary, therapy that worked toward simply restoring the previous equilibrium—"I want to go back to what I was before"—would lead the client to obey to the parental "Be perfect" and "Be strong" messages and would certainly not save them from their own nightmares. The disturbance that dreams of distress offer to clients thus becomes an opportunity to explore the need for the child part of their personality that rebels against returning to the adaptation imposed by the script. Additionally, there are nightmares that manifest an even deeper level of the client's script, which are what in TA we call injunctions. We will return to this original theory of Novellino's in Chapter 6, which will focus precisely on script dreams. The choice to face one's nightmares and work with them constitutes the premise for a script analysis aimed at building a more mature personality. Novellino writes in this regard:

The prize is real script healing and in-depth deconfusion. In this sense, nightmares can offer important openings to unconscious processes that otherwise would remain neglected […] Therapeutic work with nightmares represents an effective tool for achieving better integration of the patient's personality and offers to him or her more flexibility in the ongoing interplay between his or her openings and enclosures. Understanding and using the psychodynamics of nightmares in appropriate phases of therapy and with patients who are interested in doing so provides a powerful means of revealing script mechanisms that might otherwise not be uncovered. However, deciding to confront our patients' nightmares (and sometimes our own) or to avoid doing so, intentionally or not, may also depend on the profound acceptance of a different way of understanding that person who, for a briefer or longer period, becomes our patient. The human being, in order to grow psychically, sometimes must be able to confront demons.

(Novellino, 2012, p. 284)

Relational transactional analysis

Sills and Hargaden's (2002) relational approach provides a useful framework for the treatment of personality disorders and overall vulnerable people. While not explicitly addressing dream analysis, these authors argue that, by identifying the purpose of analysis with the integration of the split parts of the self, such integration can and should be conducted through a

> relationship where the therapist is willing to hear the non-narratable story that arises from the internal object world of the infant and can come into play only within the transferential relationship.
>
> (2002, p. 28)

In Beatrice's case, used in the book as the main example of the relational model of therapy, dreams are described in the last stage of the journey.

> Beatrice began to have dreams of churches and cathedrals. She described elaborate and graphic details conveying a sense of beauty, space and riches beyond compare. The therapist felt spiritually affected and increasingly deeply connected to Beatrice. In recounting the dreams, Beatrice connected with a sense of joy and sensuality as she explored the images and their meanings with the therapist. When the therapist mirrored back to Beatrice the rich sense of optimism, promise and connection between them.
>
> (2002, p. 197)

The large spaces of churches and cathedrals are contrasted with the client's feeling of living inside a prison cell and the image of the dollhouse in which she had subsequently locked herself away out of fear of facing life. The personal themes and illustrations with which the client's life is metaphorically and symbolically defined are significant as are the therapist's insights and emotions. Nothing, however, is suggested about dream work from a technical standpoint.

William F. Cornell

William Cornell's work is regarded as particularly significant for his studies on the integration of verbal therapy with body therapy. In recent years, Cornell has dealt with the relationship between transactional analysis and Wilma Bucci's multiple code theory, offering a model of communication in therapy focused on the sub-symbolic level, which brings together an attention to gestures and the body and an attention to oneiric communication. In both cases, in fact, the therapist opens themselves up to an engaged listening experience and to the client's Child as well as their own, facilitating, in our view, the creation of a deep connection between client and therapist, and, with it, access to the client's inner world, the exploration of their more archaic needs and their familiarization with emotional experiences in the here-and-now of the therapeutic session.

Cornell has been working for many years to integrate his Reichian training as a body therapist with that of a transactional analyst. In a text published in 2015 he describes working on a dream with a client named Simon. Simon, a young man living with elderly parents, had a very passive attitude toward life, had abandoned his studies, left a girlfriend and had no friends. One day, during an individual therapy session, he brings up a dream so narrated by Cornell:

> Simon dreamed that in a session he rolled to his side, and I came over to sit at his back, my hip and thigh against his spine. We wondered together about the dream, Simon associated to it, I offering my associations and speculations, when suddenly Simon rolled to his side and asked me to move over to sit with him as in the dream. I did.
>
> Simon's body began to tremble and he began to cry. He was stunned by the warmth of my body and his sense of the strength in it.
>
> He found himself thinking of this father's weak and withering body, which he found disgusting [...] Every few sessions Simon now asked me to sit with him, as I had in the dream. He felt it helped him separate his experience of his own body from that of his father's.
>
> (2019, p. 79)

Here is a way of working on dreams that integrates the corporeal approach with the talking cure. Cornell observes that "Reich realized that verbal interpretations were limited in their effectiveness in disrupting or shifting character organization" (2015, p. 79), which manifests itself in transference dynamics.

Richard Erskine

Erskine's integrative approach is very helpful in laying the foundation for an effective therapeutic relationship in which alliance-building is based on attunement and empathy. There are no specific contributions to dreamwork in his writings, but his invitation to therapists to create a climate of acceptance and alliance is certainly helpful for dreamwork as well.

Erskine suggests paying close attention to attunement with the client. Guiding our clients to change the deep-seated decisions that depend on dismissive attachment relationships requires relational therapies.

However, surely the most useful aspect of Erskine's work concerns the study of the process of script formation and how to deal with it in therapy. Erskine has devoted many articles and publications to the study of the unconscious relational patterns that constitute the script protocol and that are uniquely revealed in dreams. It was for these works that he received his third Berne Prize in 2018.

In his acceptance speech for the prize, he stated that:

> Clients' emerging stories reflect the physiological survival reactions, procedural memories, implicit experiential conclusions, explicit decisions, and parental introjections that compose a life script. Through our intersubjective dialogue, the client's previously inchoate emotions and rudimentary experiences become configured into a consistent, comprehensive, and integrated life-narrative—an essential component of a script cure.
>
> (2019, p. 10)

In the dialogue between therapist and client, a reflection on relational needs is always very useful. In an interview with PerFormat in 2018, Erskine mentioned that the need for safety in the relationship, "to be in the presence of someone that you know is not going to hurt you physically, who is not going to humiliate you, put you down or demean you in any way" (2018, p. 27), is the most important thing, and a necessary condition for the client to feel free to express themselves.

Ray Little

From Ray Little we have learned to view ego states as interacting systems—in the Parent–Child pair—that tend to hold themselves in a bond of loyalty, identifying a threat in therapy.

Approaching dreamwork with such an understanding helps to avoid attacking the defenses the clients need to maintain in order not to lose the primary sense of security necessary to survive. Therefore, dreams could serve to restore the intrapsychic balance unintentionally attacked by therapy. Little writes:

> One of the goals of therapy could be described as supporting the resolution of this struggle. This can be done by opening up the closed system [...] with the therapist being available for the Child to connect with as a new object, thus enabling the Child to emerge and work in therapy to free itself from the old bond with the Parent.
>
> The relationship between the Child and Parent may also involve a bond of loyalty.
>
> (2006, p. 10)

Using dreamwork to transition from recurring relationships to necessary relationships is the goal we seek to facilitate change, by paying close attention not only to the evolution of dream content, but especially to the small variations that can be seen in the narrative structure and emotional dimension with which the dreamer recounts their dreams to us.

Co-creative TA

To Graeme Summers and Keith Tudor we owe the focus on the process of co-construction of meaning that occurs in therapy whenever the therapist engages the client in an open and creative dialogue.

Again, we do not find in their texts any direct guidance on dreamwork, although they do contain some useful pointers on the respectful and open attitude to discovery that is particularly fruitful for dreamwork.

The concepts we find most useful in this regard are those of Integral Adulthood, We-ness and co-creative empathy.

> The integrating adult, which builds on our original ego state model and idea of adult expansion, is a concept that Keith went on to name and develop more fully in a chapter published in 2003 in which he represented this ego state as a series of overlapping circles (see Figure 1). We are aware that some colleagues do not like this representation of the integrating adult and find it too "messy." Our point in representing it in this way is to emphasize the moving and changing nature of this aspect of the psyche and personality. In other words, it is an aesthetic representation of an ontological reality—or, at least, our perspective on and of this essence of things.
>
> (2021, p. 12)

> We-ness, which although not new in the broader field of psychology, was new to TA and is a concept that Keith has further developed in an article arguing that "we are" (rather than "I'm OK–You're OK") is the fundamental life position.
>
> (2021, p. 11)

Overall, the idea of co-creative empathy is related to the atmosphere of openness and exploration that must be generated in the individual or group therapy session to create an environment conducive to the discovery and reactivation of the Creative Child, the same dreamer who writes and rewrites the script.

The PerFormat method

Our approach to dream analysis has been described in a number of works already published in English and Italian (Tangolo, 2015, 2017, 2018, 2022) and mainly takes up the Bernian method, following its original psychodynamic matrix. Our interest in the application of Fosshage's technique to dreamwork brings us closer to the approach used at the Milan school of TA and, overall, as far as the individual setting is concerned, we use a model of psychodynamic transactional analysis inspired by the work of Michele Novellino.

We place significant attention on the present moment in therapy and consider dreams as narratives whose understanding is co-creatively and sloppily defined (BCPSG, 2010) by the relational exchanges that occur between client and therapist in specific and local ways.

In a group setting, we have developed an array of original techniques and methodologies that are thoroughly described in our manual devoted to group therapy (Tangolo & Massi, 2022). We are working on a research protocol that integrates transactional analysis with CCRT (Luborsky & Cristoph, 1998), one that we find fertile for further developments in the analysis of transference in both group and individual therapy also because of the attention given to dreams. Essentially, we believe that the language of dreams allows us to access the richer inner world of our clients, recovering the energy of the script-creating Child, the same energy that was infused in the survival strategies enacted in the face of an often-hostile world. Recovering the Dreamer opens us to the possibility of having an emotionally capable co-therapist to bring into the therapeutic work the energy and motivation needed to open up to important changes. It is as if we can activate a little playwright, who, like Shakespeare, generates storms and shipwrecks and midsummer night's dreams in order to find their own way to survive and return from the islands of dreams to the reality of wakefulness, thus giving meaning to the struggles we often have to face already in childhood and certainly in adulthood.

After all, as Prospero says in *The Tempest*: "We are such stuff / As dreams are made on, and our little life / Is rounded with a sleep" (Act 4, Scene 1, 156–158).

References

Berne, E. (1957). *A Layman's guide to psychiatry and psychoanalysis*. New York: Simon and Schuster.

Berne, E. (1964). *Games people play: The psychology of human relationships*. New York: Grove Press.

Berne, E. (1966). *Principles of group treatment*. New York: Oxford University Press.

Berne, E. (1972). *What do you say after you say hello?: The psychology of human destiny*. New York: Bantam Books.

Boston Change Process Study Group. (Ed.). (2010). *Change in psychotherapy: A unifying paradigm* (1st ed.). New York: W.W. Norton & Co.

Bowater, M. M. (2016). *Healing the nightmare, freeing the soul: A practical guide to dreamwork*. Auckland: Calico.

Cornell, W. F. (2015). *Somatic experience in psychoanalysis and psychotherapy: In The expressive language of the living*. New York: Routledge, Taylor & Francis Group.

Cornell, W. F. (2019). *At the interface of transactional analysis, psychoanalysis, and body psychotherapy: Clinical and theoretical perspectives*. London; New York: Routledge, Taylor & Francis Group.

Cornell, W. F. (2020). Transactional analysis and psychoanalysis: Overcoming the narcissism of small differences in the shadow of Eric Berne. *Transactional Analysis Journal*, *50*(3), 164–178. https://doi.org/10.1080/03621537.2020.1771020

Erskine, R. G. (2018). Interview with Richard Erskine. *Percorsi Di Analisi Transazionale*, *V*(1), 36–48.

Erskine, R. G. (2019). The life script trilogy: Acceptance speech on receiving the 2018 Eric Berne Memorial Award. *Transactional Analysis Journal*, *49*(1), 7–13. https://doi.org/10.1080/03621537.2019.1544773

Goulding, M. M. C., & Goulding, R. L. (1979). *Changing lives through redecision therapy*. New York: Grove Press.

Hargaden, H., & Sills, C. (2002). *Transactional analysis: A relational perspective*. New York: Brunner-Routledge.

Ligabue S. (2005). *Dedicato ai sogni*. Milano: La vita felice

Little, R. (2006). Ego state relational units and resistance to change. *Transactional Analysis Journal*, *36*(1), 7–19. https://doi.org/10.1177/036215370603600103

Luborsky, L., & Crits-Christoph, P. (1998). *Understanding transference: The Core Conflictual Relationship Theme method*. American Psychological Association.

Moiso, C. (1989). Cenni su un possibile rapporto tra neuroscienza e analisi del copione nell'interpretazione dell'attività onirica [Notes on a possible relationship between neuroscience and script analysis in dream activity interpretation]. In M. Gaudieri & L. Quagliotti (Eds.), *Il sogno nell'analisi transazionale clinica*. Napoli: Marotta, pp. 63–66.

Moiso, C., & Novellino, M. (2000). An overview of the psychodynamic school of transactional analysis and Its epistemological foundations. *Transactional Analysis Journal*, *30*(3), 182–187. https://doi.org/10.1177/036215370003000302

Novellino, M. (1990). Unconscious communication and interpretation in transactional analysis. *Transactional Analysis Journal*, *20*(3), 168–172. https://doi.org/10.1177/036215379002000306

Novellino, M. (2010). The demon and sloppiness: From Berne to transactional psychoanalysis. *Transactional Analysis Journal*, *40*(3–4), 288–294. https://doi.org/10.1177/036215371004000313

Novellino, M. (2012). The shadow and the demon: The psychodynamics of nightmares. *Transactional Analysis Journal*, *42*(4), 277–284. https://doi.org/10.1177/036215371204200406

Rotondo, A. (1989). Sogni e stati dell'io [Dreams and ego states]. In M. Gaudieri & L. Quagliotti (Eds.), *Il sogno nell'analisi transazionale clinica*. Napoli: Marotta editore.

Scilligo, P. (Ed.). (1990). *Gestalt e analisi transazionale: Principi e tecniche. [Gestalt and transactional analysis: Principles and tecniques]*. Roma: LAS.

Summers, G., & Tudor, K. (2021). Reflections on cocreative transactional analysis: Acceptance speech for the 2020 Eric Berne Memorial Award. *Transactional Analysis Journal*, *51*(1), 7–18. https://doi.org/10.1080/03621537.2020.1853345

Tangolo, A. E. (2015). *Psychodynamic psychotherapy with transactional analysis: Theory and narration of a living experience*. London: Karnac.

Tangolo, A. E. (2017). Group imago and dreamwork in group therapy. *Transactional Analysis Journal*, *45*(3), 179–190. https://doi.org/10.1177/0362153715597722

Tangolo, A. E., & Massi, A. (2018). A contemporary perspective on transactional analysis group therapy. *Transactional Analysis Journal, 48*(3), 209–223. https://doi.org/10.1080/03621537.2018.1471288

Tangolo, A. E., & Massi, A. (2022). *Group therapy in transactional analysis: Theory through practice*. New York: Routledge.

Thomson, G. (1987). Dreamwork in redecision therapy. *Transactional Analysis Journal, 17*(4), 169–177. https://doi.org/10.1177/036215378701700407

SUGGESTION

The history and culture of dreams

Interest in the world of dreams spans throughout time and involves every human culture. Anthropologists, philosophers, and historians have dealt with these themes with great passion. The journey could be boundless and adventurous. We shall merely point out authors who deserve to be used as guides to accompany us in this vast quest: Carl G. Jung, James Hillman, Sidarta Ribeiro, Silvia Rosa, and Vittorio Lingiardi.

In his anthropological search for symbols and archetypes, Jung investigated the analysis of dreams by exploring themes of the collective imagination beyond the history of the individual, opening psychoanalysis up to new knowledge.

We encourage the reading of *Man and His Symbols* (1964), a popular text and Jung's last work, which he decided to write after having a dream, as described in Freeman's introduction to his book. Jung had been persuaded to be interviewed by British television, and after the interview he dreamed that he was standing up to speak to a large audience enraptured by his words, no longer cooped up in his study speaking only to psychiatrists. The creation of the work took place collectively, with contributions from several of his collaborators. In the book Jung clearly explains the usefulness for the dream analyst of knowing the symbols of the collective unconscious and also recounts a personal dream he told Freud when they were still working together. In this dream, Jung explored a house in which he descended from one floor to the next, tracing backward the history of all mankind so as to arrive at a prehistoric cellar. Jung later confesses that he lied to Freud about his free associations because he feared he would not be understood and accepted by his master. Insight about the dream occurs when he breaks away from the pretense of reading dream images only in terms of individual conflict.

In our quick journey we also want to suggest reading James Hillman's work *The Dream and the Underworld* (1979), in which an extraordinary analysis of the language of myth helps us build a bridge between philosophy and analytic psychology. Hillman observes that sleep (*Hypnos*) and death (*Thanatos*) are twins for the ancient Greeks, and states that even for the Indian Atharvaveda, dreams come from the realm of Yama, the lord of the dead (p. 32). Eros, too, is a brother of Thanatos and descends from the progeny of night, Hillman again argues, quoting Freud himself from the *Introduction to Psychoanalysis*. In a similar fashion, for Hillman, dreams "are part of her great brood, which includes Old Age, Envy, Strife, Doom, Lamentation, Destiny, Deceit" (p. 32). The author also quotes Plato, who in the *Sophist* (266c) states that dream imagery is comparable to shadows, "'when dark patches interrupt the light,' leading us to see a kind of 'reflection'" (1979, p. 54). Shadows, after all, give depth to objects we see in light.

Hillman then goes on to criticizes the optimism of psychotherapies that want to illuminate dreams with daytime language and find in them a chance to keep the underworld under control.

In his fascinating work *The Oracle of Night: The History and Science of Dreaming*, neuroscientist Ribeiro traces back the history of the interest in dreams that has been common since prehistoric times to every known human culture. Ribeiro asserts that prehistoric dreams were not so dissimilar to ours because our brains have had the same structure for at least 315,000 years. Totem traces and cave drawings would represent the dream world of our ancestors. The scholar also traces a link between the beginning of the practice of ritual burials, grief for the dead, and dreams. The dead we long for appear in dreams, but dreams also contain the capacity for imagination that contributes so much to the construction of the world to come both in writing and in the creation of more articulate societies such as that of the ancient Egyptians in the Mediterranean.

Silvia Rosa (2020) argues that

> the *Oneirocritica* by Artemidorus Daldianus, a monumental work in five volumes dating back to the second century CE, is a key-text in the reading of dreams that has retained its authority until the early modern era and whose traces, in epitome, are still present in many dream interpretation texts of the popular tradition circulating to this day.
>
> (p. 22)

Freud had already cited the work of Artemidorus, although he did not dwell on the cultural history of dreams.

Rosa adds that

> in Artemidorean Greece of the second century A.D. the origin of the dream (the answer to the question *Where do dreams come from?*) was located outside of the dreamer: The dream contained a message from

the cosmos itself and the dreamer, by disposing themselves to receive it, could learn to interpret it—better if with the help of a competent diviner—and extract any useful information about themselves and their own context and, in particular, about the future, precisely in relation to their own context.

(p. 23)

So, the widespread idea was that dreams were an epiphany, a divine revelation; one need only think of the cults of Asclepius and Apollo of which we find archaeological traces in the remains of temples where people went to dream in order to receive in a dream the god's answer to their worries and anxieties. The oracle spoke in the dream and the priests interpreted it.

This view of the dream as a voice coming from outside persisted even in the Christian and medieval eras. Just think of the dream of Emperor Constantine, also pictorially represented by Piero della Francesca: In fact, Constantine recounts that it was in a dream that he was instructed to become a Christian in order to win the battle.

Then, in the Middle Ages, the idea that dreams could be of demonic origin also resurfaced, taking up and resignifying beliefs from ancient times. Even the devil was believed to be able to enter people's dreams producing the *incubus*, a term derived precisely from "incubate," which meant sexually possessing a "succubus," usually a woman.

Rosa then leads us into the thinking of later centuries by showing how naturalistic thinking about dreaming, vision, and the imagination came about, weaving in references from philosophers and cultural historians, and preparing us to understand how in the 20th century, with Freud, a scientific interest in dreaming could be found.

Recently, in his latest work, psychoanalyst Vittorio Lingiardi (2023) offered once again a historical journey that, in keeping with our own path, starts with the origin of Western thought and ranges from myth to philosophy, concluding,

I do not believe in prophecies, but I love the dreams of the ancients because they pose fundamental questions about the boundary between fantasy and reality, the inner world and the outer world. With Penelope, literature inaugurates its debt to the dream. With the Platonic myth of the cave, it makes it a philosophical object. If it was an angel who convinced Joseph to marry Mary and the flight to Egypt was guided by a dream, if Maya, the mother of Buddha, became pregnant after she dreamt of a white elephant, is not the debt of religions towards dreams also great? Freud constitutes his doctrine from the dream of Oedipus Rex; psychoanalysis owes much to the ancient world.

(p. 48)

References

Hillman, J. (1979). *The dream and the underworld.* New York: Harper & Row.
Jung, C. G. (1964). *Man and his symbols.* Garden City, N.Y: Doubleday.
Lingiardi, V. (2023). *L'ombelico del sogno: Un viaggio onirico [The navel of dreams: A dreamlike journey].* Torino: Einaudi.
Rosa, S. (2020). Il sogno nel tempo. Una prospettiva storico-culturale [Dreams over time. A cultural-historical perspective]. *Percorsi di analisi transazionale, VII*(3), 19–36.

4
OUR METHOD OF DREAM ANALYSIS IN DIFFERENT SETTINGS

Introduction

Our method is essentially to welcome a client's dream narrative as a gift that brings something new into therapy, a perspective that adds something to the usual narratives of daytime experience.

Welcoming it, without the immediate pretense of understanding its meaning, is the first duty of the analyst, and the client (as well as the group, if the telling takes place in a group setting) is also involved in this experience.

Thus, listening to a dream means accepting the gift that the most emotional and deepest part of ourselves—or someone else—makes to our rational mind, a gift that we accept as we accept the story that a child may decide to tell us. A dream, then, is heard by also opening our mind to visualize the images it evokes through words. The first thing we do is thank the dreamer for sharing their intimate experience, as we would thank a child handing us a picture and telling us about it. The child may decide to describe the drawing as a story or perhaps as multiple stories, and so a sign may become a snake, a path or a thread. The way that a drawing might reference multiple objects, multiple meanings and therefore multiple stories is identical to how dreams work. The key to approaching dreams is therefore an attitude of listening, acceptance and wonder. Only then can we ask ourselves what message does the dream convey.

The techniques we use and will illustrate below have been pioneered by us and developed by integrating several contributions that are fundamental to us. With respect to transactional analysis, we have learned much from the work of Bowater, from the co-creative method of Tudor and Summers (2000), and from Cornell's work (see also Chapter 3). In the area of psychoanalysis, we owe much to Fosshage and Resnik.

Why work on dreams in therapy

There are several reasons why we consider dreamwork useful in therapy.

First of all, many patients ask it of us, since they might be upset by the anguish and the repetition of nightmares and disturbing contents that make it hard to sleep and often come with sudden awakenings.

Second, because dreams represent a form of psychic expression that is essential for self-exploration and therefore important for the work that therapist and client conduct together to dissolve conflicts and make the intrapsychic world more orderly and familiar.

Third, because dreams help to cope with and reprocess traumatic experiences, as we now know thanks to much scientific and clinical evidence.

Finally, we work on dreams because they represent the form of knowledge and adaptation that is most useful to mediate between our deepest affective needs and the external world, with all the limitations and frustrations that this encounter constantly generates. Inside our dreams is the wisdom of the inner curator, whom we will call Protective Parent, as well as the cunning, the creativity, the life impulse of our Free Child. Inside our dreams we can discover how our life script came to be, how and why we made survival decisions that simultaneously caged and saved us from the dangers we once perceived as threatening to our lives.

How to prepare analysts and clients to dreamwork

The analyst who works with dreams is first and foremost a person who is in touch with their own inner world, and therefore who listens to, transcribes, and uses their inner dreamer to both understand themselves more and receive messages about their clinical work. We will talk more about countertransference dreams and the use of dreams in supervision later. For now, we will just say that it is necessary for the analyst to work on themselves in order to provide clients with a model to follow and an openness to the dream world.

Thus, there must be a dream transcription notebook in the analyst's room as well as in the client's room.

Today, with ever greater frequency, dreams are audio recorded and shared, perhaps through messaging apps such as WhatsApp, but we recommend transcribing them manually in a notebook. The activity of manual transcription is as important as journal writing, and the manual character of writing promotes a reactivation of memory.

We can instruct our clients to keep a notebook of dreams and thoughts regarding the analytic journey that has just begun, and to those who do not remember their dreams we can provide reassurance that after some time from the start of the analysis they will begin to remember them.

We can also invite them to focus on a short relaxation activity before falling asleep, through which they may give themselves the pre-hypnotic command to remember dreams. This method often works, as does the decision to wake up in the middle of the night at a specific time before the alarm.

In any case, the approach to each person's inner dreamer is very personal and it is best to be encouraging, but also extremely respectful of each other's differences.

There are people who also have a very vivid memory of nightmares and dreams from when they were children and are very interested in sharing these memories.

In each family, then, there are different approaches to sharing dreams: there are families where dreams are recounted over breakfast, others where dreams are just nightmares to get rid of, and others where there is no sharing at all.

Schooling, readings, comic books, fairy tales, movies, and songs also contribute to generating a specific culture that tends to accept or reject the content of dreams.

In the conversations through which we get to know our clients, it is important to learn to explore these cultures of reference, the images, sounds, and stories that have accompanied their construction of self.

We are what we eat, what we breathe, what we hear, what we see, we are the experiences that made us human, the music, the sounds, the hugs, and the wounds we have been inflicted with as well as those we have inflicted on others. Stored in our minds are so many experiences that we have categorized and that make us who we are today. In dreams, as in our adult choices of colors and clothes, what surfaces is a synthesis of many experiences and paths.

The visual dimension of the dream is a powerful vehicle of information that latches on to other sensory experiences, sometimes to sounds, smells, tastes, or tactile sensations, but, in each of these cases, there are still emotional connections that activate us by arousing fear, anxiety, terror, disgust, curiosity, and pleasure.

There are even people who find themselves being profoundly moved while dreaming, when they experience love for someone they have lost in life.

The correct attitude of the analyst is the curiosity of the explorer, the respect of the anthropologist and the person who also understands the sacredness and spirituality of the dream as a universal human experience even before a psychic experience.

In the case of dreamwork with psychotic patients, special care, and caution must be employed in relation to the fact that the boundaries between dreaming and wakefulness are blurred, and the interpretative tendency regarding any prophetic messages could further confuse the patient. Resnik, a great psychoanalyst who worked with psychotic patients, states that:

> On the other hand, in psychosis the frontier of the dream is eliminated. Everyday life, waking life, the non-dream is invaded and inhabited by dream elements: this is the alienation of "the space of life." It is a spatial phenomenological element: dream thought "in" the dream and dream thought "outside" the dream. The work of the reader, the interlocutor who reads and interprets the dream, is above all a work of

translation: the translator must know the language that he translates as well as the language into which he translates.

(Resnik, 1982, p. 74)

The different settings

Working through dreams in psychotherapy makes sense if both therapist and patient believe that it can serve the purpose of the therapy itself, a purpose that usually concerns relief from a symptom, recovery from a mental illness, or resolution of a conflict. Only rarely does the person undertaking therapy have a purely cognitive and analytic goal, and thus dreamwork can be part of the path if there is actual utility in achieving the contractual purpose of therapy.

From the point of view of knowledge, of intellectual stimulation, dreams are a fascinating entry into the emotional world of the other, but if we do not understand their usefulness for the purpose we want to achieve through the sessions, it is better to refrain from introducing their themes.

Of course, if our client brings up dreams in a spontaneous way, they should always be welcomed, because surely there is a reason for them to do so, a reason that makes this narrative a gift that needs decoding. So, we recommend that at the beginning of each treatment the therapist welcome any narrative from their client, without urging them in particular to bring up their dreams.

Only when exploring the client's sleep functioning can we ask if they remember their dreams, if they have sudden awakenings from nightmares, or if they have the perception of disturbed sleep.

This is particularly true when the client is not yet ready to work together with the therapist, but tends to approach the dream analysis like a child who wants to passively receive the unveiling of the secret about their life.

The games that might be activated, such as "Professor" (Berne, 1964, p. 151) or "Psychiatry" (Berne, 1964, p. 154) might lead us into a territory of idealization and subsequent devaluation of therapy that is not helpful at all. Berne's chapter on games in the doctor's office, in his previously cited text (Berne, 1964, p. 141) is always an excellent reference for assessing whether the technical choices we make with our clients are problem-solving oriented, or whether they are pastimes that maintain the illness, nurture the symptoms, and can lead to playing with negative scripted payoffs.

Working together

Indeed, dream analysis necessitates a willingness on the part of both therapist and client to listen to this particular and mysterious language, which is sometimes truly obscure and perturbing. If our client gives us the dream as a narrative so that as therapists, we might explain it to them and they might gain some knowledge about themselves, or resolve through our interpretation their own anxieties—as if they were standing before a magician or an oracle—it may be useful to analyze this passive attitude, and the exploration of their magical expectations may become the central theme of the session. If the therapist feels uncomfortable with the dream narrative, they must always ask themselves whether their discomfort arises from the client's magical expectation, or whether they themselves would like to feel like a magician or an oracle. In the latter case, this tells the therapist that there are obstacles to be removed before they can be two Adults working together in exploring the unconscious.

The principles

Dreams are a mental product of our client and, therefore, they alone can learn to recognize within the dream a series of messages that might be useful to them.

It is not possible to access the dream "objectively," as it was dreamed: we access only the memory of the dream reorganized by the dreamer into a story that is reconstructed with verbal language while awake.

Similarly, there is no single meaning to be attributed to dreams. However, dream imagery and its history can be traced to a plurality of meanings that might be associated with the dreamer's history and the dreamer's archaic and current emotional world.

Thus, one of the purposes of dreams is certainly to process daytime emotions, reprocess traumatic or at least undigested and unabsorbed experiences, but there is also the dreamer's intent to find options and ways of coping with a current problem.

A number of studies recently published by members of the International Association for the Study of Dreams (Bulkeley & Domhoff, 2010; Hartmann, 1998; Siegel, 2003) have found that most of our dreams are closely related to emotional concerns associated with here-and-now events and situations in our lives. In many cases, the dream brought up in therapy will therefore be implicitly or explicitly related to the object of our contract with the client (Bowater & Sherrard, 2011). In addition, dreams represent a potential resource for providing insight to client and practitioner alike, and thus become a way of bringing into the helping relationship aspects that are perhaps more difficult and hostile to present "directly."

The technique

1. The present moment

"I had a dream"; "I want to tell you a dream I had this week/last night." These are the words which often open a therapy session, especially when a person is troubled by the content of their dreams or the emotions associated with them. For the therapist, it is crucial to remain present to themselves and to the client-dreamer while welcoming their desire to bring us such a gift. For the therapist, maintaining attention to the present moment means asking, "How do I feel in listening to the dream? How does the narrator breathe, move, speak?" Listening to the voice, noticing when it is plaintive, shrill, interrupted and broken, or warm and deep is a fundamental aspect that we must not overlook, because these elements constitute the sub-symbolic language that contains the narrative. We often react unconsciously to these elements, for example, missing pieces of the story because we tend to doze off following a hypnotic voice, or because we are not captured by the story, which seems insulting or boring to us, and therefore we find ourselves fatigued. Similarly, we can observe that the client gets lost, stops, is also not interested, but seems to have the need to fill an empty space, nonetheless. In other cases, on the other hand, the client is so involved that they seem to step into a series of virtual rooms in which they move away from us and lose themselves, perhaps entering another world from which we feel excluded.

2. **Listening to the narrative**

Dream-listening is a complex endeavor. Some therapists have an advantage because they have stayed more in touch with their Child ego state and are immediately ready to tune into narrative thought and produce their own images while listening to any story. For those who are more centered on the logic of secondary thinking and the Adult ego state, the oddity of the dream can be as annoying as a conversation with a child who tries to explain their drawing in a hundred different ways, in turn annoyed that the interlocutor does not grasp the obvious in their signs.

3. **Listening repeatedly to enter the dream space**

More often than not it is useful for both the dreamer and the listener to repeat the dream narrative a second time. This practice is beneficial when approaching a different world, one where the coordinates of wakefulness and the laws of logic do not work anymore.

If the dreamer has the dream transcript, they are invited to reread it by focusing on the physical sensations and emotions they feel in rereading or retelling the dream.

If the dream is not transcribed, the listener may notice that the same story is told using new words, new emphases in the punctuation, and new details that the dreamer will say they just remembered.

4. **Entering emotions evoked by dream imagery**

If the atmosphere of the conversation has already become "dreamlike," that is, suggestive and imaginative, it becomes easy to invite the dreamer to listen to the emotions they feel in the present.

One might ask if the emotions are the same as those they remember feeling during the dream or upon waking, and might suggest taking note of the concordances or differences. If the emotions are the same, one might invite the dreamer to perceive them with greater intensity. One way to help them is, for example, to re-describe the dream scenario using the same words they used (if needed the analyst can take notes while listening to a dream) and observe what happens to the dreamer during this immersion. The process of emotional immersion is very useful for people who have trouble recognizing their own emotional state, and can become an opportunity for a small emotional literacy exercise following the dreamwork. It does not hurt to feel anxiety or to reexperience the distress of the dream; if anything, it aids the dreamer in finding an opportunity to get in touch with and express an up until that point unexpressed intrapsychic part.

5. **Exploring with the dreamer**

We stand by the dreamer in the exploration of their fears or anxieties, and therefore, maintaining an exploratory attitude means walking hand in hand within their inner world.

Exploring means proceeding slowly, following the breath, the gaze, and the bodily tensions of the dreamer, who may be sweating, contracting, squinting and looking beyond, and still coming to terms with unknown dimensions of their self that may perturb them.

It is like being in the company of a child while they watch a scary movie or listen to a story or play with their monsters. One has to stay close by, sometimes a step behind, to allow the dreamer to move forward and find a passage first.

6. **Tracing emotions back to current experiences**

The next order of business is to explore the meanings that the newly discovered emotions hold for the dreamer at that moment in time, at that stage of their life and therapy.

The dream has arrived now, so if there are messages to be heard, deciphered, and understood, we assume that such messages must be useful for the present and the future.

Retracing dreamwork to transference and all the other themes discussed in therapy—if significant at that time—is a part of the work that is done by going back to the language of the Adult.

A powerful experience has just been shared with us, and we can use it to shed light on an open question we have been working on for some time.

Usually, this happens spontaneously, without the need for special prompting, and if it does not happen it is best that the therapist not force this process.

One can say: "Let's stop here, we will figure out later whether this dream of yours can be useful to us, but right now we cannot go any further."

7. Tracing imagery and story back to the dreamer's other narratives

If, on the other hand, we have other dreams or narratives from the dreamer that are easily traceable to the themes of the new dream, then it is appropriate to explore what emerges from their "putting the pieces together" together with the client. Sometimes it is extraordinary to observe how the latest dream may add clarifying pieces to the mysterious puzzle we are putting together.

8. Communicating the suggestions picked up by the listener-analyst

During the above work of reconnection, the analyst may choose to tell the dreamer what in their stories struck or made an impression on them, always taking great care to specify that what they picked up may also be something of their own and that has perhaps nothing to do with the client.

9. If in group, invite group members to enter the dream space with their own emotions

Various activities can be done in a group setting to use dreamwork as a stimulus for the group itself, but we will further discuss this in the chapter devoted to groups. Thinking about the usefulness of having a listening group, for the dreamer, the therapist can engage the group in two different moments: when exploring the emotions elicited by the dream (in step 5) and when working on tracing back (in step seven). A syntonized group is an excellent amplifier of the oneiric atmosphere and can be of great help, especially for people who are more inhibited and struggling with the recognition of their emotions.

10. Stop at the moment that most intrigues us or that is most charged with emotional experience

Dreams can be a treasure chest of riches, a container of emotions as well as options for dealing with problems and suggestions from the inner curator, and therefore we may become stunned or overwhelmed by an excess of references. There is no point in over-analyzing and giving too many messages to the dreamer. After a while we might get lost and end up intellectualizing and ruining valuable work.

As therapists, we must always remember that we need to put forward only stimuli that can be received, understood and digested by our client in the present moment of the session. If, complacent with our findings, we decide to talk too much, or offer too many avenues, we will end up like those hosts who go so far as to make their guests vomit their dinner because of an excess of food that cannot be refused. The pleasure of a good dinner is to get up feeling gratified, joyful and light, able to take a walk, have a conversation and maybe get a good night's sleep.

11. **Choose the level of dream analysis that meets the client's need in the here-and-now**

As mentioned earlier, bringing a dream into therapy is the client's choice, perhaps encouraged by a therapist who likes to work on dreams. This exchange, therefore, contains elements of transference, which we will explore in the relevant chapter. In any case, we need to take into account the relational context in which the dream is brought up: Are we at an early stage where the person wants to make themselves known? Do we have a client who wants to surprise the therapist, to frighten them or please them? Are we in an established alliance stage where we are working together? Or in a stage of reprocessing past traumas? Or are we toward the end of the journey, when themes of separation and grief tend to emerge?

Our suggestion to therapists is that they frame the offering of the dream within an understanding of the current stage of therapy and pre-established goals, so as to lead the client toward the resolution of their conflicts and symptoms.

In Chapter 5 we shall describe how dreams may be used in an individual psychotherapy setting, while Chapter 11 will take a closer look at how to deal with them in a group setting. We will also devote several chapters (6 to 9) to the kind of dream content that is typical of different moments in psychotherapeutic work.

An example of different ways of dealing with the same dream

We now present a dream that was treated in two different ways by analyst and client within the frame of a recorded didactic simulation. The purpose of the "double simulation" is to emphasize, for educational purposes, the possible differences and declinations in how to deal with a dream within a helping relationship aimed at producing real changes toward the client's well-being. Specifically, we will explore here two modes of intervention: In the first part, we will describe a cognitive approach aimed at promoting client empowerment and, in the second, an exploratory approach aimed at promoting a deeper knowledge of the client's self and their shadow-parts.

In regards to the *difference* in how dreams are treated with respect to the two agreed-upon goals, it is important to point out that the practitioner, in the case of cognitive work, always has a well-defined contract with the client, whether it be related to identifying a problem, gaining awareness about a problem or consolidating a change that is taking place in the here-and-now. In this context, dreamwork is brought back by the practitioner to the issues being discussed. *What does our contract entail? What are we talking about? Does this dream you have brought me have anything to do with the issue at hand? May I remind you that you are bringing it to me in a context where you and I are working on a predefined contract of this kind?*

Therefore, in this case, it is good to keep in mind the contractual dimension of one's work, and invite the client to focus on the relationship between their narrative and the contract in place. It is very likely that this connection exists: sometimes it is very clear and explicit, other times it has to be looked for, since it is less obvious, and that can be the object of the work.

Supportive and empowerment work in the first simulation

In the case addressed in the first simulation, the connection is evident: we have a client whose therapeutic contract aims at providing her with the necessary support to deal with a job change, the consolidation of new choices, and all the anxiety that these entail; at the same time, the dream speaks of a new house purchased by some unknown person. The clinician picks up on the possible presence of script elements in the dream, but does *not* start working on such elements immediately.

Here, the practitioner focused purposedly on two aspects, namely:

- Clearly identifying the initial anxiety;
- Underscoring the positive emotion tied to an open attitude toward all new things (emotion that is free from the script)

All this without specifically touching on archaic and scripted aspects, on which incidentally the dream invited to dwell. The practitioner may also have picked up on these relevant aspects concerning the past (the client being "told" by *who knows who* that that is her house, which she bought but did not choose). Working on this first part could have led toward still confusing aspects within the client's Child. But all this is not the subject of the contract, so it is left out of the session's work.

Instead, the therapist stays within the framework of the contract, which means that yes, it is certainly useful to show the discomfort, the restlessness and the fear of the new, to give a more specific name to the restlessness and anxiety expressed at the beginning, but it is also important to reinforce the fact that her fear did not prevent the client from making the changes she set out to make, and she is successfully increasing the free space available to her. Thus, the therapist moves toward empowering the client's Free Child and Adult. And indeed, what the client asked of the clinician was to "support" her in this phase of change. As a matter of fact, this is an acceptable and valid contract, and consists precisely in empowering certain parts and certain resources of the client.

If, for example, after buying the new house, the client had gone back to live in the old one with a major sense of guilt, at that point the practitioner could have intervened by suggesting the presence, in this behavior, of archaic conflict elements, such as to recommend further work in a different setting.

So the path described above, in relation to this dream, can end in two ways:

1. the practitioner "crystallizes" the fact that the client's fear has not been blocking her and that she is able to live her new life, although elements of "confusion" are still present at a deep level;
2. if, on the other hand, the client's behavior goes in the direction of boycotting her current life because "the leash is short" and she feels she has to go back (e.g., she has panic attacks or similar manifestations every time she enters the new house and, as a result, has to go back to sleep in the old house), the practitioner is tasked with leading the client toward a new contract that has psychodynamic work as its goal.

First simulation: *The dream about Francesca's house.*

Let us imagine that the client, after several meetings, comes to the session recounting a dream ...

Francesca (client)*: I dream of a house on the hills. I know this hill very well, it's the one where I've always lived and where two couples of my long-time friends live now. I dream that I am on this hill and I spot this house, and I am told, by someone I cannot identify, that that house is the house I just bought. So, I find out that I also live on this hill and I remember looking out the window and seeing only the green mountains and all the other hills.*

I see this house and I am amazed at how big it is. It doesn't match in every way the house I would have wanted, which is actually the one I chose in my life, a more modern one. But I dream of discovering this house, exploring it, and being amazed at how beautiful it is, how bright, and how much I like it even if it doesn't match my expectations. Not only that, I enjoy discovering that every time I look there is something more than what I thought, like one more room, and then behind a door I discover that there is a small opening that leads to another unexpected space.

With respect to this indefiniteness, this lack of clear boundaries, I remember that in the dream I take great pleasure in exploring and seeing that there are other walls where I can put paintings, other spaces where I can arrange my things. So, the dream closes with this very feeling of pleasure in imagining myself filling all these nooks and crannies, these walls. The feeling that I will have a lot more time to do it, so it won't all end right away, since for example, I don't have just one wall available to put a painting. And that's where the dream ends.

Emanuela (analyst): *You're smiling while you bring me this dream. How did you feel when you woke up?*

Francesca: *I woke up with this feeling of pleasure in the discovery, so a pleasant feeling. And I am still experiencing it.*

Emanuela: *So, this smile of yours matches precisely the pleasure you felt in waking up and the pleasure you felt in narrating the dream, because you got back in touch with it by telling it to me.*

Francesca*: I liked narrating it. But it didn't feel this way from the start. The beginning of the dream was ... maybe unsettling, since I found myself in a situation that was not what I imagined for myself. So there was definitely an evolution of sorts, an emotional one even, within the dream itself, and then the conclusion kind of lingered with me, since I was discovering something I wasn't expecting and that actually was becoming something enjoyable.*

Emanuela*: I was wondering, since you decided to tell me the dream, if it also had something to do with the reason why you came to me in the first place. You told me you wanted to reflect on the changes that are happening in your life at the moment.*

Francesca: *Now that you mention it, on a small scale the dream represents what I'm experiencing in my life, in general, so I find the same changes in my job, in the city where I live, all the changes that I was initially attracted to but also worried by. And that's why I needed some support. There was a moment, at some point, where I didn't want these changes any longer, and I almost rejected them, like in the very beginning of the dream I rejected the house.*

Emanuela*: I found it very interesting that your dream portrayed the initial trouble you came to me with, and the fact that you're experiencing conflict regarding some of the changes you're making to your life. So, it's as if the dream is using metaphors to tell us, in the first part, what are these conflicting feelings that you're asking support for, while the last part of the dream might be telling you that you found an answer to your inner conflict, to your disorientation. Is that so?*

Francesca*: Yes, it is. While you were speaking I was thinking that maybe rather than unsettlement it is fear of the unknown.*

Emanuela: *The dream clarified what was the initial conflict.*

Francesca*: I also realized that this fear is the same I've been feeling in my real life, and that I always thought was caused by small issues regarding an unstable job, the inability of getting closure on what was my life before. But maybe in reality it was a fear of walls I didn't know how to fill, of something I didn't know. Now I'm in a new stage of my life, and all thanks to what came after, when I realized that I wasn't losing anything, but in fact I was gaining something, like this house which gives me new things to find each time. I was also thinking that I've always had a strong need to* control everything around me, but I don't know if this has anything at all to do with the dream.

Emanuela: *What I'm getting from it, is the definition of an initial situation of discomfort which looks very similar to the one you found yourself in when we met. You were feeling a discomfort, a kind of unsettlement, because you were doing many things, some belonging to your old world and some to your new world, and this created a conflict, between your old city and your new city, your old life and your new life, buying a house/not buying a house. Afterwards, during our treatment, you actually implemented those changes and now, about this feeling of unsettlement, you say: "I realize that it was fear of the unknown, and that it has to do with several things in me." In any case, what I saw and I accompanied you in seeing is that this unsettlement which you're now identifying as fear, didn't actually block you in any way. You changed what you needed to change and now you've got more space for yourself, like in the house of your dream. In order to withstand change, the new, the empty wall becomes not just something that scares you but also an opportunity.*

Francesca: *Then maybe what you're describing is exactly the control I was talking about earlier, that I thought I had and that helped me overcome fear. While in this exploration of the house, I'm letting myself go a little, which is also the same thing I've been doing in my life, as far as experiences go. Things are not going exactly as I expected, but that is okay. I've accepted it.*

Emanuela: *You cannot control change: Sometimes it comes in the form of surprises, and these might also be enjoyable ones. To describe it in AT terms, we would say that perhaps the dream is a rundown of your therapeutic journey. It's telling us that we reached the end of it. In the dream I'm seeing a Little Professor, that is, an Adult to your Child that built this story, and this Little Professor is telling me that you went from a situation of general unsettlement to one of pleasant surprise. So, then, you're not just scared that not everything can be controlled or controllable in your life, but in fact you're tolerating that lack of control, and you also find interest and curiosity in the fact that there are still rooms to discover and walls to fill. Given all this, I think that what the dream is telling us is that your journey with me is coming to an end, since you appear to no longer need me and you have rekindled inside you the will to explore the world. And even if sometimes you feel scared, or uncomfortable, or unsettled, you're still more curious than scared, and fear and curiosity can go hand in hand: They are the energy of the explorer as well as their caution, because we all bring some degree of fear with us when we enter a new territory. That's quite inevitable. The important thing is that it doesn't stop you from doing what you want to do.*

Francesca: *No, I don't feel like there's something blocking me from this change. And while you were talking I felt a little sad imagining something* ending, like our sessions, but I also told myself, maybe confirming that what you're saying is true, that maybe there is going to be a picture of our sessions up on one of those walls. So I can take this experience with me.

Emanuela: To sum up, I believe that, as far as the Adult is concerned, you have actually implemented a series of concrete behavioral changes, you moved from one city to another, to one job to another, and you consolidated some new experiences.

I would say that perhaps there was a conflict, when we first met, between Parent and Child, because it was as if your inner Parent was always telling you "Be careful" because you didn't know, you had no control, and that was an element that, from the Child's perspective, caused some unsettlement in you. Despite this theme of worry within the Parent–Child dynamic, you did do many new things, you didn't let yourself be stopped in your behavior, and as a result your life gained many new rooms, a new house even, and new experiences. And the dream is telling us that you didn't just do these things, but that more rooms are popping up inside you, more walls, and the fact that not all of them are full isn't something unpleasant, but an opportunity. So we can end this leaving some walls blank.

The explorative-psychodynamic work in the second simulation

Given the fact that the dream is the same as the one in the first simulation, the object of the work, in this case, is a contract related to the analysis of the script, and therefore not solely focused on "sustaining the current change," but including work on the emotional aspects of the change. In this case, the focus of dream analysis will be directed toward connecting old dream contents and processes with new ones.

It is thus a work that, from an analytic point of view, amplifies the themes related to the archaic dimension of the dream: the way in which the script conflict is represented.

The main questions that the therapist asks, in this context, are: How is the script conflict represented in the dream? What is the strategy the client is adopting to cope with this conflict?

In this sense, the dream contains several relevant elements. These appear, in particular, in the first scene, which tells us about the script strategies used in the operation of "unbinding from home." In the final scene, we see an increase in options, in opportunities, resulting from further exploration.

The second half of the dream undoubtedly speaks of the psychotherapy journey. This is suggested to us by the continuous discovery of room after room, of "rooms within rooms," a dimension of further deepening that actually corresponds to what the client is doing in the present: seeking her own freedom not so much in a "mileage definition" of distance as in an emotional *permission* related to defining herself in a different way from the "conforming way" of the beginning. So, the message is something along the lines of "let's find out what's inside me."

At this point, endless—or at least many—possibilities for emotional exploration open up. The therapist's choice was to follow the patient into the emotion that is evoked by the sadness of the blank wall.

It would have been possible to follow other paths. From the point of view of psychodynamic work, emotional redecision won't be able to take place if the client is unable to tolerate the "emptiness," as in the case of the wall yet to be filled. In this sense, it is important that the therapist does not reproduce, in the healing relationship, a "leash" dimension, risking guiding the client too rigidly in the exploration of the dream.

Thus, the client makes emotional contact with one specific emotion among many, the same one stemming by the impact with the blank wall. The therapist seizes the opportunity and stops there. Once there, we enter an extremely delicate space in which the therapist must accompany the client to explore her old and new emotions with great respect. The element that is going to be empowered here is one that finally allows the client to get to follow her own "leads," to choose her own rooms, to be with her own blank walls, to try hanging pictures on her own walls and feeling that she's increasing her own possibility of choice.

To summarize, in this kind of work there are several simultaneous levels that require to be interwoven:

- the first is the content level: the script content and the new content, both to be analyzed;
- the second is that of script emotions, archaic emotions, and current emotions;
- the third is that of emotions related to transference, that is, the inherent dimension of "I'm the one you're telling this story to," which also includes the modeling of a new, restorative Parent, and which ensures that such a client does not risk approaching therapy from an attitude of adaptation.

Regarding the specific emotions brought into the session by the client, one dimension to work on may be the one related to the fact that the emotion of sadness evoked by the empty wall is, precisely, an *ancient* emotion. At that point, the client is back in the Child, and we can work with this, even at the level of the transference dimension: the client feels this emotion and reports it to the therapist; the therapist lets her off the hook, remaining present. In other words, the therapist stays with the client in a moment when the latter is experiencing loneliness: This already means that she is no longer alone. Sharing this intimacy without the erasure of sadness means being able to narrate sadness. The therapist might then work on this level, exploring the client's emotions in the face of this reality, asking her how she feels in the new closeness with her, exploring the transference dimension. This moment of transition, of unblocking, can be defined as *a moment of clarification and change (insight)*.

Second simulation of the same dream analysis: Francesca's house

Francesca is in her second year of individual psychotherapy and brought as the object of the therapeutic contract a desire to change many things in her life in which she felt stuck: she wanted to find a new job, move to another city, and free herself from her family of origin, defining and separating herself from that context. She made many behavioral changes during the first year of therapy; she was able to do the things she wanted to do (i.e., move to a different city, find another job) and even bought a house.

Right now we are also working on the emotional aspects and conflicts with respect to the choices she has made and is making. In this context Francesca recounts her dream.

Francesca (client): *Last night I had a very vivid dream. I find myself in a country house that is clearly on the hills around my childhood home, in which I lived most of my life before moving away. It's a hill I know intimately, since two couples of my long-time friends chose to live there. I find myself in this house that someone (I don't know who) tells me is the house I just bought. So I find myself living there.*

Emanuela: *So the house in the dream is on a hill near your family of origin, but it's not the house you grew up in. And someone inside the dream tells you that you just bought this house, but you cannot see this person and you don't know who it is.*

Francesca: *Somebody told me I bought it and I'm seeing it for the first time. I recognize the familiar hills. I know, with respect to these hills, where my childhood home is, but I do not know this house. I open the door and it's a beautiful house. It's not the house I dream for myself, but it's a wooden house, very bright, and I start exploring it. I wander around the rooms and even if at first I feel some hesitation—since this is supposed to be my home, I'm worried I'm going to find myself in a place I don't like—but I discover that this exploration is actually a pleasant experience. Not only that, but something else happens: at some point, the house, which looks pretty definite, starts offering me new spaces, like when I discover an opening behind a door which leads to another room, and so I continue this exploration with curiosity and pleasure.*

Where I think there's a wall I find a door instead, a door that leads to yet another room, so the house is even bigger than what I believed it to be in the beginning. The dream ends while I'm thinking: "Will I have enough time to fill this house? There's so much space, so it's going to take a while," but I mean it in a positive way, as if I "have many chances" to put myself in it before it becomes something more definite and complete.

Emanuela: How did you feel while you were dreaming? What kind of emotions accompanied this story?

Francesca: Several ones. In the beginning I was reassured by the soft green hills, the familiar scenery. So I felt calm, peaceful. But this shadowy figure who tells me "This is your house" is unsettling to me, because then I feel like I have to accept that this is my house. I remember feeling troubled by the fact that I was not the one choosing this house, but that someone else was choosing it for me. So, I enter this house I don't know, and I'm worried and unsettled while I start wandering around the rooms of a place that, at the moment, I don't feel belongs to me.

Emanuela: Let's take a closer look at the first part of the dream. There are two very different emotions, since you're saying you feel calm and peaceful when looking at the hills, but then you feel unsettled when someone tells you that the house in front of you is actually yours, that you bought it, but you didn't choose it. Does this contrast say something about you?

Francesca: A few things come to mind: the first is the need for peace, quiet and safety which always kept me on the familiar hills, one of the reasons why I'm here with you. This peace [...] it's like there's a part of me that finds peace in the known. So the unsettled feeling is tied to the exploration of something I don't know, a house I don't know. But it might be due to the fact that somebody else decides for me in which house I should live and I can only adapt to what's being decided for me.

Emanuela: Do you think this is another thing that says something about you? The fact that somebody else is choosing this house for you?

Francesca: Yes, actually, it makes me think of me adapting to something I've always been subjected to: It was very difficult for me to get myself out of this role of the adapted Child and finally want to choose something for myself. It's as if the dream represented the part of me that finds peace but also uneasiness in the familiar.

Emanuela: The first scene is telling us something very insightful. It struck me how the hills are familiar to you, but we cannot see your childhood home, while we can see your friends' houses and another house that somebody tells you you bought, even if you didn't know you bought it. I think that it's as if this is your first attempt at getting away from your family, but you're not going very far. It reminds me of your first job, the friends you had there, as if it was for all intents and purposes a "I'm leaving my family but I'm staying here."

Francesca: When I woke up, I remember thinking: "I would never live there." Also, ever since I was a child, I've always had this idea that I would leave one day, and so I fantasized about having the freedom I never actually allowed myself in my everyday life. My fantasy did not go beyond those hills. So what I felt was something more than just unsettlement—maybe the distance from my parent's house, but actually it wasn't even that strong.

Emanuela: Thinking back to all the issues you brought into therapy, I believe that when we met you were in the first part of the dream. You worked, you already had an adult life of your own, but you still felt the pressure of having to adopt a conformist lifestyle, also when comparing yourself to your friends. Everyone was getting married, having kids, and everyone was still together with their first partners. You felt pressured to enter in an Adult role that was defined by others and not yourself.

Francesca: And I still don't want it.

Emanuela: For example, one of the things I noticed while you were telling me about the dream today—but also, in general, you often adopt these kind of body movements—is that you were shaking your head a lot, as if saying "No," while toward the end of the dream you were often nodding "Yes."

Francesca: Nice. I didn't even notice it.

Emanuela: This is something I found happening at times also in your narration. It's as if inside you there's a strong conflict between feeling pressured into stepping in the role of the Adult as defined by others, a way to be an Adult that is structured by others, on the familiar hill; so being an Adult in a "standard" way, at least according to the social expectations of your environment ...

Francesca: Standard, yes, and always under my mother's influence.

Emanuela: It seems to me a very good realization to have, in the first scene of the dream. So, what happens later in the dream is a process of inner discovery, an exploration of rooms, openings; and instead of leaving the hills you enter the house and you discover so many new inner dimensions. Does this ring any bells?

Francesca: While you were talking, I felt a sigh of relief coming up, especially at the idea of the possibilities. This is what makes me breathe more easily. This need of mine not to stop; I don't want to stop, I need to go beyond, to discover, to feel alive. If I stopped, I'd feel how my mother always wanted me to be.

Emanuela: This thing about rooms might have something to do with your therapeutic journey, your inner journey. Many rooms are being discovered, in a dimension where it's not their size that gives you a sense of autonomy, but the fact that you're the protagonist of every opening and closing of the rooms, of filling in or tolerating the blank, empty walls. It's an inner journey, so it doesn't matter how many miles you're putting in between you and your old world.

Francesca: When you were talking about the blank walls I also thought about something else: this intense need I feel to fill up my life with genuine connection, which maybe will be my next goal in therapy, in relation to change, unbinding, the roles [...] but there's something more here. Maybe

when you talked about tolerating the emptiness I thought about loneliness and my wish to build true, intimate connections with people.
Emanuela: *What are you feeling now, saying these words?*
Francesca: *When you talked about emptiness I felt sad because of the loneliness I had felt in the past, And by not leaving and adapting to what others wanted of me I kind of covered up this loneliness. So getting away from my family actually made me more free and I don't feel lonely anymore. I tolerate these empty walls but I also want someone to be closer with, without leashes, with only the pleasure of being together between us. So, sadness, but at the same time desire and trust.*
Emanuela: *On this, your body also tends to say "Yes," so I believe we're on the right track. Your dream is telling us that going through this sadness and loneliness defines you as a free person [...] that is, a separate person [...]*
Francesca: *I feel some kind of warmth in my chest, hearing you say that.*

Comparison and summary of the two simulations

Let us now return to the comparison between the two sessions. Comparing them, it is interesting to note that in the first one, at the end of the client's account of the dream, the practitioner questions her about her emotions with the following words: "You're smiling while you bring me this dream. How did you feel when you woke up?" To which the client replies that she woke up with a pleasant feeling, which still lasts. The "emotional check-in" at the end of the first session thus seems to want to bring out, from the outset, a different emotion than in the second session (serenity and smile from overcoming the difficulties of change in the first case, sadness from the "blank, empty wall" in the second).

We can ask ourselves to what extent the first mode of work—which does not access the exploration of the archaic content and emotions related to the "blank wall"—can nevertheless succeed in "preserving" this sadness without the risk of erasing it by superimposing on it the "smile" related to the success of the client's resource-strengthening intervention.

To understand this, it is useful to explore the different levels of intervention on which are focused the two contracts.

In her here-and-now the client actually feels well, because the promoted change has actually taken place. In the second case, too, the well-being associated with this achieved goal is clearly discernible. In the second simulation, however, at the same time, an ancient loneliness and sadness has been accessed. Therefore, the client's well-being in the present does not represent the erasure of a *present* sadness. "Today," the client is well, but, if we investigate further, "underneath," what remains is an ancient sadness that the helping relationship is able to bring out.

At the same time, as shown in the two examples above, the possibility of a multiplicity of readings of dream analysis also well illustrates the distance that, to date, has been created, even at the theoretical level, from the orthodox psychoanalytic interpretation originally theorized by Freud. Indeed, this new perspective, different from the Freudian approach, does not seem to contemplate a single, right, true, objective interpretation of the dream. Here we have (at least) two ways, two readings, and also two different emotional outcomes, which in turn lead to two ways of leaving each other at the end of the session, that are substantially different, relationally speaking, although both "true."

The specificities of the two types of intervention also find an effective explication in the goal of the contract and treatment planning. The starting questions are:

1. What is the client asking for?
2. What is best for the client?
3. What is the practitioner's role in this specific helping relationship?

There are times in life when it is more appropriate to opt for one type of intervention over another.

In this sense, we can end by saying that an ethical approach to the helping relationship requires the practitioner to prioritize what, at any given moment, a person needs in order to cope with life: a path to empowerment? An exploration of archaic experiences? A coach to help them "do" things? A counselor to help them clear their head? Or a psychotherapist to help them remove ancient obstacles?

References

Berne, E. (1964). *Games people play: The psychology of human relationships*. New York: Grove Press.

Bowater, M., & Sherrard, E. (2011). Ethical issues for transactional analysis practitioners doing dreamwork. *Transactional Analysis Journal, 41*(2), 179–185. https://doi.org/10.1177/036215371104100215

Bulkeley, K., & Domhoff, G. W. (2010). Detecting meaning in dream reports. *Dreaming, 20*(2), 77–95. https://doi.org/10.1037/a0019773

Hartmann, E. (1998). *Dreams and nightmares: The new theory on the origin and meaning of dreams*. New York: Plenum Trade. https://doi.org/10.1177/036215378001000306

Resnik, S. (1982). *The theatre of dream*. London: Tavistock Publications.

Siegel, A. (2003). *Dream wisdom: Uncovering life's answers in your dreams*. Berkeley: Celestial Arts.

Summers, G., & Tudor, K. (2000). Co-creative transactional analysis. *Transactional Analysis Journal, 30*(1), 23–40. https://doi.org/10.1177/036215370003000104

5
DREAMS IN INDIVIDUAL PSYCHOTHERAPY

Introduction

Among the most accredited and recent theories on the functions of dreaming generated in the field of neuroscience, one of the most extraordinary, in our opinion, is that which considers dream production as a function of the human mind aimed at promoting negotiation with people of one's affective world. We can define Antti Revonsuo's Social Simulation Theory (SST) as a theory consistent with the relational paradigm that has been established in psychoanalysis since the 1980s and that today guides theory and research in psychotherapy across various theoretical models. To define this paradigm with a slogan, we borrow the words of philosopher Martin Buber (1923/1937) who in his work entitled *I and Thou* declared: "In the beginning is relation" (p. 18). Infant research and particularly the groundbreaking studies of Daniel Stern (1985) have shown that the child is relationally competent from birth. Not only that: The self emerges from the internalization of the relationship with the caregiver. We become who we are after internalizing interactions with others; we are our relational history. First comes the *we* and then the I.

Berne's ego states model

With his transactional analysis, Eric Berne can rightfully claim a spot among the "relational" theories, not because there has been a *relational turn* within this theory (Lingiardi et al., 2011), but because it was *born* relational. By defining ego states as portions of the self, states of mind, Berne describes a tripartite model of personality in which one part of the self consists precisely of the Other within us. Berne calls this part Parent, which stands for the set of ego states that arise from the introjection of the child's affectively significant figures, or the attachment figures, to speak plainly. However, the Parent does not contain merely the attachment figures in one's family context. It contains the entire social, cultural, economic, and political world within which we have been immersed since birth, which has more or less consciously influenced us and whose impact cannot be overlooked, as Sedgwick points out in his recent book *Contextual Transactional Analysis* (2020). In order to explain this mechanism of introjection, the author observes that: "Within transactional analysis our favored way of explaining how the world comes to be part of us is to talk about Parent ego-states" (2020, p. 63). The other two parts that make up the personality according to Berne are the Adult and the Child. Each represents a set of states of mind complete with their own, mutually consistent emotions, thoughts, and patterns of behavior. Each represents a uniform pattern of experience, a way of manifesting a part of the personality at a given time. Pertaining to the Child are emotions, thoughts, and mannerisms peculiar to a person's childhood. What we have been, our emotional and most important experiences remain forever imprinted within us, whether we have conscious memory of them or not, since they belong to the domain of implicit memory. The third component of personality identified by Berne is the Adult. The result of smooth emotional evolution, it is the part of us that is completed by overcoming the Oedipus complex, which in psychoanalytic language represents the internalization of limitation, the awareness of one's finitude, and the renunciation of childhood omnipotence. Therefore, the Adult is that part of the mature ego that is able to deal autonomously with the present, and the tasks of daily life, being aware of its own resources and shortcomings. For a person to function healthily it is necessary for the Adult to be predominant, to "hold the executive energy," to use a Bernian metaphor, or to remain firmly at the helm, using another metaphor borrowed from the nautical world. This way, the person does not live reproducing someone else's life—domain of the P, or Parent—nor do they live stuck in the past, endlessly reproducing ancient object-relational patterns—domain of the C, or Child. In a functioning personality there are bridges between ego states, and the Adult is integrated with the other parts (Trautmann & Erskine, 1981), engaging in fruitful dialogue with Parent and Child, and synthesizing from this relationship a functional response to the environment, making decisions, solving problems. As Lingiardi (2019) argues, "Inner coexistence asks us to stand in between spaces and cross bridges built, more or less laboriously, in the archipelago of our identity"[1] (p. 10). He continues: "In short, we are made up of many. We start here, then, from the idea that good psychic functioning is the result of the encounter, soft or heated, never opportunistic, of multiple states of the self"[2] (p. 10). Therefore, to have a good psychic balance means to be composite and complex, where "complexity" etymologically indicates the coexistence of multiple parts. Consequently, the psychopathology of personality can be read as the lack of dialogue, of bridges, as Bromberg (2006) puts it, between the different components of the self. Developmental traumas result in cracks on the ground of identity: the deeper and earlier the emotional

---

1 My translation.
2 My translation.

breach is, the deeper the cracks will be. Berne (1961) uses the metaphor of the stack of coins to explain the relationship between traumatic experiences and personological frailty: If the defective coin, that is, the negative traumatic experience, stands at the base, even if the other coins added on top are "good," the stack that results will be highly unstable or, even worse, fall. Similarly, a singular very defective coin that is added to many other "good" coins will cause all the coins on top of it to fall over. The unstable coin stack, or even the one that falls over, is for Berne the more or less severely disturbed personality structure. Fragmentation, splitting, and dissociation are defense mechanisms that characterize the victims of severe early relational trauma: in order for the coin stack not to collapse in on itself, that is, in order to survive, parts of the ego states, or even worse, *entire* ego states, are disavowed, stripped of their power and removed from consciousness. As we shall see later, this mechanism of exclusion can be crystallized, as in the case of dissociation, or intermittent, as in the case of splitting. What remains constant is the incommunicability between the different components of the self, the absence of integrated dialogue between Parent, Adult, and Child.

The psychopathology of ego states

To explain psychopathology, Berne considers the boundaries between ego states. If the boundaries are weak, the Adult will be contaminated by Parent and Child. This means that the Parent's prejudices and rigid frames of reference might influence the secular and rational processing of information coming from external reality, leading the self to incongruous and exaggerated emotional reactions peculiar to the Child, such as irrational fears or phobias. An example of this double contamination of the Adult by Parent and Child might be the anxiety experienced by a young woman, who grew up with the parental message that the world is a dangerous place, whenever she is about to board a plane for a trip abroad with friends. However, if the boundaries are too rigid, there is no dialogue between the various parts of the self. In this case, as we saw above, some parts of the ego states may be excluded in favor of others. A child's psychological development proceeding without major hiccups—meaning that is characterized by relational experiences with caregivers made up of a healthy oscillation between moments of syntonization, rupture and subsequent repair—leads to the construction of a good internal balance: Boundaries between ego states are well defined and the Adult, dialoguing with Parent and Child, remains more or less firmly at the helm of personality. On the contrary, we can speak of early relational trauma in cases where repeated relational ruptures have not been repaired, and because of them the child has experiences that are excessively painful with respect to their ability to process them. These experiences can go from neglect, a significant loss of reference figures, up to actual abuse (Beebe & Lachman, 1988, 2005). Berne (1972) argues that, as a result of these experiences of micro- and macro-trauma, the child will move through the world avoiding with all their might any contact with parts of themselves and relational situations that would force them to feel pain again. However, when left unsatisfied, the need for love, support, and trust does not disappear even if it seems so, rather it becomes fixed, Berne says, stuck inside the Child ego state, like a ghost that refuses to leave the living in peace until it takes care of its unfinished business. This survival mechanism takes the name of *life script* and it is the most important cause, according to Berne, of an unconscious idiosyncrasy to change:

> If I have learned that I will be fine by giving up parts of myself—those parts that would express forbidden needs—then I will not change my ways, even at the cost of experiencing major limitations, having a distorted view of myself and others or manifesting overt symptomatology of mind and body.

Giving up parts of oneself is the price to be paid for survival. The more severe and early the traumatic experiences the greater and more significant will be the parts of the ego states that become fixed, split, or dissociated. The life script will consequently be characterized by more or less defensively organized life plans, with varying levels of autonomy and integration among the multitude of ego states making up the personality.

Dreams as the ego states' talking parts

In the spring of 2020, when lockdown had just been declared in Italy due to the coronavirus pandemic, we were following our patients remotely. During one of such sessions, Mario, a middle-aged man with anxiety depressive disorder, appeared calm and thoughtful as he explained to me that he felt perfectly able to cope with the emergency situation with a good amount of common sense—yes, sure, he felt an understandable uncertainty about the future, a hint of worry, but nothing more. Toward the end of our meeting, he tells me that a few days earlier he had a nightmare that upset him. Some aliens sneaked into his house in the middle of the night—not by forcing the door as any burglars would do, but by going through the walls—before approaching his bed threateningly as black shadows. He woke up suddenly, distressed. The dream analysis reveals that the dreamer is the frightened Child: a different psychic reality, entirely separate from the vigilant Adult sitting in front of me. Freud claims that when the dreaming is done by a Child ego state, dreams show us recovering our lost omnipotence and realizing desires, while in nightmares we encounter monsters, aliens, and witches, or fall victim to natural disasters that make us feel small and powerless. In this case the dream is an expression of the part, or parts, of us that we cannot contact while awake. If the psychic reality contacted during the day is that of the Frightened Child, it is more likely that the dreamer is a problem solver, such as the Adult, or a wise Parent showing the way, as in dreams in which angels, deceased parental figures, or seers and prophets appear. The material of which dreams are made of is largely composed of metaphors, and while some of them are shared culturally, the meanings they convey are multiple and personal. For example, a classic dream imagery in psychotherapy is the journey. But which scenario, which fellowship—sometimes the therapist is there—or which vehicle is used to travel depends on the imagination and imagery of the dreamer's mind: Cars, cruise ships, airplanes, spacecraft are just some of the vehicles that symbolize our patients' inner journey into the deepest meanderings of the self.

Malinowski (2021) argues that it is through dreams that the mind processes and crystallizes meaningful emotions, expressed with a different intensity than in wakefulness. These are not only negative emotions. Positive emotions can also be the protagonists of dreams:

> We need to remember which experiences were horrible and which were brilliant, so we can remember how to avoid the former and seek out the latter again in the future. So we're dreaming of both ugly and beautiful memories, perhaps so that we can remember them. In this way, memory consolidation and emotion-processing go hand-in-hand.
> (2021, p. 49)

In dreams we can see the emergence of latent emotions still unprocessed, the resurfacing of submerged worlds. Dreams are the expressions of fragmented, misrecognized, disowned ego states that lie beneath or beyond consciousness (Bromberg, 2006, 2011). Interrogating them activates a modulating and integrating internal dialogue between ego states. If the psychic reality of the dream interacts with waking reality, the Adult ego state—which in itself is self-awareness—expands (Summers & Tudor, 2000, 2021) to contain all our multiple contradictions. If there is a place where contradictions coexist—as André Breton evoked in 1929's *Second Manifesto of Surrealism*—there is no doubt that that place is the dream. However, since dreams are a boundless universe of imagery and meanings, it is important that the therapist does not end up like Major Tom, the mythical astronaut in David Bowie's *Space Oddity*, who, having interrupted all contact with Earth, gets lost in space. As we saw in Chapter 4, when we interrogate dreams in therapy, we must always ask ourselves what is the purpose of the interrogation, and, among the endless avenues we might pursue, which one is the most useful at any given moment, based on the goals agreed upon with our client.

Getting to know a city by getting lost in its alleys

Every dream conveys an indefinite number of symbolic messages, and infinite are the readings that can be derived from its analysis, whether it be an evolving narrative, or a single image—such as a photograph or a short film—or a movie. Working with dreams requires giving up the search for linearity, causality, and scientific evidence and being able to stand in uncertainty, to move in complexity, in the presence of multiple parts (Tangolo & Massi, 2022). The open and creative stance required may frighten the young psychotherapist who is about to work on dreams. Diagnostic framing and the achievement of verifiable and observable work goals are fundamental aspects of a work that is not just effective from a psychotherapeutic point of view but also from an ethical point of view. However, beyond this, aiming for a linear and causal epistemology to understand psychic processes remains a mere illusion. As rigorous master of psychodynamic transactional analysis Michele Novellino (2010) (mentioned in Chapter 3) says, to be a good therapist one must learn—also—to stand in uncertainty. And that means accepting that we are not always clear about what is happening at the process level in the encounter with our patients at any given moment. What is this person, through their actions, communicating about themselves, about their needs? Why are they talking to me about this very thing, right now? The answers will come, as long as the therapist does not adopt a defensive posture and fill with words or actions the moment to which it is difficult to attribute meaning. This clinical phenomenon is called *sloppiness* (Stern, 1985; Novellino, 2010). It refers to the spontaneity and unpredictability inherent in the encounter between patient and therapist who must co-construct worlds to share. This is why the process of therapy is necessarily sloppy, that is, approximate and imperfect in its inevitable mistakes and repairs. To overcome the anxious search for certainties it is not appropriate to stop asking questions. On the contrary, it is precisely the therapist's job to ask and ask, in order to extend the panorama of the possible and approach what lies beyond awareness. Beyond such a relational attitude, working with dreams does not require theoretical and technical skills much different from those that the therapist already possesses since the clinical interview, and it is common for psychotherapists of different psychotherapy approaches without specific training to use dreams in clinical practice, as demonstrated by the study conducted by Scherdl and colleagues (2000). However, transactional analysis offers the therapist a methodological map to navigate the endless sea of messages that the unconscious conveys through dreams, in search of those most useful to the therapeutic goals of the individual patient and, above all, at that specific time. Let us, then, get to know this map.

Strategic stages of therapy

When the goal of psychotherapy is a deep restructuring of personality, the model of transactional analysis involves going through four strategic stages, each with specific tasks and distinctive characteristics. It is important for the therapist to orient themselves on the map of the therapeutic path, and know where they stand at any given point in their work with the client. Of course, as we mentioned above, every process is unique and sloppy, as is every encounter between two individuals and every encounter of an individual with themselves, and it is not possible to think of the succession of each stage in a predetermined and linear way. Indeed, it is possible to regress to an earlier stage in the journey or to perform the entire cycle of stages several times, deepening the level of analysis each time, in what is sometimes represented graphically in therapy as a downward spiral (Hargaden & Sills, 2002). Let us now look at the characteristics of each stage.

Therapeutic alliance

For therapy to work, everyone must do their part. The therapist must put their skills at the service of the client, and the client must be willing to bravely put themselves on the line. But this is not enough. Whatever the goal, it can only be achieved if a coalition is built among those engaged in the work. What has to work for therapy to be effective is, above all, the coming together of two people who make a pact, the cohesion that forms between client and therapist, an expression of the feeling of belonging to the smallest group of which one can be a part of, i.e., the couple (Tangolo & Massi, 2022). This first stage is called the therapeutic alliance. A common factor in all psychotherapies, whether short or long, the alliance is fundamental to the success of the process and, when it is lacking or for some reason becomes disrupted, it is the main cause of patient discontinuation (Horvath et al., 2011). A good alliance is built when an atmosphere of trust, mutual respect, curiosity, and sincere interest is created in the therapy room. At the social level, this can be quite easy to achieve: The client is suffering and is genuinely interested in getting help to ease pain and recover a lost sense of agency. The therapist is there to help those in front of them, is passionate about their work and human encounters, and has the tools they need to make a contribution. From a social point of view, these positions encourage the creation of a contract. However, on a psychological level, not always conscious, there may be forces working in the opposite direction that end up boycotting the possibility of change brought about by the beginning of therapy (Tangolo, 2018). As the biological sciences teach us, all changes jeopardize the survival of the individual and come at a significant energetic cost, and this is also true of changing the way we represent ourselves, others, and the world we live in. Due to this, maintaining homeostasis is always the top-most priority. This mechanism is known to psychoanalysts as transference: "I expect and anticipate experiences akin to those I have had in the past." As in, if it happened once, it will happen again (Clarkson, 1995). Many clients are very motivated, willing to change, and eager to find a person to help them with this. However, they do not trust that this can happen, because they are convinced that nothing can change. Joseph Weiss together with the San Francisco Psychotherapy

Research Group developed the *control-mastery theory*, according to which the patient unconsciously subjects the therapist to a series of tests in order to prove that they can be trusted, that they are the right person to disconfirm their own pathogenic beliefs about themselves and others (Weiss, 1993). Passing tests fosters the establishment of a solid transference alliance, and conversely failure of one or more tests reinforces script beliefs that are sometimes traumatic and can lead to the abrupt termination of therapy. In transactional analysis we call "psychological games" the relational dynamics that unconsciously lead to the confirmation of one's script, and testing the therapist is an example of this. Keeping these aspects in mind shields the two protagonists from easy enthusiasms and subsequent ruinous disappointments. A careful therapist who takes a good history knows very soon what relational patterns the client will reproduce in their relationship with them, and this will protect them from perpetuating dysfunctional dynamics, from entering a psychological game mechanism that would undermine their chances of recovery.

One element of whether or not we have built a good therapeutic alliance is countertransferential in nature: We feel more relaxed in our chair, more spontaneous, freer to explore. We simply spend time with the person in front of us more willingly. We invite you to try your hand at an exercise in this regard. Look at your schedule, and consider a day of the week in which you are busy in your clinical practice. As you go over all the marked appointments—11 o'clock, 4 o'clock, etc.—try to make contact with your emotions. Imagine you are on a rollercoaster: thinking about some meetings weighs you down, thinking about others makes you feel relieved. Consequently, try to comment on it with things like "I will have a good day on Thursday," or on the contrary, "It will be a tiring day," basing yourself off the meetings you have rather than the number of hours you have to work. This fatigue or relief is not associated with the appointment time and only partly with your patient's psychopathology. Rather, these countertransferential reactions are associated with the degree of alliance you have built with these people. When the alliance has been established, there is ease in conducting the session, since the client's defenses—and yours as well—are lowered: Sharing a dream is no longer a leap in the dark, as in the very first encounters; it now becomes a need, a time of relief and participation.

Decontamination

If in the first period of therapy the therapist's concern is to pass the patient's tests so that they feel safe within that relationship, going forward the focus of the work will become more cognitive in nature, and will aim to bring out and confront those rigid patterns of reference, those distorted views of self and the world that are expressions of the contaminations of the Adult by Parent and Child. As a matter of fact, by "decontamination" we mean the process of liberating the ego state of the Adult from the interferences of the Parent and

Child. As we have seen above, when the Adult is contaminated, the options for problem-solving are limited, if not absent. We always tell our trainees that when a patient sees no way out of their problems it means they have a severely contaminated Adult, because there is always a way out, even though it may be difficult and painful to undertake. A typical contaminated statement we often hear in therapy is, "I can't leave my partner because we have children," as if the presence of children precludes a separation. Decontamination work helps the person define the problem in a new and addressable way: In this case, for example, "I don't want to separate because I'm afraid it would hurt my children." Although the way out still appears blocked, this second statement is more realistic, more Adult; it is in fact an expression of a personal emotional experience that leads to a choice and is not an externally dictated impediment. Here is where it is easier for the therapist to feel more empathically closer to the client than before, more mentally active, more reflective. They, too, can find ways out, can explore the client's pathogenic beliefs, provide them with useful information in the search for possible, rational, and concrete solutions. In this sense, decontamination is the work of reformulating and empowering the individual, of becoming aware of one's personal power, of recovering one's own agency, but also of accepting one's limitations and difficulties, all aspects that in fact characterize the part of our personality that Berne calls the Adult: from the Latin *adultus*, one who has grown up. Even when faced with the prospect of separation, albeit the most final and painful separation possible, as in the case of death—one's own or that of affectively close people—each person has a small margin of choice. Choosing how to live out their remaining time, for example, choosing how to say goodbye, what to leave behind about themselves, and what emotions to take away: resentment or guilt rather than gratitude and thankfulness. If, as we have just seen, Parent contamination of the Adult takes the form of prejudices and generalizations that block the Adult's ability to adopt healthy and functional coping strategies, Child contamination is responsible for phobias, unrealistic fears, or delusions (Berne, 1961, 1972). Again, examples are numerous. It may happen during a session to hear the client say, "I'm afraid something bad will happen if I leave my home," or "I'm sad because my husband gave me a diamond but if he had really loved me he would have known that what I really wanted was a trip." As if loving means reading someone else's mind. In this case, the magical thinking of the Child leads the individual to illusorily think that they can have indefinite power of control over people and events or, conversely, to feel totally powerless. Investigating the client's expectations can help them realize the irrationality of certain attitudes and re-establish the wavering reality check.

Analyzing dreams at this stage of therapy aims to investigate such expectations. The monsters the dreamer battles against in dreams can be read as beliefs of the Parent or illusions of the Child that, like Scylla and Charybdis for Odysseus, hindering him from reaching his Ithaca. At the same time, the intuitive solutions found by the dreamer or provided to them by benevolent and wise characters can be seen as a freer Adult taking back the helm with the cooperation of the other parts of the personality.

The decontamination process is potentially endless because each of us has varying degrees of contamination of our Adult. However, the greater our psychological well-being and autonomy, the more defined the boundaries of this part of the personality will be. When good decontamination work has been done, on average 8–12 months after the first interview, psychopathological symptoms are in remission and in general the patient's quality of life is much improved. It is at this point that we are ready to enter the third stage of therapy.

Deconfusion

Up until this point, we have focused on the pathological limitations in the client's life that have been caused by the prevarications of the Parent and Child over the Adult. When the boundaries of the latter are freed and strengthened, the therapist can count on a new ally to go and unlock the issues fixed in the Child ego state. Deconfusion is the deepest and most emotional stage of the work that leads to the resolution of the central conflict fixed in the Child ego state, the conflict which, as we mentioned above, was generated by the failure to meet basic relational needs that are fundamental to the child's psychological survival. This slow and sometimes painful transition leads to healing, which for Berne does not mean erasing trauma by getting as adults what we lacked as children—love, support, closeness, trust. Healing for Berne means letting go of the rope that keeps us tied to our traumatic past in a desperate search for a compensation that we will never find. In this sense, healing means growing up, accepting that Santa Claus does not exist, that what we have experienced is unfortunately in some ways irreparable. Healing also means understanding on a deep emotional level that now that we are grown up we have a right to go after what we did not have as children and that our happiness depends on us. To achieve this full autonomy we need to make space, grant dignity, and integration to the fragmented ego states. At such an advanced stage of the therapeutic process, the emotional stimuli are numerous and the stress on the Child intense. This is the stage when conflicting relational dynamics related to the traumatic past are re-actualized through psychological games, enactments, and dreams. If it is true, as we have written many times, that the dreamer can be any part of our submerged personality, it is now plausible that through dreaming we express the dissociated parts of the Child ego state, the ghosts of the self, as Onno Van der Hart and colleagues (2006) call them. We know from Schredl et al.'s (2000) research that the stronger the emotional intensity of an experience, the more likely it is to show up in dreams. To work effectively at resolving emotional blocks related to traumatic early relational experiences, the right timing of intervention must be carefully chosen. To this end, in our working model we adopt what we call the *gnocco* technique. *Gnocco* is a type of Italian pasta the size of a grape and the consistency of a pancake, made of flour and potatoes. The Italian cooking recipe calls for "throwing" the *gnocchi* into a pot of boiling water and removing them after a few minutes, after they rise to the surface of the water. In therapy, we work with what comes "up to the surface," that is, with the psychic material that, consciously or unconsciously, the patient brings to us through multiple codes of communication (Bucci, 1997), such as the sub-symbolic one of enactment, or the symbolic non-verbal one of dreams—the channel of dreams becomes verbal only when it is narrated. Dreams are in fact visual and embodied; here the metaphors are not told, as in verbal language, but seen and experienced (Malinowski, 2021). The therapist's task is to keep the flame burning and the water temperature high so that the *gnocchi* can be cooked. Stepping out of the metaphor, it is important for the therapist to cultivate an empathic relationship, remain emotionally syntonized, and adopt a curious and interested attitude toward the client. Scraping the bottom of the pot in search of clinically interesting material fixed in the Child, such as trauma or relational fractures, appears today to be a violent attitude that opens up ethical issues. Conversely, to stand by and watch the *gnocchi* on the surface of the water without picking them up means not only missing a therapeutic opportunity but even reinforcing the patient's script. It should be emphasized here that the Hippocratic admonition taken up by Berne, *primum non nocere*, cannot be translated as doing nothing. And a dream brought to us in therapy is a *gnocco* that has come to the surface. So yes, it is good to wait, but only up to a certain point, in order to avoid getting stuck in the fear of getting it wrong. When doing dreamwork at this stage of depth therapy, the thinking minds of client and therapist meet and spark a dialogue, both intrapsychic and interpersonal, conscious and unconscious, that generates greater coherence and integration of the ego states. This is what Bromberg (2006) calls "mutual awakening."

Re-learning

When the deconfusion process has evolved, about three years after the beginning of therapy, the patient appears lighter, looks better—their facial muscles are relaxed, their posture softer, they smile more, they take better care of themselves—they seem more courageous and purposeful, and they can answer the question "who am I?" At the behavioral level they experiment with new possibilities, expand their space for action, go on a long trip or peacefully stay at home during a rainy Sunday without the usual *horror vacui*. New beliefs and softer, less rigid reasoning replace old, limiting and contaminated patterns of thinking. Such breakthroughs are an expression of the change and healing that has occurred. However, this is a delicate moment for the client who may feel fragile and uncertain: They have lost the certainties guaranteed to them by the role the script had reserved for themselves, and they have not yet acquired the security of the achieved autonomy. It is as if they are swinging in the middle of a Tibetan bridge, distant from the bank behind them, while the one in front of them is still far away. At this point, the fourth and final part of transactional-analytic psychotherapy can begin. Re-learning refers precisely to the stage where the client is encouragingly accompanied by the therapist and the therapy group to face life in this transitional phase. Berne (1961, 1966) urges psycho-therapists not to hastily end therapy. The patient who is not ready will feel fragile, unsupported, and unprotected, and may go into destructive regression. Instead, it is helpful to take time. Time for the changes that have taken place to crystallize and time for the client to enjoy their achievements. Only after these steps will the time be ripe to prepare for separation. As Tangolo (2018) says, "The end of therapy is both a graduation party and a tearful goodbye at the station" (p. 86). Emotions are complex, multiple, and nuanced; there is sadness but there is also joy, pride and gratitude. Sometimes old fears come back, but what changes is how they are dealt with.

At this stage of therapy, it is typical for dreams with a recurring theme to have a new conclusion, or for epic dreams to inhabit the nights of those who did not dream before, such as patients with depressive symptomatology (Schredl et al., 2000). In other cases, true closure dreams may make their appearance (Dry, 1980; Tangolo, 2015): these are typical end-of-therapy dreams that contain universal images of building renovation or completion.

We have seen how dreams make the greatest therapeutic contribution when analyzed specifically based on the stage of therapy the patient is in. It is possible for dreams to evolve and change in content as the therapeutic process advances, just as the same dream can be dreamed at the beginning, middle, and end of therapy and lead to ever-new knowledge, discoveries, and fruitful conversations between the different parts of the self. To better understand this aspect, let us introduce Alexander to the reader. Alexander, a 40-year-old man who has been in treatment for four years because of a severe obsessive-compulsive disorder, comes to his last group therapy session bringing a dream. Alexander says that a panther appears in the middle of the sea where he blissfully had been diving. The dream goes on like this:

> *The panther jumps with a leap into the boat where I was, and with a jump I manage to reach the edge of another boat nearby, then I fall into the sea, so does the panther, I can't get on the boat, I try to jump into another boat but I can't get on it; while still in the water, with my left hand seizing the edge of the boat to climb on board, I am attacked by the panther, who grabs my arm. In one corner I see Francesca (therapist) quietly strolling along the outside of the bar near the rocks and looking out to sea.*

The therapist is depicted here as detached and "calm," as opposed to the dreamer fighting his monster, just as in the adventure film *Life of Pi*. However, when questioned about the emotions experienced in the dream, Alexander does not feel anguish nor does he feel that the therapist is emotionally distant or indifferent, as might have been the case if the dream had happened during the alliance-building phase. Alexander now feels fear and pride at the same time because the imagery of the therapist standing quietly on the shore assures him that he will make it on his own, that he will be able to face the challenges that life presents to him from now on. Let us now see an example of the evolution of dreams in the different stages of therapy.

Dreams in the different stages of therapy: a therapeutic tale

Susan is a young psychologist in her 30s who is training as a psychotherapist. During her training years she decides to begin a personal therapeutic journey with the aim of deepening her self-knowledge in preparation for her future profession, but also to process the untimely death of her father, to whom she was very close, and her conflicting relationship with her mother. Susan is a cheerful and intuitive woman with a brilliant and creative mind; yet during her sessions she seems very composed: She sits straight, chooses her words carefully, answers by saying what she thinks when asked how she feels. She intellectualizes and rationalizes to control her emotions. It is as if she is afraid of being intrusive in the therapy space that is hers and hers only. When I share my observations with her, she replies, "I have to think about it." Susan thinks, thinks on her own, and only after she has done so does she bring me the results of that process. From the information I gather about her life history, the picture that emerges is that of a very crowded family: There are her siblings and, above all, her mother's family of origin, from which her mother has never been separated and for which she cares thoughtfully, neglecting the new one. Susan's father seems to react to his wife's absence by distancing himself from her and devoting himself full-time to his job, while Susan herself feels neglected and unimportant. During her adolescence, the discovery of her father's illness brings her even closer to him; their relationship becomes more intimate and exclusive. She will be the one to entirely take care of him until his death, thus recovering her centrality and being able to feel loved by him.

We know that the central conflict theme around which the script has been constructed is easily identified already in the first few sessions, through careful and focused listening and observation. However, especially when the patient is more defensive and adapted, it is the dreams brought during the first meetings that contain their metaphorical enactment. And that is why it is never too early to welcome a patient's dreams.

And that is how Susan can bring a dream she had the night before to the first meeting:

I am in school and have to take an exam, and one of the questions is about the new law issued by the Ministry of Health. I write in a fragmented way on pieces of things, edges of objects; I feel that time is tyrannical and I don't have the space to write; they are waiting for me to hand it in, but while I'm taking the exam I'm also deeply heartbroken and crying because they have just told me that you (therapist) died suddenly. I feel abandoned, I don't know why I try not to let them see me crying; I feel that my grief is different from the others'.

In such a dream, we see the symbolic emergence of some of the themes that will be most meaningful to Susan throughout her therapeutic journey. However, the main priority at this stage is alliance-building. Therefore, it is necessary to interrogate Susan's dream in search of her main relational concern. To identify it is to place oneself in a position to pass the initial test that, according to Weiss's (1993) control-mastery theory, the client administers to the therapist. From the dream we can infer that Susan feels that she is under examination, and to pass this test she is required to have knowledge of healthcare: This is not surprising since her therapist is also a member of the school of psychotherapy—Ministry of Health in the dream—where she is training to become a professional, precisely in the healthcare field. Susan needs time to "write herself." Here, Susan is unconsciously expressing a request that the therapist not be tyrannical—like time, and who knows who else—and that she try to wait for her. There are many things she will talk about, which will need to be collected and put together, since they are "fragmented," confused, scattered. In the second part of the dream comes a further and deeper relational concern: abandonment. The moment she lets go and opens herself up to the relationship, the therapist suddenly dies. Here we can already see Susan's script response to loss: "My pain is special but I cannot show it to anyone, I have to be strong. What is the point of expressing grief if there is no one who can take care of me?" In this case building a solid therapeutic alliance with the patient looks like, on the therapist's part, paying special attention to the delicate moments of transition, to the suspensions of therapy, to the closing of the session, to everything that could unconsciously remind Susan of irreparable loss and abandonment. But there is also another aspect that requires special care: When Susan brings her pain to the therapist, they have to be there for her and be strong enough to contain it. This gives a restorative response to her renegade need to be wanted and supported. After a few weeks, Susan brings a new dream to therapy:

I'm getting ready to leave, I'm wearing something I think I might need: mask, oxygen tanks, and some strange equipment. My trip involves descending below a flat surface, like a solid lake. I feel like I'm gearing up for the trip. From the outside, I must look very funny indeed. All the while on TV there's a documentary about a sewage engineering project that involves tunneling underneath the earth. A guy on TV says something like, "I'm getting ready to descend to the deepest depth." And then there's me inside a metal cage harnessed from above, preparing to descend. The rope allows me to go back up whenever I want, the cage protects me.

The journey to the deepest part of herself, the part where the sewage is collected—the dirtiest, most putrid parts—is about to begin. Susan is well equipped to safely deal with this descent: She has her mask and oxygen tanks with her, but, not only that, she is inside a metal cage and has a rope at her disposal that allows her to return to the surface—to defend herself—whenever she wants. Susan feels safe: The first goal of building a good alliance has been achieved.

Susan lives with her partner in a town a few hundred miles away from the home where she grew up. About a year after starting therapy, the dream setting becomes that very house:

I find myself in my own home, not realizing it right away but feeling that something has changed. My parents' room is no longer a bedroom; there is a carpet, a couch (nice and uncomfortable), it is smaller in size and there is something new, like a closet. I think I can't sleep there anymore, that all references to my father and my parents' married life have disappeared, and so has my existence! My father is there, like a passive spectator, he doesn't react, I don't interact with him. I realize that my brother's room also lacks a bed and nobody can sleep there anymore, so that the only "sleepable" room left is mine, and I feel lonely. I am bewildered at first, then angrier and angrier; it seems my mother has moved back in with my grandmother, I get angry with her, I accuse her of deciding without consulting me, I tell her this is my house; she says she didn't do it; I shake her, I get angry, then I move on to my uncle: He did the work, so I accuse him of being a meddler. But it's still not enough; my grandmother appears, I tell her, "You have ruined at least three generations, my mother's and my uncle's, mine and my cousins', I hate you."

In the "house" under renovation, the emptied rooms and the helpless father can be read in terms of the contamination of the Adult by the Parent: "Others are dangerous because they steal emotional bonds." Parallel to this is the Child contamination of the Adult expressed in the form of a pathogenic belief: "It's all your fault that I'm alone," accompanied by an emotional experience of helplessness and anger. Other similar dreams characterize this stage of therapy: they are filled with scenes of prisons, situations of restraint, beds to lie in that are already occupied by others; with characters evoking parental figures metaphorically represented by foreign, demanding, and inaccessible Directors and

Ministers. The decontamination work will lead to freeing Susan's Adult so that she does not confuse receiving attention with receiving love, and regains confidence in her ability to maintain stable emotional relationships without fearing that others will destroy them. Having dealt with this more cognitive phase of the therapeutic process, it is time to address the conflicts fixed in the Child ego state. By that time Susan's obsessive defenses were lowered to make way for the parts of the Child ego state in which trauma is engrained: The abandoned Child—once neglected and deprived—could finally be expressed. The dumplings finally come up to the surface and are ready to be picked up through transference work—"Will I be special to you?"—and countertransference—"You are great, you can do it on your own"—the processing of enactments, psychological games within the therapeutic relationship, and dreams. In the third year of her therapeutic work, Susan brings the following dream to the session:

There are several rooms in a long corridor; outside the door I see boxes with small packages inside, I am curious, I want to take hold of the things inside. I ask everyone if I have lived there before, I feel something like doubt, I don't remember, I am missing a piece. Maybe I don't know why they are there. We sleep, the next day we have to go to school, we wake up early, we are farther away than usual. There's a little girl in a stroller, she's small, she's crying. My mom is there too, I don't know why she's there but she seems involved in caring for the baby. When I try to pick the baby up from the stroller I notice she is strapped in, so I have to unbuckle her. The stroller is small compared to her size. So I think, tonight I'll take her to sleep with me on the big bed, and I'm a little scared as I say this, I'm afraid she might fall off the bed or who knows what, but I feel it's the right thing to do no matter what my mom thinks.

Analyzing the dream it becomes clear that the long hallway with the many rooms is a metaphor for Susan's mind, while the boxes outside the room are parts of herself to be taken hold of with curiosity and a sense of bewilderment—*I don't know why they are there*. Then there's a change of scenery. The first to appear are Susan's closest colleagues from the psychotherapy school, then a crying child and finally the mother "involved" in the child's care. The crying child is a recurring theme in Susan's dreams. However, a new element appears in this dream: Before now she has felt helpless in the face of that childish call, while on this occasion she decides to take the child with her to bed, regardless of her mother's wishes. In making this new decision, Susan experiences fear. She is wondering if she will be able to take care of this part of herself. For the patient, this dream represents an epiphany. Indeed, it reveals the profound change that is taking place within herself: The misunderstood parts of her ego states are being welcomed and integrated into her personality, which is increasingly complex, that is to say, composed of multiple parts. Here are Susan's words describing this therapeutic transition:

> The dream comes at a really difficult time for me. The encounter with my vulnerability was kind of like an earthquake. Insomnia plagued me every night, I was filled with relentless anxiety. With myself, I had no patience at all: I couldn't stand not being able to function, I constantly felt naked and exposed, and the encounter with my fellow therapy group members had taken on the appearance of danger and threat. I just wanted to hide until someone magically fixed me. At first I felt misunderstood even by you: You kept saying things like 'Of course you can work, you'll only appear more human, you'll feel more, you'll discover new things,' 'Right now the group can be so helpful to you.' I was thinking, 'Can't you fucking see how bad I'm feeling? That I cannot do it? That I cannot be with others, cannot help others?' Until then I had never experienced a parent who doesn't get worried and I wasn't sure if this was okay. I was mistaking love for worry and the wound of un-recognition was knocking at my door. Your calmness was my Copernican revolution: There I found the security I needed. Your encouragements are carved inside me; they helped me discover that my most fragile part (the endangered Child) has a right to exist and to accept warmth from others. The dream of the stroller anticipates this transition. I remember the relief I felt when I woke up, as if a new sense of trust had made its way inside me: the possibility of accepting her and being a more patient and loving mother to such a distressed child.

The last strategic stage, *re-learning*, is characterized by Susan's work in group. During this period the following dream makes its appearance:

> *I'm with my dad on the streets of a city, and I have a feeling that they brought him back to life: He was dead and they saved him. And he actually tells me that a year has passed from that moment, that a year before, that very week, he had been saved, resurrected. While everyone thinks he is dead, I have the feeling that I am the only one who knows that he was resurrected. Strolling along the street I see S. and G. chatting on a step in front of a door, as if they had been out drinking. I am so happy, I see them and say "Oh, hi. This is my dad; dad, meet S., G." He is in his tank top, that is, his relaxation mode outfit, and I am more than happy to introduce him to them, like, he is the one I have told you so much about.*

Immersed in a festive atmosphere, Susan resurrects her father, discovers that he is alive within her—"I have the feeling that I am the only one who knows that he has been resurrected"—walks with him, and with joy and pride introduces this part of herself to her groupmates.

In conclusion, we could see how fruitful it was for the evolution of Susan's therapeutic journey to connect dream work to the specific goal of each strategic stage. We also noticed that during the therapy process it was not just the type of dream analysis that changed. It was Susan's dreams themselves that changed, evolving over the course of her journey: The conflicting themes with dark and uneasy "Goya-like" emotional overtones slowly gave way to joyful discoveries and fruitful encounters characterized by pastel-colored emotional hues. In the following chapters we will take a closer look at how to recognize and work on script dreams, transformation dreams, and finally dreams related to the healing process.

References

Beebe, B., & Lachman, F. (1988). The contribution of mother-infant mutual influence to the origin of self and object representations. *Psychoanalytic Psychology*, 5(4), 305–337.

Beebe, B., & Lachman, F. (2005). *Infant research and adult treatment: Co-constructing interactions*. London: Routledge.

Berne, E. (1961). *Transactional analysis in psychotherapy*. New York: Ballantine Books.

Berne, E. (1966). *Principles of group treatment*. New York: Oxford University.

Berne, E. (1972). *What do you say after you say hello?* New York: Grove Press.

Bromberg, P. (2006). *Awakening the dreamer: Clinical journeys*. Mahwah: NJ: The Analytic Press.

Bromberg, P. (2011). *The shadow of the tsunami and the growth of the relational mind*. London: Routledge.

Buber, M. (1937). *I and thou*. Edinburgh: T. & T. Clark.

Bucci, W. (1997). *Psychoanalysis and cognitive science: A multiple code theory*. New York: Guilford Press.

Clarkson, P. (1995). *The therapeutic relationship in psychoanalysis, counselling psychology and psychotherapy*. San Diego: Singular Pub Group.

Dry, B. (1980). Psychoanalytic definitions of cure: Beyond contract completion. *Transactional Analysis Journal*, 10(2), 124–130.

Hargaden, H.,& Sills, C. (2002). *Transactional analysis: A Relational perspective*. London: Routledge.

Horvath, A. O., Del Re, A. C., Fluckiger, C., & Symonds, D. (2011). Alliance in individual psychotherapy. *Psychotherapy*, 48(1), 9–16.

Lingiardi, V. (2019). *Io, tu, noi. Vivere con se stessi, l'altro, gli altri [Me, you, us. Living with one self, the other, others]*. Milano: Utet.

Lingiardi, V., Amadei, G., Caviglia, G., & De Bei, F. (2011). *La svolta relazionale [The relational turn]*. Milano: Raffaello Cortina Editore.

Malinowski, J. (2021). *The psychology of dreaming*. London: Routledge.

Novellino, M. (2010). The demon and sloppiness: From Berne to transactional psychoanalysis. *Transactional Analysis Journal*, 40(3–4), 288–294.

Schredl, M., Bohusch, C., Kahl, J., Mader, A., & Somesan, A. (2000). The use of dreams in psychotherapy: A survey of psychotherapists in private practice. *Journal of Psychotherapy Practice and Research, 9*(2), 81–87.

Sedgwick, J. (2020). *Contextual transactional analysis*. London: Routledge.

Stern, D. (1985). *The interpersonal world of the infant*. New York: Basic Books.

Summers, G., & Tudor, K. (2000). Co-creative transactional analysis. *Transactional Analysis Journal, 30*(1), 23–40.

Summers, G., & Tudor, K. (2021). Reflections on co-creative transactional analysis: Acceptance speech for the 2020 Eric Berne Memorial Award. *Transactional Analysis Journal, 51*(1), 7–18.

Tangolo, A. E. (2015). Group imago and dreamwork in group therapy. *Transactional Analysis Journal, 45*(3), 179–190.

Tangolo, A. E. (2018). *Psychodynamic psychotherapy with transactional analysis: Theory and narration of a living experience*. London: Routledge.

Tangolo, A. E., & Massi, A. (2022). *Group therapy in transactional analysis: Theory through practice*. London: Routledge.

Trautmann, L., & Erskine, R. (1981). Ego state analysis: A comparative view. *Transactional Analysis Journal, 11*(2), 178–185.

Van Der Hart, O., Nijenhuis, E., & Steele, K. (2006). *Haunted self: Structural dissociation and the treatment of chronic traumatization*. New York: W.W. Norton & Company.

Weiss, J. (1993). *How psychotherapy works: Process and technique*. New York: Guilford.

6
SCRIPT DREAMS, RECURRING DREAMS

Introduction

Anthropological studies have shown us the extent to which the theme of dreams defines a society, its culture, its languages, and its way of sharing fears and desires. Without repeating too many of the studies already mentioned (Silvia Rosa, Jung, Hillman), we refer here to the idea that the repetitive themes that define an individual's anxieties and constitute the internal relational pattern with which one faces life are conditioned by one's environment, family, the era in which one lives, and the language one speaks. In fact, we know that no man is an island and that we are built as a jigsaw puzzle from many influences and experiences that make us similar to our contemporaries and neighbors, even if we remain unique in the way we respond to the stress we are subjected to. Script dreams are recurring dreams that contain for each individual the deepest emotional conflicts, fears, and traumas they have ever experienced; they are specific to each person, but at the same time they may contain imagery and themes related to the historical and cultural context in which the dreamer lives. We will look at recent studies conducted in Europe during the COVID-19 pandemic, but we will also deal with common themes related to the years of the Third Reich in order to refer to eras that have strongly influenced the expression of collective anxieties. Times of war, pandemics, and collective changes certainly determine how whole countries and their peoples express feelings, particularly anxieties and fears, according to archetypal patterns. Solomon Resnik states that mythic discourse is a "cultural dream" and that dream discourse is a "personal myth" and that both "are expressed by means of a metaphorical logos, specific symbolic mediations" (1987, p. 74).

Environmental and historical influences

Context, historical time, and the different systems of relationships in which each individual is born and grows up are the elements that influence and determine the way we are, think, feel and behave much more than we would be led to believe. As Berne wrote in his book on life scripts:

> The forces of human destiny are foursome and fearsome: demonic parental programing abetted by the inner voice the ancients called the *Daemon*; constructive parental programing, aided by the thrust of life called *Phusis* long ago; external forces, still called *Fate*; and independent aspirations, for which the ancients had no human name, since for them such were the privileges mainly of gods and kings.
>
> (Berne, 1972, p. 56)

And again:

> The script scene began long ages past, when me first oozed out of the mud and began to transmit the results of its experiences chemically, through genes, to its descendants. This chemical branch culminated in the spider, who spins his strange circular geometry without instruction [...]. In his case, the script is written in fixed molecules of organic acids (DNA) [...]
>
> In man, too, the genes determine chemically some of the patterns he must follow and from which he cannot deviate [...]. Many a man with the chemistry of a great ballet dancer spends his time dancing with other people's dishes in a lunchroom, and others with the genes of a mathematician pass their days juggling other people's papers in the back room of a bank or bookie joint. But within his chemical limitations, whatever they are, each man has enormous possibilities for determining his own fate.
>
> (Berne, 1972, p. 63)

Berne often seems to fluctuate between the idea that we are beings strongly determined by genetic and historical-environmental conditions and the possibility of self-determination as individuals, that is, being free to choose and modify our script. He often writes that we do not know whether we are playing music that we have created ourselves or whether we are playing music that has already been created as with a pianola with perforated paper rolls, or like we would say today, with MIDI recordings.

How much, then, we as people are determined by context is a theme that takes on a philosophical character. Heidegger in his 1927 masterpiece *Being and Time* wrote that we do not choose the fundamental parts of existence: We are thrown into the world, we do not choose to be born, and we do not choose when to die. However, we are projecting beings and therefore it is in the essential human condition of being-in-the-world and *Dasein* that lies our possibility of choice: Shall we lead an inauthentic or authentic existence? An authentic existence would thus entail taking into account in one's choices the limitation of death and the condition that drives us nonetheless to realize a project in life.

The 20th century was a time of great tragedies and great transformations in the world. Between the terrible world wars and the globalization of recent years, however, cultural threads have connected every corner of the earth. The 20th century was also the century of psychoanalysis, of the appearance on the global scene of previously unknown and peripheral peoples. Distant religions, languages, and traditions were all brought together. The desires, myths, and dreams of the human beings of our time have been profoundly enriched and altered by the infinite stimuli that mass communication, music, cinema, television, and the internet, have delivered to everyone.

Today, after two decades of the new 21st century, we unfortunately still face great collective tragedies such as climate catastrophes, pandemics, and new wars, and thus reflections on individual scripts and environmental conditioning are dramatically topical. With this in mind, we reread Charlotte Beradt's text, *The Third Reich of Dreams*, the result of research conducted by a journalist in Germany in the 1930s and published in the United States in 1968. The afterword by Bruno Bettelheim, a survivor of the death camps, is particularly useful for today's readers. One can dream of being free when in captivity, but when a regime kills even the thought of rebellion and the possibility of dreaming, that is when humanity dies.

Thus wrote Bruno Bettelheim, the psychoanalyst of myth and fairy tales, the unforgettable author of *The Uses of Enchantment*, commenting on Charlotte Beradt's book:

> It is a shocking experience, reading this volume of dreams, to see how effectively the Third Reich murdered sleep by destroying the ability to restore our emotional strength through dreams. Beyond physical rest, sleep is refreshing to us because in our dreams
> we can feel and do those things we dare not attempt in reality […] But many subjects of the Third Reich did not dare to do this. Even in their dreams they told themselves, "I must not dare to act on my wishes" […] Thus the regime was successful in forcing even its enemies to dream the kinds of dreams it wanted them to dream: those warning the dreamer that resistance was impossible, that safety lay only in compliance.
>
> (p. 151, 1968)

And he goes on: "Thus has tyranny robbed men of their sleep and pursued them even in their dreams, long before and long after Macbeth" (p. 152, 1968).

Even Sartre, in 1941, rewriting an ancient tragedy by Aeschylus, *The Coephoras*, in a modern version of *The Flies*, describes a murky atmosphere of dreamlike dreariness of a world with no more sun or dreams but perturbed by the ghosts of the dead, by guilt over perpetrated family murders, and by the presence of the flies, which torment the living as obsessive thoughts torment those who no longer have hope.

The life script, the internal relational schemas

By life script we refer to the internal object-relational schemas with which we approach life and which are made up of beliefs constructed in our childhood about ourselves, our relationships with others (what kind of responses to our needs we can expect from others) and what life may hold in store for us. We briefly described the history of this concept in Chapter 3, within that of the development of transactional analysis.

In recurring dreams and nightmares we can find significant traces of the script or, better yet, the script matrix, which contains the protocol experiences (the attachment experiences) that might provide therapist and client with the key to understanding strange and bizarre relational balances, which are absolutely not logical and functional according to the rules and laws of secondary thought process.

A great 20th-century writer, Arthur Schnitzler wrote down his dreams throughout his entire life in a diary that was recently published (2013). He was a contemporary of Freud, a physician, a poet, a playwright, and a writer who lived in the same Vienna and in the same era as the founder of psychoanalysis. Today he is best known for the beautiful novella *Rhapsody: A Dream Novel*, which inspired Kubrick's film *Eyes Wide Shut*. Reading his dream diary, a complex and exhausting endeavor, allows us to identify along with the brilliantly painted portrait of an era, the great intellectual's scripted themes: the theme of the double—which links him to Freud in an imaginary competition—the inordinate narcissism, the obsession with death. To give a few examples: "I am at a reception with Goethe, who is small, inapparent [...] I'm wearing Schiller's cloak, and I hold out my hand to him" (p. 10). And, toward the end of his dream diary, in 1930: "I dream that I am on a train, passing a cemetery, embankments, and I have the painful feeling that I will never read my biography"[1] (p. 221).

In *What Do You Say After Hello*'s chapter on adolescence, after discussing Wanda (see Chapter 3), Berne mentions a patient who told him she had dreamed of entering a tunnel because she was being chased. Whoever was chasing her could not follow her into the tunnel, but she knew that there were still dangerous people on the other side. So she could not let go, could not go forward nor backward, and to save herself she clung to the tunnel walls. Berne notes that this is a representation of the script scenario in which the patient asks

---

1 My translation.

the therapist to help her learn how to be more comfortable in the tunnel, even though healing would mean getting out of it (Berne, 1972, p. 153).

One of the most prominent transactional analysis therapists and an influential exponent of integrative psychotherapy, Richard Erskine wrote in 1980 that the script is

> A life plan based on decisions made at any developmental stage which inhibit spontaneity and limit flexibility in problem-solving and in relating to people. Such script decisions are usually made when the person is under pressure and awareness of alternative choice is limited.
>
> (1980, p. 101)

With Zalcman, Erskine developed a useful model for analyzing the coping system (1979) that easily allows one to visualize how prior beliefs and emotional experiences constitute a closed system that therapy goes to undermine, offering the chance to access all reparative possibilities that life has in store, but which are rejected by very frightened and suffering people.

Describing the racket-system model, Erskine considers dreams to be akin to fantasies that give support to script beliefs.

He also described (1979, 2019) how script beliefs are beliefs that people have about themselves, the world, and the responses they expect from others. Such beliefs have an unconscious root and are then confirmed through thoughts, emotions, fantasies, and reinforcing experiences. We can then consider recurring dreams as fantasies, experiences which reinforce deeper beliefs about ourselves and life.

Script dreams

Thus, script dreams are recurring dreams which are filled with themes of anguish and decisions that express attempts to cope with a conflict with seemingly constant characteristics. As stated in a study by Schredl and colleagues, published in 2022: "The majority of adults (50% to 75%) report that they have had at least once recurring dreams in their lives" (Schredl et al., 2022).

A renowned neuroscientist specializing in sleep and dreaming phenomena, Sidarta Ribeiro, recounts the dark atmosphere of his childhood nightmares, which reoccurred every night and always ended distressingly with the appearance of witches and a creepy scream that awoke him. Ribeiro writes:

> Months before the appearance of the first nightmare, one Sunday at sunset, the boy's father died, struck down by a heart attack. At first, his mother reacted serenely, but a few months later, now a widow with two children to bring up, working every day and taking university courses in her spare time, she fell into a violent depression. It would

be months before the boy's younger brother asked where his father was. It was in this context of family suffering that the terrible recurring nightmare of the witches appeared.

(2021, pp. 21–22)

The child who later became a neuroscientist was aided by psychotherapeutic care to transform his recurring dream.

Many people have a repetitive theme in their dreams, a theme that has accompanied them since childhood or adolescence, or dreams that recur with the pathos of sudden interruptions and suspended anxieties, open questions that we hope to resolve overnight.

As we read further in Schredl and colleagues:

As negatively toned recurrent dreams overlap with nightmares, for example, being chased, falling, death of the dreamer (Gauchat et al., 2015), the findings that recurrent dream frequency is correlated with stress, neuroticism and lower levels of well-being fits in with current models of nightmare etiology.

(Schredl et al., 2022, p. 237)

Thus, then, there are those who always dream of being chased without ever seeing by whom, those who dream of escaping danger by flying away, those who search for something with great anxiety without knowing what they are searching for. A 2014 study by Robert and Zadra (in Schredl et al., 2022) identified 12 categories of recurring themes in dreams. Schredl gives a summary of these:

The categories include the following 12 themes: being chased (dreamer is being chased by another character, but not physically attacked); physical aggression (threat or direct attack on one's physical integrity by another person, including sexual aggression, murder, being kidnapped, or held captive); interpersonal conflict (conflict-based interaction between more than two characters involving hostility, opposition, insult, humiliation, rejection, infidelity, lying, etc.); environmental anomalies (bizarre or implausible events that occur in the environment of the dream); evil presence (seeing or sensing the presence of, or being possessed by, an evil force, including monsters, aliens, vampires, spirits, creatures, ghosts, etc.); accidents (the dreamer or another person is close to having, or is involved in, an accident, including vehicle accidents, drowning, slipping, falling, etc.); disasters/calamities (plausible events ranging from relatively minor anomalies, such as afire or flood in one's home or neighborhood, to major disasters, such as earth-quakes, war, the end of the world, etc.); failure or helplessness (difficulty or inability of the dreamer to reach a goal, including being late, lost, inability to speak, losing or for-getting something, making mistakes, searching something or someone, and being locked up); insects/vermin (the presence of an infestation, bites, or stings of insects, rats, snakes, etc.); health concerns and death (presence of physical illness, unwanted pregnancy, health problems, or death of a character or the dreamer); fears/worries (the dreamer is afraid or worried about someone or something with or without an objective threat); and others (includes idiosyncratic as well as rare themes such as being naked, being self-critical, being in an unhealthy environment, and not being able to find a toilet or being ashamed to use a toilet.)

(Schredl, 2022, p. 239)

Above all, it is at the beginning of a psychological journey that people begin to remember their dreams more, because their introspection and attention to their inner world increases.

Margaret Bowater describes the recurring dream of her 60-year-old client Florence, a dream she has been having since the age of 5 and that she shares in a group therapy session devoted to dreamwork:

I am a large fruit fly, conscious of who I am. I am hovering, as fruit flies do, in their particular jagged up and down motion, around a metal dustbin that is in the fore-ground of the London house where I lived most of my earliest years, specifically, in the front of the dining room near the door. Many other fruit flies hover around this dust bin. There is moldy food in the metal serrated dustbin, which has no cover, and there is a sense of decay, old furniture, and life not being lived there. I am observing the fruit fly that is me and watching it.

(2010, p. 96)

Bowater observes:

Reflecting now on the context of her life at the time the dream first occurred, Florence began to make connections in response to questions from the group. She had been born during the Blitz in a working-class suburb of London, when her parents were under severe strain during World War II. Her paternal grandparents had disapproved of her mother as being of a lower class, and Florence had been evacuated with her sister to a "posh evacuee home" where they were disdainfully treated as lower-class children. Florence even recalled her sister looking in a mirror and describing herself as "you horrid horrid ugly little thing."

(2010, p. 96)

Script themes in adult dreams

When we work with a patient in therapy, we pay attention not only to the dreams that are reported to us as being absolutely identical and repetitive throughout the course of the client's life, but also to the repetition of very similar themes that are represented in different scenarios. In a way we consider these as script dreams, because the recurring elements outweigh the differences and the feelings that accompany the dreams are almost identical.

The individual constructing the dream feels the same emotions, reports that they are in the same social role, that the ending is always the same, and they bring the same despondency to therapy, sometimes even a sense of surrender and defeat. Identifying script themes is very important to get to know our patient more deeply, and usually, as the therapeutic journey goes on, some of the strangest and bizarre elements in their dreams become more and more understandable and interesting. In this sense, it is advisable to suggest to our patients that they keep a dream diary, as it is important that the therapist keep a log of their patients' dreams in their notes. Recurring themes, small differences, strategies the dreamer deploys to solve the same problem are all useful for analysis: In dreams, we rehearse for life.

Among the dreams we heard in therapy

The dreams we shall describe below belong both to the classic type of dream that always repeats itself and to the type of dream that in different forms appears at specific moments of adolescent and adult life with the recurring themes that we call script themes, because the role that the protagonist plays is always very similar, although the scenarios change from time to time. For the sake of therapeutic work, however, it is very interesting to observe whether, in the repetition of certain themes, there can be noticed small and subtle changes that foreshadow the opening of the closed system. Thus, collecting dreams during the course of therapy becomes a signal of the implicit, emotional process of opening up and finding solutions to recurring problems and impasses.

Gina: "There is no place for me"

I'm sitting at a table with my parents, my brother and my sister. It seems like we're at lunch or dinner. They are talking, discussing quietly, and I'm trying to fit into their conversations but I can't because they don't listen to me and don't seem interested in what I'm saying.

After making several attempts to introduce myself into the conversation, I realize that it is useless so I decide to pull a kind of curtain in front of me, disappearing from the scene. I wake up and feel anger but also a slight sense of sadness. The thought I have as soon as I wake up is "There is no place for me."

At the end of the day, the last thought I have before falling asleep is "There is no place for me anywhere," and suddenly I realize that it is the same sentence I started the day with, after the dream.

So I thought that it wasn't random, that there had to be a connection, since I'd said that sentence to myself twice, and it upset me a little bit but also made me think.

In session I said that I remembered why I'd said those things to myself before I fell asleep but then I recalled what had happened during the day.

I had gone to a community for psychiatric patients to leave a resume and ask if they were looking for staff, but the response had been negative. The thought, then, was probably related to the difficulty of finding a job.

I think the dream speaks of my script, but it is also an experience I had several times when I was a child. It is interesting how circular this day is, ending with a "conscious" reflection that retraces the steps of the morning dream.

Analysis of Gina's dream in therapy

Such a dream reflects the existential position of the dreamer. We are talking about a person who, for example, and rather recently with respect to the dream, happened to misremember the location of a first business meeting that was important for her. Also significant is the dynamic of this act of self-sabotage in which she "gave up her place." The designated location of the meeting was a stone's throw from her home. Gina created a very complicated condition for herself (one that took her a great deal of effort) in order to be able to exclude herself. Moreover, having arrived at the wrong venue, although she had the resources to activate herself, she became passive by deferring to the initiative of her coworkers talking to her on the phone from the other venue.

At the beginning of her therapeutic journey, her difficulty might have appeared related to a specific moment in her life. But as she went on, the belief that there was no place for her, appeared as stable, constant.

On the contrary, when episodes of inclusion and success occur, she erases them, because they clash with her reference system. The dynamic actually resembles that of a self-fulfilling prophecy.

It is interesting that Gina, both in life and within the dream, actually takes a place for herself, but takes up the role of the victim. As in the case of that day at the meeting. What is the secondary benefit of such a dynamic? Surely that of experiencing a known, familiar condition, admits Gina, who adds, "rather than *prendermi il posto*, I accept that I have a place that someone else has assigned me." The advantage may be to be able to find someone else to take care of her, so that she can take a place for herself, feel welcomed, but not from a position of independence. Even in groups, she waits for someone to speak to her, to ask her a question. She acts on the suggestion of others. In the dream dinner she closes the tent, does not call the attention of others.

Gina's script as inferred from her dream

Gina has the emotional belief that she cannot choose and that there is no place for her.

In transactional analysis we might say she experiences two levels of impasse, of blocking conflict. The first-degree impasse consists of the conflict between her need to be accepted and the internalized voice of parental origin that sends her messages such as "Please people" and "Try hard." In other words, in order to be accepted, she has to show that she is trying hard and pandering to the expectations of others. Associated with this conscious, and therefore known, conflict is a deeper level of conflict of an emotional kind, not quite conscious and verbalizable, which in transactional analysis we call the second kind: Gina feels like there is just no place for her in the world, that she cannot choose, and that others do not want her. In terms of transactional analysis we might say that Gina has the injunction "Don't be yourself," "Don't be important." Gina has the unconscious perception of a Witch Parent who could threaten her life if she behaved differently, no matter how much she might want to. Her theme then becomes:

> Either I stay behind the scenes hoping to be called to the stage of life, or I try to step up and still be inconspicuous, so as not to incur the wrath of those who do not want me in the competition.

Luca and psychiatric illness

The following is an anxiety dream from a young bipolar patient aged 21. The patient is a young man who has had two major depressive episodes with a psychotic outcome. He recalls the dream as such:

I am on a mountain and I have to plant an olive tree on a plot of land where there are chestnut trees. The ground is full of stones, I see two wild boars, I start to run, I stumble, one boar comes at me, then rolls into a ditch, the other boar I manage to shoot.

Luke's reading of the dream leads him to interpret the two boars as his two depressive-psychotic episodes.

His symptoms first start when he is 17 years old. After getting drunk and smoking hashish he has a psychotic break: He locks himself in his room and no longer wants to go out; he believes his mother wants to kill him. His parents call the police, the mayor, and the doctor, and they have him committed into a psychiatric ward for an Involuntary Psychiatric Treatment. The therapist meets him after this hospitalization, following which he begins pharmacological and psychological treatment.

Afterwards, Luca finishes high school, gets his surveyor diploma, recovers from psychotic confusion, refrains from using alcohol or hashish since he realizes he cannot sustain those substances, starts a pharmacological treatment, and goes to therapy, but still lives in fear of a possible relapse.

At the time of his dream he is doing an internship, and he associates the first boar with the past breakdown, while the second with the sense of control he feels he has now.

The therapist notes that there is also the fact of planting an olive tree where there are chestnut trees and stones in the ground: As if Luca is manifesting a tendency toward the impossible, a feeling of being different from his environment. The olive tree among the chestnut trees also represents his laborious attempt to assimilate. Luca is an introverted and solitary young boy. Substances helped him fit in into the group through those "initiation rites," which, however, cost him his psychophysical health. The first crisis had occurred in the midst of a party for the village's *palio*, during a collective celebration. Anxiety remained associated with the link between acceptance and the psychological price to be paid.

Luca's high school graduation exam

I dream that I was at my high school graduation exam. In math I got a failing grade, but I'm not worried. In literature I also got a failing grade, even though I thought I did well. After the exam I appeal the Literature mark. I win the appeal and pass the exam.

The dream narrative continues: *I'm on my way home to my parents to tell them I have done poorly on the test, when I see the surveyor where I used to work, and my first girlfriend holding models of a house.*

Sometimes Luca worked on dreams, other times he simply recounted his dreams at the beginning of the session because he preferred this mode of communication. He was unaware of the moment of dysphoria related to the manic crisis that had led to his hospitalization. The same defenses that had led him to deny his mental suffering would also be reactivated later on, when he would fancy himself a genius creating new mathematical laws. In this case, the dream seems to dwell in the intermediate territory between depressive awareness of reality (the negative marks) and its denial (the appeal and victory).

Luca's life script as inferred from his dreams

Luca is an adolescent with a psychotic onset and therefore comes with major dissociative aspects. With respect to his script, in transactional analysis we would say he has bipolar functioning as described by Loomis and Landsman (1980, 1981) and Tangolo and Massi (2022). The inner parental voice is split into polarized messages between "You can do anything" and "But it will never be enough" to which correspond responses from the Child's ego state that are in turn split between a manic sense of omnipotence and a depressive anxiety with a sense of hopelessness, guilt, and emptiness.

Berta and Virginia, two therapeutic journeys running in parallel

On a winter afternoon, two new patients schedule a first interview: Virginia at 4 p.m. and Berta at 5 p.m. For an entire year they come and go without meeting each other in the therapist's office. Between the two there is an invisible thread of depression and guilt that is difficult to understand.

Virginia

Virginia is a woman in her 50s. She comes to therapy for a recurrent depression disorder that has never been treated. She's a hard-working teacher and mother of one. She has always faced her bouts of depression with the psychological drive that in TA we call "Be strong." She cannot be weak nor let herself feel the fatigue and sadness inexplicably invading her.

In her childhood she experienced the severe depression of her mother, with whom she had a very conflictual relationship. When she starts therapy her mother has recently died.

She says: "I have a strong sense of guilt for hating her. But I would also like to heal from my depression so as to resolve this conflict with her that is still very much open." As an adult Virginia discovers the terrible secret that had marked her family history. Her mother had been Jewish, so during the time of the racial laws she had decided to marry a Catholic and convert to Catholicism in order to escape persecution. Both her mother (Virginia's grandmother) and brother, however, had died in concentration camps. Shame and guilt had driven her mother to hide her grief as well. These events had resulted in a depressive withdrawal in Virginia's mother. Virginia was born immediately after the war, but her mother had remained in this "silent" depressive state and had never told her daughter about the tragedy and the broken bond with her origins.

The patient says,

> I hated her because she made me live in this depressive bubble. Today I understand why. But at the time my life was very difficult, marked by this depression, which for me was the rejection of my very existence: I felt as though she did not want me.

Berta

At 5 p.m. Berta sat on the couch still soaked in Virginia's tears. Also a teacher in her 50s and the daughter of a Nazi officer, she too had recurrent and untreated depression. Berta associated her depression with her harsh relationship with her father and the pain she felt at knowing he had been a Nazi. In both patients' cases the depression was, albeit indirectly, related to historical macro-events. Berta said that her parents had separated when she was still a child and she had been forced to spend summers in Germany with her father and his second wife. She feared her father, who was violent and cold, and still recalled how he demanded that she finish every piece of food on her plate when at the table. One day Berta vomited the food she had swallowed against her will, and he forced her to eat her own vomit. Later, as an adult, Berta had married and had two children, but she felt very guilty for being strict with them. She painfully recalled that she had forced her very young son to eat after having vomited and felt that the violence she had suffered had infected her. Shame and guilt had sunken their teeth in her as well. We might call this "second-generation depression."

It was interesting for the therapist to see them at the same time. They were two women in their 50s, living in the early 2000s. Born after the war. With this conspicuous "historical" past on their shoulders.

As an outcome of therapy, the Jewish patient, Virginia, would later go to the synagogue to look for traces of her family to reconstruct their history. She would start attending synagogue again as an element of reconciliation. It should be noted that Judaism is transmitted matrilineally.

Virginia's first dream: the lion inside the house

Inside a house there is an arena with a lion. (It's worth noting that Virginia's family came from Rome and only later moved to Florence). *The lion is hidden behind a short wall. My husband says, "Be quiet or it'll get angry." I think about going outside. The lion turns around, looks at me and growls. I'm afraid and leave.*

Virginia's second dream: "At the Rhino"

I am with a group of coworkers. They tell me: let's go to a place called the Rhino. I don't like it because rhinoceros have many layers of skin, one on top of the other. I am like the rhino.

Virginia's reflections in therapy

Virginia claims that these two dreams are allegories of her anger. She says, "I am very angry. I was very angry at my mother. I'm angry because this was the story of my life." The hidden lion is a symbol of her smoldering anger. Additionally, the lion inside the arena might be a reference to Christian martyrdom. Following this line of thought, her anger toward her mother's conversion might be connected to the lion, with which she, now daughter of a convert, must fight in the arena. For her, becoming a rhino meant covering herself with many layers of skin so as not to feel her own fragility and fear, but also to hide behind an appearance of strength and arrogance in order not to feel like a possible victim.

Berta's dreams

Berta's dreams are always very meager and repetitive; she reports being faced with a plate full of vomit that she has to eat. She hears her father's voice giving her orders, but does not see his face.

Virginia and Berta's script as inferred from their dreams

Virginia and Berta both carry the burden of parental guilt and the history that victimized them, as little girls who found no joy in childhood. Virginia's mother grieved the loss of her family members to the Holocaust, but she also bore the guilt of hiding and converting to Catholicism out of convenience. Berta's mother had been the companion and accomplice of a Nazi, with whom she had conceived a daughter. Berta's father was authoritarian and violent and had never disavowed his past and ideology.

Where the two women differ is that Virginia is angry and rejects the role of the victim; she is always angry with her mother, who does not look at her, and in feeling rejected by her she finds the reason for her constant contentiousness and belligerence. Berta, on the other hand, feels like the awkward, weak Italian daughter, unable to meet her father's expectations; she identifies with the losing side. Virginia places herself in the role of the rebel and Berta in the role of the hyper-adapted person.

Sara's dreams: repetitive themes in adolescence

The first dream: the hang glider

Sara is an 18-year-old anorexic patient. She recounts:

> *I dream about an airplane falling into the sea. I almost fall into the water but someone catches me. The water isn't deep, but beautiful, green. I am actually on a hang glider. I am the hang glider guy. I don't ask for help. I just let myself be rocked. Like I'm on a swing. I don't know if I'm alive or dead.*

The patient comments, "The hang glider I see in my dream is colorful, tangled, with all the wires entangled around me and the cliff." Emerging quite clearly here is the desire for lightness, the fear of constraints, the yearning to have a light body that can fly, but also fall.

The second dream: sinking and rising again.

I was at the home of a newborn child. I see her again a little later and she says, "Good thing you were here." The baby's dad was there too and he was worried. He says, "You can make it."

Second scene. I'm on a sinking ship but I jump onto a dock in the harbor and save myself, and I think, "I wonder how happy mom is that I managed to survive." I climb up on a cliff overlooking the beautiful blue sea. I lie there in the sun next to a boy.

Third scene. I get on a helicopter with a friend. My friend is eating a slice of pizza that she lets me taste, we fly over a chalet in the mountain. Then I find myself in the water and in danger of drowning, but I manage to get out.

Interestingly, each time Sara has an upward momentum, she then proceeds to fall back into the water. There are repetitive elements: the cliff, falling off the boat, falling off the hang glider, the risk of drowning, the fear of not surviving.

Sara's script as inferred from her dreams

Sara had begun to lose weight when she was a teenager. She was the only child of a mother with an eating disorder. Born to this young, 18-year-old woman who had an equal but conflicted relationship with her, Sara's birth had meant the forced end of her mother's adolescence. The theme of falling, of being in the water also recalls the (symbiotic) relationship with her mother. The patient said that the water she falls into is not water she is afraid of, "I manage to get out, and walk away." This in itself is not a positive element; on the contrary, it attests to the fact that Sara is not afraid of her weight loss. She sees only the transgressive dimension of it. The analysis of the feelings experienced in the dream is also interesting. Sometimes anguish can be associated with evolution, change (fear of dying as fear of living). Other times a feeling of peace, contentment, and a lack of fear may be negative symptoms. Sara faces the period of separation-individuation with an underlying fragility and conflict: She wants to separate from her mother, but cannot secure a clear bodily boundary and balance in her relationship with her and the world. Without knowing it, she explicitly repeats the stages of her mother's failed development.

Laura and the end of love: repetitive themes, today as yesterday

Laura comes to therapy at 32 years old, while she works as an occupational psychologist. She decides to go the analysis route because she is in great pain over the end of a romantic relationship. In the first few sessions Laura discloses that she uses cocaine and alcohol every weekend. She rather quickly makes the decision to stop substance use and begins a healthier and more athletic life. Her family is composed of a psychotic mother who has always rejected any treatment and who is enabled and overprotected by her husband, Laura's father. During the first months of therapy she brings up this dream:

> *I go to work but have to escort some company employees to a visit at the occupational physician's office. The setting looks like a royal mansion. I wait outside on a bench. An acquaintance of mine (who is involved in occupational safety) walks by and says, "You never work, do you? What are you doing here?" I reply that actually I am working.*
>
> *Then I see that it is a beautiful sunny day and a parade passes by right in front of me, as if for a patron day, or carnival. The people go all around in circles, around the mansion. Everyone is wearing masks. My ex-boyfriend appears. He's wearing make-up and he looks very handsome dressed in 1920s style. He comes up to me, he looks like that time when we went to a carnival party together and I did his make-up and made him dress like this. I was the one who did his make-up then, he looked so handsome to me. We walk and I ask him to get back together, but he tells me it's really over. We walk together for a bit, then he walks away leaving me near a low wall. I wake up feeling very upset.*

Laura's script as inferred from her dream.

In the session's work, what emerges is that the conflict Laura was experiencing with respect to the end of her relationship with her boyfriend was similar to the conflict she experienced with her parents. In a subsequent session, Laura says:

> We dress up, pretend to be a normal family, put make-up on mom to hide that she is sick, and pretend it is a beautiful sunny day. As long as the fiction stands, it seems to everyone that they're fine, even if it takes alcohol or cocaine to sustain it,

The dream contains repetitive elements, and that is the reason why we have considered it a script dream, because although it is in its unfolding a dream appearing only once at the beginning of the therapeutic journey, it seems to summarize the underlying themes of Laura's relational life and her fear that behind the façade of pretense and social adaptation lies her mother's madness, which her father has always covered and contained.

Cecilia's graves

Cecilia set her dreams in cemeteries. The recurring aspect was indeed the scenery, the setting. I found out after several months of therapy that she and her mother were actually in charge of managing their town's small cemetery and that Cecilia always swept the gravestones and arranged the flowers. So, the environment that always appeared in her dreams was indeed familiar to her.

First scene
I'm in Rome alone, looking for my tomb. I'm told it's near the church. So I go to the ancient brick church, with porticoes and columns (Santa Maria in Cosmedin, a church I love very much). I look for my tomb and can't find it. I follow the edges of the building to the right and see a big tree with green leaves and dead leaves underneath. I'm on the phone with a friend and tell her that I cannot find my grave. I explain to her that where there used to be a restaurant there is now a café, but I also see the restaurant, with opaque windows, small tables and chairs, dust between the shutters. The phone call continues and I tell her that my injunction to "Do not exist" is so strong that I don't even have a grave of my own.

Next scene
I go into the café (unpleasant feeling) and get an ice cream because that's all they have. I see men talking on stairs. These look like subway stairs, and I'm coming down these stairs with an ice cream in my hand. They tell me that my grave might be below, I see a staircase fading into the darkness. It's a wide one, but to me it looks narrow. So I go down with the pink-white ice cream I used to eat as a child, but after the first few steps I feel dizzy and decide to keep going, but backward. I have a feeling that it's very steep, but I don't see it. I wake up with the sound of the alarm clock and a wave of relief.

Cecilia's script as inferred from her dreams

Cecilia is 35 years old when she undertakes therapy; she works as an educator and does not allow herself to be a psychologist no matter how much she has the professional qualifications to do so. She is single because she has been in a romantic relationship for 15 years with a married man who is always promising to leave his wife for her, but always postpones the decision by prioritizing the needs of his children and the difficulty of dealing with a divorce in their small provincial town. Cecilia has a conflicting and ambivalent relationship with her mother with whom she identifies (her mother does not love her father and he possibly has a clandestine lover). Cecilia sees her father as depressed and withdrawn from relationships and her brother as her parents' favorite child, the only one they would have wanted. She often feels like the one who should not be there, who has no place of her own and who can get some happiness only by stealing it here and there. Cecilia lives with latent depression and as her mother she is a cemetery caretaker, always ready to sweep gravestones and care for dead loves that are not allowed to be expressed. Her therapeutic journey will involve freeing herself from the bonds of forbidden love that make her somewhat similar to Aida, the character in Verdi's famous tragedy, which Cecilia loves dearly. Let us remember that, in Verdi's tragedy, Aida spontaneously makes herself a prisoner in the crypt where her lover Radames has been sentenced to be buried alive.

Treating the script and getting rid of recurring dreams

Undertaking psychodynamic psychotherapy helps to free oneself from the distress generated by repetitive dreams that are always associated with unresolved themes in our personal lives. This is how one begins to remember with increasing specificity the themes of dreams and the emotions associated with them. Then, as self-awareness increases and both the experiences of waking life and the shadows of nightlife are shared with the therapist, we start to discover that we can give different endings to our nightmares, monsters might begin to be defeated or disappear, and other scenarios might emerge to make our nights richer with characters: The way we experience emotions, as well as our daytime life, are changed and enriched. Openness to change is one of the most visible effects of successful psychotherapy.

The most recent research confirms that the cessation of script nightmares and dreams occurs as psychological conditions improve and thus is one of the effects of successful therapy:

> The cessation of recurrent dreams has been found to correlate with a positive development in psychological well-being (Brown & Donderi, 1986).
>
> (Schredl, 2022, p. 237)

> Persons with higher scores of openness to experience report longer dreams (either because they can remember them better, the dreams were actually longer and more complex, they simply write more, or a combination of any of these), and these longer dreams have higher chances to include bizarre elements. This finding is also important for dream content analytic studies in general as it indicates that persons with specific trait levels (high openness to experience)—and high dream recall (also found in the present data set)—report longer dreams and, thus, generalizability of such studies might be limited.
>
> (Schredl, 2022, p. 246)

Therapy as a process of growth and development is unending. Therapy which focuses on script cure is complete when the behavioral, intrapsychic and physiological restrictions which inhibit spontaneity and limit flexibility in problem-solving and relating to people are removed. Beyond script is the realm of personal growth which includes the successful movement through developmental passages, expanding creativity, understanding life purpose and enhancing psychic and spiritual growth.

(Erskine, 1980, p. 106)

References

Beradt, C. (1968). *The third Reich of dreams*. Chicago: Quadrangle Books.

Berne, E. (1972). *What do you say after you say hello?: The psychology of human destiny*. New York: Bantam Books.

Bowater, M. (2010). Redeeming the fruit fly: Redecision work with a recurring dream. *Transactional Analysis Journal*, *40*(2), 95–98. https://doi.org/10.1177/036215371004000203

Brown, R.J., & Donderi, D.C. (1986). Dream content and self-reported well-being among recurrent dreamers, past-recurrent dreamers, and nonrecurrent dreamers. *Journal of Personality and Social Psychology*, *50*, 612–623.

Erskine, R. G. (1980). Script cure: Behavioral, intrapsychic and physiological. *Transactional Analysis Journal*, *10*(2), 102–106. https://doi.org/10.1177/036215378001000205

Erskine, R. G. (2019). The life script trilogy: Acceptance speech on receiving the 2018 Eric Berne Memorial Award. *Transactional Analysis Journal*, *49*(1), 7–13. https://doi.org/10.1080/03621537.2019.1544773

Erskine, R. G., & Zalcman, M. J. (1979). The racket system: A model for racket analysis. *Transactional Analysis Bulletin*, *9*(1), 51–59. https://doi.org/10.1177/036215377900900112

Gauchat, A., Séguin, J. R., McSween-Cadieux, E., & Zadra, A. (2015). The content of recurrent dreams in young adolescents. *Consciousness and Cognition*, 37, 103–111. https://doi.org/10.1016/j.concog.2015.08.009

Loomis, M.E., & Landsmann, S.G. (1980). Manic depressive structure: Assessment and development. *Transactional Analysis Journal*, *10*, 4.

Loomis, M.E., & Landsmann, S.G. (1981). Manic depressive structure: Treatment strategies. *Transactional Analysis Journal*, *11*, 4.

Resnik, S. (1987). *The theatre of the dream*. London: Tavistock Publications.

Ribeiro, S. (2021). *The oracle of night: The history and science of dreams* (D. Hahn, Trad.). New York: Pantheon Books.

Robert, G., & Zadra, A. (2014). Thematic and content analysis of idiopathic nightmares and bad dreams. *Sleep*, *37*(2), 409–417. https://doi.org/10.5665/sleep.3426

Schnitzler, A. (2013). *Sogni: 1875–1931* (P. M. Braunwart, A c. Di; F. Rosso Chioso, Trad.). Milano: Il Saggiatore (German edition: Schnitzler, A. (2012). Träume: Das Traumtagebuch 1875–1931 (P. M. Braunwarth & L. A. Lensing, Eds. Göttingen: Wallstein.)

Schredl, M., Germann, L., & Rauthmann, J. (2022). Recurrent dream themes: Frequency, emotional tone, and associated factors. *Dreaming, 32*(3), 235–248. https://doi.org/10.1037/drm0000221

Tangolo, A. E., & Massi, A. (2022). *Group therapy in transactional analysis: Theory through practice*. New York: Routledge.

SUGGESTION

Kafka, insomnia, and dreams

Kafka is the 20th-century writer who most inspired the dreamlike scenarios of our time. From *Amerika* (forced emigration, being lost, and without a homeland) to *The Trial* (a mysterious accusation, being subjected to an incomprehensible trial, and then sentenced to death without knowing why), through *The Metamorphosis* (waking up as a cockroach and being confined by family members like a monster inside a room) to *The Castle* (a mysterious authority that dominates and shirks knowledge renders the protagonist's life senseless, squeezed between a job for the count and not belonging to either the village or the castle). In Kafka's works we find metaphors for the tragedy of contemporary existence. That is why we discuss it between nightmares and script scenarios. Kafka unintentionally left us diaries, letters and dreams (he had asked his friends Brod and Dora to burn all of his unpublished writings) in which we can find the common threads of this work that also appear in the generous biography written by his friend Brod. Kafka was a German Jew who lived in Prague and died in 1924 of tuberculosis right before he could witness the tragedy which overcame Europe shortly after: His sisters and his beloved Milena, like many of his friends, died in concentration camps.

An Italian edition of a collection of his dreams, edited by Gaspare Giudice (1990), made it easy to follow the repetitive script themes that we find in his novels and short stories in symbolic form.

Life as a theater, where everything is representation

Kafka wrote extensively on the theme of life as a theater in which we may discover ourselves as extras—individuals with little possibility of influencing the course of personal and historical events. In his dreams, the theater appears frequently, often in a situation in which he is with someone to see a play. While at the end of the play it seems that everything catches fire because sparks are flying on the audience, Kafka writes

> Then a gentleman rises up out of this mass, walks on it towards the lamp, apparently wants to fix the lamp, but first looks up at it, remains

standing near it for a short while, and, when nothing happens, returns quietly to his place in which he is swallowed up. I take him for myself and bow my face into the darkness.

(1949, pp. 121–122)

His relationship with his father and with himself

Dreamed recently: I was riding with my father through Berlin in a tram-car [...] We came to a gate, got out without any sense of getting out, stepped through the gate. On the other side of the gate a sheer wall rose up, which my father ascended almost in a dance, his legs flew out as he climbed, so easy was it for him. There was certainly also some inconsiderateness in the fact that he did not help me one bit, for I got to the top only with the utmost effort, on all fours, often sliding back again, as though the wall had become steeper under me. At the same time it was also distressing that [the wall] was covered with human excrement so that flakes of it clung to me, chiefly to my breast.

(1949, p. 201)

In *Letter to His Father* (1970) he also wrote:

But since there was nothing at all I was certain of, since I needed to be provided at every instant with a new confirmation of my existence, since nothing was in my very own, undoubted, sole possession, determined unequivocally only by me—in sober truth a disinherited son—naturally I became unsure even of the thing nearest to me, my own body.

(1970, pp. 89–91)

The impossibility of finding happiness and belonging

For Kafka, love is almost always a tragedy and a passion that becomes increasingly powerful with distance and the impossibility of consummation. From Felice to Dora through Milena, perhaps his great love, Kafka's dreams also contain the theme of the unattainability of happiness. The letters to Milena are among the most beautiful love letters of the 20th century, and among them we also find a typical dream:

Recently I had another dream about you, it was a big dream, but I hardly remember a thing. I was in Vienna, I don't recall anything about that, next I went to Prague and had forgotten your address, not only the street but also the city, everything, only the name Schreiber kept somehow appearing, but I didn't know what to make of that. So I had lost you completely.

(1990, p. 41)

The premature relationship with death

The theme of death is found in several dreams, described in a form very similar to how it would appear in his short stories and novels, as in *The Trial*, where Mr. K. is condemned and killed as if in a play, and in the absurdity of the situation feels shame and guilt.

> I awoke to find myself imprisoned in a fenced enclosure which allowed no room for more than a step in either direction. Sheep are folded into pens of this kind, though theirs are not so narrow. The direct rays of the sun beat down on me; to shield my head I pressed it against my breast and squatted down with hunched back.
>
> (1949, pp. 363–364)

The metamorphosis of the body and hypochondria

In a recent book on Kafka, *Franz Kafka, The Jewish Patient*, Sander Gilman reads Kafka's neuroses in their somatic dimension, and his hypochondria as typical of a cultural neurosis of certain Jewish bourgeoisie in an anti-Semitic world. The author writes that "the Jewish patient is obsessive, the search for the disease comes to reflect the same nervousness as do all other factors in the Jew's life" (1995, p. 65). According to Gilman, the anxiety of the Jewish people in an increasingly anti-Semitic world contributed greatly to the spread of mental problems, hypochondria and neurosis.

When Kafka fell ill with tuberculosis in 1917, he wrote to his sister Ottla that the physical illness was the result of a mental illness inherited from his mother's family. Gilman (1995) writes in this regard that "his illness was the result of his nervousness, an inherited hypochondria in real illness, as real as the heart disease of his father" (1995, p. 95).

In a 1920 dream written to Milena in a letter, he returns to the theme of the body and metamorphosis:

> We kept on merging into one another, I was you, you were me. Finally you somehow caught fire; I remembered that fire can be smothered with cloth, took an old coat and beat you with it. But then the metamorphoses resumed and went so far that you were no longer even there; instead, I was the one on fire.
>
> (1990, p. 203)

In the dream reports, diaries, and letters we understand the individual dimension of Franz's human drama, his physical sense of inadequacy for life, his comparing himself with his father's vitality and robustness, his conviction that he could not have a family and children and that he was seriously ill. In the famous *Letter to His Father* (1970) we read:

> I was, after all, weighed down by your mere physical presence. I remember, for instance, how we often undressed in the same bathing hut. There was I, skinny, weakly, slight; you strong, tall, broad. Even inside the hut I felt a miserable specimen, and what's more, not only in your eyes but in the eyes of the whole world, for you were for me the measure of all things.
>
> (p. 19)

In literary works, the individual tragedy becomes universal, and in the final theme of *The Castle* we can read the same nonsense of inauthentic existence described by Heidegger in *Being and Time* and by Musil in *The Man Without Qualities*. But the condition of Gregor Samsa, who awakens as a cockroach after having been a professional salesman devoting his life to the maintenance of an entire family, can also be read as the revelation of a man's estrangement from the entire human community with respect to which he is no longer able to recognize himself as an equal.

Walter Benjamin wrote, in an essay published ten years after the writer's death, that "Kafka's world is a world theater. For him, man is on stage from the very beginning" (1996, p. 804). Benjamin reminds us that toward the end of *The Trial* K. asks the two gentlemen in top hats who come to pick him up what theater they are acting in, and they are at once mute and stunned by the question.

The dreamlike atmosphere is powerful in short stories such as *The Metamorphosis* and in the three great novels *Amerika*, *The Trial*, and *The Castle*. It is difficult to tell where one is asleep and where is awake, like Gregor Samsa does not know whether he is dreaming or awake when he discovers himself transformed. From the guilt and shame that fuel the drama of human life there seems to be no escape.

At the end, of *The Trial*, when K. is killed, the last words of the novel are very strong: "it was as if the shame of it must outlive him" (1956, p. 229).

We can describe Kafka's script as constructive and successful because of the novelist's creative genius, the depth of his thinking, the extraordinary loves and friendships he experienced. At the same time, however, we can also find aspects of a tragic script in him, perceivable in the sense of inadequacy so powerfully described in *Letter to His Father*, in his request to his friend Brod and his late companion Dora to burn all his unpublished writings, in the abandonment to psychic suffering, insomnia, and depression that plagued him long before tuberculosis. Benjamin wrote:

> For just as K. lives in the village on Castle Hill, modern man lives in his own body: the body slips away from him, is hostile toward him. It may happen that a man wakes up one day and finds himself transformed into vermin. Strangeness—his own strangeness—has gained control over him.
>
> (1996, p. 806)

In an interesting essay by Barison on the relationship between Benjamin and Kafka, one can read further:

> In light of the account of a conversation between Brod and Kafka, in which the latter states that "there is an infinite amount of hope, but not for us" since we are nothing but "a bad mood of God," Benjamin realizes that Kafka set as the background of his work, among many themes, primarily the failure of modern man, and that there is no hope for present-day humanity to redeem itself from that failure.[1]
>
> (2017, par. 3)

To understand the man, it is helpful to read his biography by his friend Brod, which ends with an invitation to embrace the author's contradictions and contrasts:

> Through the chaos and the nihilism, manifest in Kafka's world, there sounds softly but unmistakably the note of love for the human creature who will "nevertheless" not be abandoned—so runs the promise—by the divine powers; he will become a blessing.
>
> (1960, p. 243)

Coexisting in Kafka, then, is the belief that there is hope and the realization that it is not for him or for an entire generation, which will in fact know the worst atrocities in history. It is difficult to maintain a constructive and successful script in an era so destructive to all humanity: Kafka died of tuberculosis in 1924 and Benjamin killed himself while trying to escape the Nazis in occupied France.

---

1 My translation.

References

Barison, F. (2017). «Un'infinita quantità di speranza». Benjamin e Kafka ["An infinite amount of hope". Benjamin and Kafka]. *Dialegesthai. Rivista telematica di filosofia, 19.*

Benjamin, W. (1996). *Selected writings, Vol. 2 (1927–1934)*. Cambridge: Belknap Press.

Brod, M. (1960). *Franz Kafka: A biography*. New York: Schocken Books Inc.

Gilman, S. (1995). *Franz Kafka, the Jewish patient*. New York and London: Routledge.

Kafka, F. (1949). *The diaries of Franz Kafka, 1910–23* (M. Brod, Ed.). Harmondsworth: Penguin Books.

Kafka, F. (1970). *Letter to his father. Brief an den Vater*. New York: Schocken Books Inc.

Kafka, F. (1988). *The castle*. New York: Schocken Books Inc. (Originally published in 1926).

Kafka, F. (1990). *Sogni* (G. Giudice, Ed.) [Dreams]. Palermo: Sellerio.

Kafka, F. (1990). *Letters to Milena*. New York: Schocken Books Inc.

7
TRAUMA, DISSOCIATION, NIGHTMARES

Pioneering studies on trauma

As is well-known, an ever-growing interest has developed around trauma over the past four decades, accompanied by a fervent debate involving many clinicians of different theoretical orientations. The spark which triggered the debate is the discussions around Freud's retraction of trauma theory in favor of seduction theory as an explanation of the etiology of hysteria. With this move, says Elizabeth Howell, Freud "buried trauma" and with it the voices of many people, especially women, who were victims of various forms of abuse and violence. The author also tells the story of intra-familial violence suffered by Bertha Pappenheim—known by the pseudonym Anna O.—the patient whom Breuer nevertheless managed to heal through the talking cure (2020). Another book by Katharina Adler entitled *Ida* (2018) gives voice to Freud's other famous patient, Dora, the writer's aunt. Despite the shift in focus from actual events to his patients' fantasies and intrapsychic conflicts, Freud continues to talk about trauma in his writings. In his 1914 essay entitled "Remembering, Repeating and Working-Through," he identifies some peculiar aspects of trauma that we still hold true today. In it he explains how trauma generates amnesia with regard to the traumatic event and how that event can reappear in some form through dream activity:

> There is one special class of experiences of the utmost importance for which no memory can as a rule be recovered [...] One gains a knowledge of them through dreams.
>
> (p. 149)

In his essay, Freud defines trauma as an overpowering that implies, in the person who has suffered it, constant effort to adapt to. He further explains that the forgotten and removed elements related to trauma that cannot be remembered are enacted. The traumatized person "reproduces it not as a memory but as an action; he *repeats* it, without, of course, knowing that he is repeating it" (p. 150). Here Freud also introduces the concept of *nachtraglichkeit*, translated into French by Loewenstein as *après coup* (in Lingiardi & McWilliams, 2017), a term that in English was translated as "deferred action." This concept is highly topical and of great relevance for those dealing with trauma in psychotherapy. By *nachtraglichkeit*, Freud refers to the well-known circumstances in which the traumatic magnitude of the event is grasped by the victim only later, when faced with situations related to the original event. This aspect is crucial because it is often through psychotherapy that the victim of trauma understands the emotional impact of what they experienced perhaps years before. Janet and Ferenczi, contemporaries of Freud, were the first to emphasize dissociation rather than repression as a trauma survival strategy, and to find in unresolved childhood trauma negative effects lasting throughout a person's entire life. Janet was the first to describe post-traumatic functioning—what we now call PTSD (post-traumatic stress disorder)—and to identify "subconscious fixed ideas" as dissociated fragments of past experience, something the mind cannot assimilate. According to Janet, people who have been victims of trauma are cognitively and emotionally stuck at the time the event was experienced, and their symptomatology can be read as a repeated attempt to complete the interrupted action. Janet focuses on the collapse of narrative memory in trauma patients. Ferenczi (1955) defines shock in terms of the annihilation of consciousness, the ability to resist, to act and to think in defense of one's self, and continues:

> Shock always comes upon one *unprepared*. It must needs be preceded by a feeling of *security*, in which, because of the subsequent events, one feels *deceived*; one trusted in the *external world too much* before; after, too little or not at all. One had to have over-estimated one's own powers and to have lived under the delusion that *such things* could not happen, not *to me*.
>
> (p. 254)

Ferenczi defines trauma—psychic shock, in his words—an experience of rupture such that there is a pre-traumatic and a post-traumatic personality, *a great suffering that cannot be overcome*. The resulting anguish is so overwhelming that to get rid of it the most radical of possibilities is self-destruction. He continues: "Easiest to destroy in ourselves is the Id—the integration of mental images into a unit: Disorientation" (p. 249). Ferenczi also speaks of dreams in relation to trauma (1955), but he deviates from Freud's thought when he argues that the return of "day's residues" (p. 238) constitutes in itself one of the functions of the dream. He speaks of the "traumatolytic function" of dreaming (p. 240): the tendency to repeat trauma is greater in sleep than when awake. Dreaming about trauma allows one to improve one's relationship with it. Thus, wish-fulfillment is not the purpose of dreaming, but rather the means by which traumatic events are processed and made more acceptable. "Every dream, even an unpleasurable one, is an attempt at a better mastery and settling of traumatic experiences" (p. 238).

The centrality of trauma today

As we mentioned above, the interest and deepening of trauma studies that have characterized research in the fields of childhood, neuroscience, and clinical psychology in recent decades have caused a real shift in perspective from the classical psychoanalytic view, linked to Freud's seduction theory and theories of intrapsychic conflict. Since the 1970s, Freud's perspective has been strongly attacked for its denial of the traumatic basis of hysteria. In contrast, Janet's and Ferenczi's conceptions of trauma, which emphasize the centrality of actual events at the expense of mere fantasies and internal conflicts, have been rediscovered and are now widely accepted. However, this epistemological veering of trauma theory is sometimes read in terms of a dialectic between two rigidly opposing positions, coinciding, on the one hand, with the prominence of the internal—fantasized conflictual object relations—and, on the other, with that of the external—actual abuse and parental failure (Greenberg, 2019). The two views, thus set in opposition to each other, generated antithetical hypotheses regarding the etiology of psychopathology, and it is in relation to this that Stuthridge (2006) states, "The question being asked here is this: Does pathology arise from real life monsters or from monsters of the mind?" (p. 270). In an interesting article published by Howard Levine in *The International Journal of Psychoanalysis*, the author defines this kind of question as *puzzling*. Acknowledging the existence of truly experienced events to explain trauma should not debase the subjective experience of those who experience them. Trauma does not affect everyone equally. As Malinowski (2021) argues:

> For some people, it is possible to recover and to continue with life without the event having a major impact on their lives afterwards. Some may even experience post-traumatic *growth* (sic): to adapt in such a way that subsequent living is improved, perhaps in terms of having a greater appreciation for life. But for others, post-trauma life can become a literal nightmare.
>
> (p. 74)

The traumatic potential of events is highly subjective and personal, and the potentially traumatic consequences of events vary according to the age, developmental levels, and psychic abilities of the individuals concerned. These consequences are also strongly influenced by the reactions of the individual's family, social, and cultural context. Working in psychotherapy on trauma always means working on the consequences that a life event or events left in the mind of the individual who experienced it. Regardless of the type of event, an experience is traumatic when it disrupts and disorganizes the psychic processes charged with the construction of meaning. To such events the individual fails to give meaning, because "*such a thing* cannot happen, not *to me*" (Ferenczi, 1955, p. 254). And it is obvious that the familial and social environments also fail in this unsuccessful attempt to make meaning. The familial and social environments can be complicit in increasing resilience or, conversely, vulnerability. Abuse or neglect may be perpetrated within the family at the hands of those who are supposed to protect, care for, and assist the child. These dramatic experiences can give rise to what is referred to in the *Psychodynamic Diagnostic Manual* (PDM-2) as "betrayal trauma" (Lingiardi & McWilliams, 2017). However, even in privileged familial and social contexts, where the child's needs are placed at the center and the child is given adequate care, adverse circumstances and negative events experienced by the child may hold potential for trauma, because such crises go beyond the ability of the child's mind to make sense of the experience. Moreover, it is the consensus of all scholars pertaining to the field of infant research that caregivers can modulate the disturbing impact of the event on the child's mind. As Fonagy (2002) would say, a lack of reflective functioning and emotional regulation in attachment figures determine a dangerous vulnerability in the child that is fertile ground for trauma. But trauma is never a direct consequence of this. What happens is that the individual's psychic functioning is weakened, inadequate, or nonexistent due to constitutional factors, inadequate external situations, and problematic affective relationships. From this perspective, it almost seems obvious that there should always be some form of trauma underlying psychopathology. And at the same time, that life itself in its unfolding continually produces potential trauma, that is to say, occasions when something overcomes the mind's ability to make sense of an experience. In this regard, Cornell (2012) writes:

> We are, by the very fact of being alive, in essence, a threat to ourselves, at risk of being too much for ourselves. The forces of human development constantly push us past our capacities to maintain a self in equilibrium. This can be experienced as traumatic, regardless of the recognition and attention of another.
>
> (p. 255)

And Howard Levine (2021) reiterates:

> What we eventually call trauma is determined by the relative strength and balance of the ongoing struggle to contain, "detoxify" and "metabolize" raw existential experience; the inevitable consequence of being sensate and alive in the world.
>
> (p. 802)

Trauma and dissociation in TA

Eric Berne has always considered the origin of psychopathology to be traumatic. In *Transactional Analysis in Psychotherapy*, the 1961 work in which he systematically introduces transactional analysis, he states that: "Pathology is concerned with the reactions of living organisms to injury" (p. 44). Additionally, he describes a traumatic ego state as a defectively shaped coin that can topple the stack of other coins above it, the latter representing the entire personality (see Chapter 5). A relational model by definition—transactional analysis stands for the analysis of communicative exchanges between people—transactional analysis defines health as the integration of the multiple parts of the personality called ego states. Repairing trauma does not only mean participating in fruitful and healthy communicative exchanges—i.e., transactions—with others. Above all, it means making contact with oneself once again and dialoguing with the different parts of the self, even those that have caused such deep and unbearable shame and pain that they have been forgotten and exiled (Bromberg, 2006, 2011). The ego states model lends itself well to comparison with recent theories of trauma and dissociation (Stuthridge, 2012; Novak, 2013). It was Sullivan who first spoke of dissociation as a defense mechanism and a specific category of the human mind called "not-me" (in Cornell, 2012). Although it is not the only one, dissociation is the main mode by which a mind defends itself against trauma. Dissociation is defined as the disconnection and discontinuity of the normal integration of consciousness, memory, identity, emotionality, perception, bodily representation, motor control, and behavior (PDM 2, pp. 195–196; DMS 5 p. 337). This "fault line within the psyche" (Stuthridge, 2012) serves to protect the victim from reliving the trauma. And, to repair the wound of trauma patients, Novak suggests an integration in transactional analysis between structural and relational work (2013). Structural work involves getting the emerging parts to communicate. This operation diverges very sharply from that suggested by Goulding's (1979) redecisional therapy, according to which the patient, by means of systematic regression within a marathon group setting, is urged to identify with the traumatized part of the Child in order to heal. Today this approach is considered risky and iatrogenic. Psychotraumatologists give clear and precise guidance to therapists who want to learn how to work with trauma: Never take the patient back to the hell from which they came from and which they survived at great cost. What helps to heal from the fragmentation of the Self is to start from the safe position of the Adult to welcome and protect the wounded parts of the Child ego state. According to Morena (2014), "we do not disturb hibernating monsters, but we are ready to chase and follow them when they wake up" (p. 121). And when they do wake up, Janina Fisher urges us to remind patients: "You are safe now—no one can hurt you—this is now, not then" (2017, p. 229). It is nonetheless important to look at, but not relive, the wounded part, because it does needs to receive attention, understanding, and compassion (Fisher, 2017). With regards to relational work, Novak explains that the journey to repair by means of the therapeutic relationship is fraught with pitfalls because of the introjection of traumatic Parent–Child patterns: The encounter with the therapist has a great emotional impact for trauma victims. When the parent is abusive, neglectful, or dysregulated, toxic, poisonous Parent–Child relational patterns are introjected into the ego states (Little, 2006; Stuthridge, 2006). Permanent changes in the psyche can occur as a result, which we call *traumatic script* and which often result in full-blown personality disorders (Mucci, 2014, 2019). Such relational dyads are defensively excluded from consciousness as a result of dissociation but can be reactivated in dreams and nightmares as well as in the relationship with the therapist through transference and enactment (Bromberg, 2006; Novak, 2013). Stuthridge (2006) identifies three typical relational patterns, each of which concerns a dyad of Parent–Child ego states: the good child (Victim) and the idealized parent (Savior); the abused child (Victim) and the abusive parent (Persecutor); the empty child (Victim) and the neglectful parent (Bystander) (Clarkson, 1987), in the case of those parents who assist without intervening to protect the child from becoming a victim of trauma, "adults [who] react with a deathly silence that makes the child as ignorant as they are required to be"[1] (Ferenczi, 1933, p. 103). The therapist working with victims of early relational trauma will transferentially take on such dramatic triangle positions at different stages of therapy, or even at different times in the same session, if the patient is very unstable.

The patient who wishes to trust another human being again has, at the same time, a need to protect themselves from intimacy, which is considered dangerous because it is within a relationship that the traumatic experience has been consummated. The relationship is desired but at the same time feared, since it could lead to reliving the trauma. Here is where what Little (2011) calls relational impasse is generated in the therapeutic relationship: The members of the dyad are poised between the resurgence of their own transference dramas, in which the other is experienced as a character in one's own traumatic script (repeated relationship) and the creation of a new reparative relationship (needed relationship). The healing process, involving therapist and patient, develops from the possibility of establishing a new necessary relationship. It is precisely in identifying this kind of deconfusion-like, reparative intervention of the traumatized Child ego state that psychodynamic and relational transactional analysis departs most from Berne's original directions. The assumption of a Martian thinking on the part of the therapist, who observes from the outside the patient's games, confronting and decontaminating the patient until the they gain the necessary insight, is no longer considered viable. From Cornell, Hargaden and Allen (2005) comes a bi-personal relational approach where therapist and

---

1 My translation.

patient interact toward healing. William Cornell, an author we constantly draw inspiration from in our work, argues that psychological games in therapy cannot be avoided but must be experienced, waded through, because they represent the closest thing to the patient's unspoken reality, to their traumatic contents recorded in implicit memory. When both therapist and patient become "blinded in the dark of our pasts," says Cornell (2016, p. 271), reflective functioning is momentarily lost, emotions are toxic, dysregulated (Fonagy et al., 2002). Distress is not contained, emotions are not linked to thought, and this causes emotional storms and acting out that can be explained by the dominance of the Child over the Adult. The reactivation of traumatic scripts in the therapeutic relationship is a co-presence of loneliness. However, the lack of encounter in the here-and-now between therapist and patient may be a more suitable framework for trauma repair than the search for explicit memories of the traumatic event in the there and then. When the Adult ego state—that component of the personality stitching together all the parts of the ego states in order to create an integrated sense of identity—is reactivated, only then the new relationship, the needed relationship, can be created. The meeting of thinking minds restores connections to disowned parts of the self (Bromberg, 2006, 2011) and enables the recovery of that lost intersubjectivity that Keith Tudor would call we-ness (2016). Despite the current and increasing emphasis on dissociation and trauma, Cornell urges that enthusiasm with respect to dissociation be curbed. Psychopathology is not all about dissociation. It is not "the new black." His invitation is, first and foremost, not to confuse the mechanism of dissociation with the disorganization and fragmentation typical of the psychotic patient. He also urges caution when putting great emphasis on relationship as a necessary tool for healing from the traumatized self. He argues that "Relational attentiveness is not a universal solvent to trauma" (2012, p. 255). It is helpful, certainly, but not essential to the development of the self or the continuity of the mind that there be someone close by to provide support or protection. In repairing a dissociated and blocked mind, we must not underestimate the encounter with ourselves and all our parts (2012).

Post-traumatic nightmares

Research shows how trauma and stress are central elements in dreams. As well as falling under nightmare disorder among the parasomnias in APA (2013), recurring nightmares with sudden and distressing awakenings associated with sleep disturbances constitute some of the most common and universal onset symptoms of post-traumatic stress disorder (Pace-Scott et al., 2015). In trauma victims, the nightmares are initially true reenactments of the traumatic event. This aspect is what mainly differentiates traumatic nightmares from other types of nightmares, for example, the highly imaginative, symbolic, and hyperassociative script nightmares we dealt with in Chapter 6, such as the ones with horror content, which function to help process emotional experiences (Barrett, 2001). In his *Libro de sueños* (Book of Dreams), Jorge Luis Borges quotes the English Romantic poet Samuel Thomas Coleridge when he says, "the images of wakefulness inspire feelings, while during sleep it is feelings that inspire images [...] If a tiger came into this room, we would be afraid; if we are afraid in sleep, we generate a tiger"[2] (1976/2015, pp. 20–21). If the dreamer wakes up distressed about the tiger, we are most likely dealing with a script nightmare. Inspired by some current life event or stimulated by psychotherapy, the shadow and the inner demon communicate unconsciously through dreams (Novellino, 2012). However, if the dreamer wakes up repeatedly, over the course of many nights, because of the same tiger appearing to them in their sleep, perhaps after having had close and shocking contact with the same animal, we are most likely dealing with a traumatic nightmare.

Most of the time, fortunately, peri-traumatic nightmares slowly disappear with time, giving way to ordinary dreams or nightmares with more varied plots. As the event is integrated, the representation of the event becomes more symbolic, and dream elements are interwoven with elements from the dreamer's recent or past life (Berrett, 2001; Hartmann, 1996, 1998).

Studies of war veterans, Vietnam veterans, or ethnic minorities persecuted during dictatorial regimes, such as the Kurdish people during Saddam Hussein's Iraqi regime, show that the greater the personal exposure to death and danger and the greater the extent of trauma, the more frequent the traumatic nightmares will be and the longer they will occur (Malinowski, 2021). Several cross-cultural studies prove that children or adolescents exposed to traumatic events commonly report nightmares that somehow recall that experience. Regardless of one's culture, the greater the traumatic impact, the more frequent traumatic dreams are (Nader, 2001). Nightmares in relation to trauma are associated with other symptoms such as sleep disturbances, difficulty in concentration and memorization. Monsters in dreams express fear and vulnerability in children and may represent some aspect of the experience as well as the perpetrator himself (Nader, 2001).

The nightmares described here certainly do not represent wish-fulfillment and do not contain the Adult's attempt to find a solution to a problem. In this case, the dreamer cannot get rid of their dream. The dream is a condemnation, a betrayal. According to some theories, the traumatic nightmare constitutes the failure of the defensive attempt to remove trauma from consciousness. Like flashbacks or the intrusion of affect, sensation or behavior, the nightmare represents a momentary weakening of dissociative defenses (Lingiardi & McWilliams, 2017). According to other theories, it is the expression of a failed attempt to process emotions so overwhelming that they cannot be processed

---

2   My translation.

(Barrett, 2001). The mind's attempt to process through dreams the traumatic experience fails completely. In any case, there seems to be a need to process the traumatic material in order to interrupt the repetition. It is certain that these sleep-interrupting dreams, violently altering the dreamer's quality of life, provoke such emotionally intense experiences that the dream is unable to perform its "traumatolytic" function (Ferenczi, 1955). It is as if the mind is stuck, like a broken record. Whether in the case of acute or chronic trauma, the recurring nightmare subjects the victim to re-traumatization by making them relive the original trauma in all its emotional intensity. For Margaret Bowater, a transactional analyst who has dealt with dreams for decades, the recurring nightmare is revelatory of a wounded psyche, and needs to be healed (2013). If that does not happen, the dreamer will keep seeing themselves as a victim, reinforcing their traumatic script. It takes a reparative experience, such as trauma-focused psychotherapy, for the record to start turning once more and the mind to evolve. Being able to bring to someone trustworthy, in a safe context, the monstrous content of one's nightmares is the beginning of liberation. Referencing his work with children who were victims of trauma, Morena (2014) declares that certain monsters brought into therapy seem more like evacuations than insights. The need of the patient, young or old, is to unburden themselves, to get rid of something painful, entrusting it to the therapist so that the sense of overwhelm, powerlessness, of feeling helpless, trapped, or defenseless is at least shared. With regard to this urgency to share, in *The Truce* (1963/2013) Primo Levi recounts two dreams. The first is a recurring dream from the years spent in Auschwitz:

> Dreams used to come in the brutal nights / Dreams crowding and violent/ Dreamt with body and soul / Of going home, of eating, of telling our story. / Until, quickly and quietly, came / The dawn reveille: / Wstawàch. / And the heart cracked in the breast.

The dream he shared with his fellow prisoners was to survive the horror of the concentration camp and return home, to eat, and tell their story. The need to share is as primary as the need to eat and to be reunited with loved ones. The second dream, reported at the conclusion of the book, is a real recurring nightmare full of anguish that, at regular intervals, sharply wakes Levi up since he returned home from Auschwitz:

> I am sitting at a table with my family, or with friends, or at work, or in the green countryside; in short, in a peaceful relaxed environment, apparently without tension or affliction; yet I feel a deep and subtle anguish, the definite sensation, of an impending threat. And in fact, as the dream proceeds, slowly or brutally, each time in a different way, everything collapses and disintegrates around me, the scenery,

the walls, the people, while the anguish becomes more intense and more precise. Now everything has changed to chaos; I am alone in the centre of a grey and turbid nothing, and now, I know what this thing means, and I also know that I have always known it; I am in the Lager once more, and nothing is true outside the Lager. All the rest was a brief pause, a deception of the senses, a dream; my family, nature in flowers, my home. Now this inner dream, this dream of peace, is over, and in the outer dream, which continues, gelid, a well-known voice resounds: a single word, not imperious, but brief and subdued. It is the dawn command of Auschwitz, a foreign word, feared and expected: get up, "Wstawàch."

(Levi, 1963/2013, p. 420)

In this nightmare, which recounts the most heinous of traumatic experiences a human being can be subjected to, there is no possibility of survival or even consolation; going back home is a dream that fades away at dawn.

When nightmares are chronic, causing interruption and actual sleep disturbances, peremptory action must be taken to stop them. There are numerous studies that have demonstrated the efficacy of therapies that focus on changing the nightmares' ending: for instance, *Image Rehearsal Therapy*—IRT—which is considered by the American Academy of Sleep Medicine to be the most effective therapy in treating such nightmares. Other examples are the *Focusing Oriented Dreamwork*—FOD—or the *Mastery Dreams*, (Barrett, 2001; Wittmann & de Dassel, 2015) as well as, to go back in time, the work on nightmares borrowed from Gestalt therapy described by Thomson in his famous *TAJ* article (1987). Such therapies, although different in some methodological aspects, have all in common the goal of training the victim to change the ending of their nightmares in order to master the traumatic event. In individual settings or with the aid of a group, such methodologies encourage the construction of scenarios for the incubation of healing dreams. The aggressors are thus rendered powerless, the fires extinguished, the virus isolated and rendered harmless. The efficacy of such techniques by which complete remission of repetitive nightmares is achieved is well-known and widely documented. However, their efficacy is greatest when the cause of the traumatic pain is easily identified. When, on the other hand, the rupture is hidden, not obvious or immediately traceable to a specific episode, as in cases of developmental trauma, abuse, neglect, bereavement, and loss, or in cases of abuse perpetrated over time and chronic loneliness, these techniques do not work as effectively. In such cases it is the whole personality that is deeply affected and damaged by the trauma. In short, when we are faced with what Judith Herman calls *Complex PTSD* (1997), focal intervention on the nightmare is not sufficient to provide symptomatic relief to the sufferer. In this case, recovery from trauma is complex and requires very long and delicate work within a psychotherapeutic journey.

Dissociation in dreams

As we have mentioned several times already, putting aside repetitive traumatic nightmares, dream production has a therapeutic function because it represents an additional space for processing emotional experiences that upset the dreamer's mind. A dream-producing mind, then, is a mind at work expressing concerns, metabolizing emotionally charged experiences, and finding solutions. For this reason, scholars agree that it is an indicator of progression that patients who previously did not dream, or rather, did not remember their dreams, at some point begin to do so, and bring their dreams to the therapist (Howell, 2020; Lingiardi et al., 2011). The fact that a patient, who previously did not dream, at a certain time begins to dream, even having bad dreams, signals the beginning of an active process of change and the overcoming of helplessness (Hartmann, 1998). Irvin Yalom's (2011) story titled *I'm Calling the Police* tells the story of the writer's encounter with Bob, a close college friend, during a party celebrating his 50th graduation anniversary. On this occasion Bob takes his friend by his arm and leads him to a quiet corner. Yalom writes:

> He leaned to my ear and rasped, "Something heavy is going on [...] The past is erupting [...] My two lives, night and day, are joining. I need to talk." I understood. Ever since his childhood spent during the Holocaust in Hungary, Bob had been living two lives: a daytime life as an affable, dedicated, and indefatigable cardiac surgeon and a nighttime life when fragments of horrific memories tramped through his dreams. I knew all about his daytime life, but in our fifty years of friendship he had revealed nothing of his nocturnal life.
>
> (2011, p. 8)

As we saw above, those parts of the ego states that have experienced trauma can be defensively excluded from consciousness through dissociation but reappear in dreams and nightmares. Dreams themselves are often referred to as dissociated states of consciousness (Barrett, 2001; Bromberg, 2006). Here the person appears adequate and well-functioning during the day, while at night they are overwhelmed and annihilated by the anxiety connected to a traumatic experience going back even years. As Mucci (2014) writes, "Trauma has no past, present or future but it is always set in a non-time in which it can be recalled over and over and which keeps the event in an eternal present" (p. 49).[3] Among the many types of trauma victims, the reliable cardiologist Yalom tells us about represents what Van der Hart, echoing Charles Myers, calls the Apparently Normal Personality (ANP), while the dreamer overwhelmed

---

3   My translation.

by memories is the Emotional Personality (EP) (Van der Hart et al., 2006). According to Bromberg, there are two privileged modes through which it is possible in therapy to build bridges between the dissociated ego states of the trauma victim: enactment analysis and dream analysis. The work of therapy is to make bearable what is unbearable and to shed light on what is disowned. What is disowned is either projected onto the therapist, acted out in therapy or dreamed (Bromberg, 2006). Through dream analysis we can attempt to understand those experiences, feelings, thoughts, and relational needs of which the patient is unaware because they reside in dissociated, excluded states of the self. As Howell (2020) argues, "Dreams provide a way for dissociated parts of the self to be noticed" (p. 172). Through the protagonist of his 1969 film *Pigsty*, Pasolini declares that the terrible nightmares that torment him at night are the most truthful thing in his life and that he knows of no other way to deal with reality. *Awakening the Dreamer*, the title of Bromberg's 2006 book, is the kind of work that leads to connecting the multiple islands of the self as they come to light through dreaming: That is how disowned emotions such as shame or fear, unacceptable thoughts or experiences such as prevarication and annihilation, find space in our true self. In patients with dissociative identity disorder (DID)—the most extreme of dissociative phenomenon—alter personalities may appear as dream characters. It may be through a dream that the main personality becomes aware of the alters and, through dream analysis, is able to make contact with them (Barrett, 2001; Mc Namara, 2019). Healing from trauma involves activating a fruitful dialogue between the client in the waking state and the dreamer/dreamers. The dissociated, hidden states of the self-find thus an autobiographical space to tell their perspective, their truth. But it is only when the absolute truth of one ego state no longer alternates with that of another that there can be a coexistence of ego states and an overcoming of dissociative defenses. This mending process is facilitated by dream work within a safe and welcoming context such as that of a solid therapeutic relationship. Stefano Morena, with regards to the role of the child therapist, states,

> To hold the thread in the narrative of a monster story is like laying the foundation for a house for the child's fears so they have a structure and will not leave him or her drifting in a terrible sea of anxiety.
> (2014, p. 119)

He concludes by saying:

> I wish to stress that dreams and monsters go hand in hand, just like expectations and disillusionment, trauma and reparation. I think that a good indication that treatment is coming to an end is when we see in our patient that vital force that allows her or him to turn terrifying monsters into a circus show, a wounded belly into a retreat protected

and made safe with her or his own hands. The child has been able to turn his or her suffering into a strength.

(pp. 125–126)

The transformation of moments of suffering into moments of strength through the sharing of monster stories is a sign of *post-traumatic growth*, as Malinowski (2021) calls it. And it affects, of course, not only children who are victims of trauma, but also adults, who were once children (Berne, 1961). Ferenczi, too, asserts something similar, demonstrating the great topicality of thought and extraordinary humanity of this pillar of psychoanalysis who, almost a century after his death, continues to enlighten us with his contributions on the impervious path into the meandering unknown parts of our patients' wounded Child. Faced with the despair of the trauma victim, Ferenczi insists that it is impossible to keep living unless:

> At the last moment some favorable change in the reality occurs. This favorable event to which we can point against the suicidal impulse is the fact that in this new traumatic struggle the patient is no longer alone. Although we cannot offer him everything which he as a child should have had, the mere fact that we can or may be helpful to him gives the necessary impetus towards a new life in which the pages of the irretrievable arc closed and where the first step will be made towards acquiescence in what life yet can offer instead of throwing away what may still be put to good use.
>
> (Ferenczi, 1955, p. 238)

A therapeutic story

Elisa is 18 years old and starts going to therapy at the suggestion of a friend, more out of curiosity than discomfort. Her terror of gaining weight and consequent control over food led the therapist (Francesca) to make a diagnosis of anorexia. During our session Elisa is proper, orderly, detached. Emotions are watered down if not completely disconnected. Elisa does not fall in love; Elisa, at most, is liked. In the first few meetings, she tells me about her family: She lives with her father, and her two older brothers live elsewhere. Her mother, a fervent Catholic, died when she was 9 from an illness that she had kept hidden as long as she could and for which she had never accepted treatment because "children always come first." Along with her mother, Elisa also loses the rest of her family: After a few months her older brother moves in with his partner, her other brother locks himself in depressive isolation, and her father has to be away from home three days a week for work. She recounts that as a child she did not go to kindergarten but stayed at home with her mother, who, officially devoted to sacrifice, had given up work in order to dedicate herself to her children. Over time, Elisa's stories conjure up a picture of her mother as an anxious, phobic, intrusive woman, who took out her fears on her daughter in order to exorcise them. Elisa's trauma script is structured around the unconscious belief that she is bad because she is the cause of her mother's death, and from this belief she develops the idea that dependency is dangerous, emotions uncontrollable and destructive. During her first year of therapy everything runs smoothly, except for the tremendous effort I sometimes have to put in in order to be mentally with her: Contact is intermittent, moments of sharing alternate with moments of withdrawal—periods of self-centering solitude. Everything runs smoothly because I cannot reach her, because we are disconnected from each other, mostly alone. In the first year of therapy, Elisa brings facts, but no dreams, since in her prevails a dissociative defensiveness and a difficulty in mentalizing. In August, a dramatic event reopens the fault line of the original trauma: a bad car accident involving friends who are with her on vacation. My own fear system kicks in when she talks about the details of the incident. Her trauma reopens mine. Five years before I met her, I too was involved in a tragic accident; like Elisa, I too lost a parent early on. Our right brains are communicating while our ability to think rationally is momentarily suspended (Schore, 1999). As a result of projective identification, I experience intense affective states. The following night I have a dream: *I am walking in an open prairie, it is sunny, suddenly in front of me there is a dizzying descent, the meadow in front of me is full of cacti, I have to go down the slope, I know I will hurt myself but I have to go.* I wake up restless.

Thomas Ogden (2005) argues that the patient needs the mind of another person "who is acquainted with the night" to help them dream those aspects of their nightmare that have yet to be dreamed. The analyst's dream does not belong to the analyst or even to the patient: It belongs to a third subject who at the same time is the patient and the analyst and yet neither of them. Using the therapist's subjective experience is crucial to nurture a mutual process that allows the patient to experience their own dissociated states of the self, but contained in the mind of another.

At the heart of this work is not interpretation but a negotiation between subjectivities (Bromberg, 2006). Two weeks later, Elisa brings to therapy her first dream, or rather, her first nightmare:

We are at my house, there are a lot of people I don't know, it's evening. You're there and at some point you start screaming, you move into the living room of this house that I don't recognize and you keep screaming. I get closer but the people around me tell me to stay away from you, they don't want me to understand what's going on. I look in from the glass door to see you from the outside and I see you're throwing things everywhere as you scream. A girl comes to me and says, "She's possessed." I want to take a closer look so I look through a window, next to me there is a boy running but I don't know who he is. I take a video with my phone. I move to the back of the house and after a while you come out. You've lost so much weight and you're all sad. You sit down and I stand behind you and stroke your hair, reassuring you that everything is okay.

In the dream, Elisa identifies with the Apparently Normal Personality, that she cares for and reassures, while the Emotional Personality (Van der Hart, Nijenhuis, Steele, 2006)—her Child ego state—fixed at the time of trauma and dissociated, is projected onto the thin, sad therapist, who finds herself in the grip of overwhelming, dysregulated emotions, by which she is "possessed." It is I who feel her fear, her shame. One day she comes in for a session and tells me, "My mom could have been cured," "I feel shame towards my family who did not do anything to stop my mom's illness." Lesser now is the use of dissociation in favor of other defense mechanisms. After two weeks, another dream:

> *I'm with G. [boy she has been in a relationship with for a few months], we are alone in a huge room. The floor is a checkerboard, with black and white tiles, but all downhill. On either side of this room there are store windows painted black. We chat quietly. Change of scene. I find myself in a museum of stuffed animals. Some of them are alive. I play with a lion. There is a very tall armchair. G. sits in it and is happy.*

Bringing the dream into the session has a constructive meaning and testifies to a previously repressed ability to think that had been formerly removed from consciousness, as well as to a therapeutic relationship experienced as a safe environment that produces an increased her threshold of tolerance to emotions. On this subject, Lingiardi and De Bei (2008) observe:

> The oneiric unconscious, which both sustains and eludes us, possesses the implicit emotional memory of every word, the one that the analysand very often does not say, not because they hide or repress, but because they have yet to learn to know and say.[4]
>
> (p. 332)

The therapist asks Elisa what animals are there in the museum. She names fawns, giraffes, lions, ostriches. Through a process of co-construction of meaning and free associations, fawns are associated with Bambi—the orphaned fawn—giraffes with curiosity, lions with strength and anger, ostriches with shame because they hide their heads under the sand. I ask her which animals she thinks are alive. Lions and giraffes. Thus, anger and curiosity are alive, parts that can be reintegrated into consciousness, into a more expanded Self.

The state of the orphaned Child ego state—Bambi—associated with the emotions of fear, guilt and shame is recognized and seen from the outside, but is still frozen, separated by an inner glass wall that cannot yet be broken.

---

4 My translation.

In the words of Lingiardi and De Bei (2008), "Sometimes I think we can do it. For as Hamlet says: 'I could be bounded in a nutshell, and count myself a king of infinite space, were it not that I have bad dreams'" (p. 324).

She experiences increasingly complex emotions while internal conflict is tolerated, showing a greater co-presence of multiple states of the Self. The structuring of a more affective Inner Parent can support Elisa's Adult in weaving stories useful to bind together the different parts of ego states into a single coherent "me." Because the Self resides in a story rather than a single ego state, not only can Elisa's present and future change, but her past too, because memory changes with new experiences (Damasio, 2000).

Collective nightmares and trauma

Over the past two years, the whole world has shared the traumatic experience of the COVID-19 pandemic. During this time there have been a great many studies focusing on the impact of collective trauma on individual dream activity. What has emerged across the board is that people have dreamed and remembered more dreams than usual—longer, more vivid, and more bizarre dreams. A study conducted by the Lyon Neuroscience Research Center found a 35% increase in dream memories in late March and early April 2020. Barrett (2020) claims that this finding can be explained by the particular combination of global crisis and more time to sleep, since REM sleep lasts longer in the latter part of sleep, which usually happens during the early morning. Sleeping eight hours instead of six means gaining 50% more dreams. In addition, you are more likely to wake up spontaneously at the end of an REM phase of sleep, which often coincides with the end of a dream in the morning. This large amount of dreams has been shared with roommates, but also online on Zoom, Facebook, and other social networks, or websites specifically used for dream-collecting. In his book *Pandemic Dreams*, Barrett presents the results of his analysis of more than 9,000 dreams collected in two months from dreamers all around the world. In Italy, a study published in 2022 conducted by Lingiardi and colleagues, analyzed a sample of 598 participants for a total of 1,037 dreams collected during the lockdown period, which in Italy lasted more than two months, in the spring of 2020. The results showed that the pandemic significantly impacted dream quality as well as quantity. In general, subjects reported dreaming more, and those with a higher level of psychological stress had more dreams with COVID-19-related themes. In some cases these were more literal dreams where the virus appeared directly; in others, its symbolic substitutes were such things as tsunamis, tornadoes, hurricanes, earthquakes, fires, and wars. These are common metaphors in dreams, not only during the pandemic but when it comes to any disaster, whereas insects and invisible monsters have been common and collective metaphors unique to the coronavirus pandemic (Barrett, 2020).

At times the metaphors used by the unconscious to express pandemic-related anxieties contain other themes experienced as conflicting by the dreamer: A phobic girl who cannot drive a car dreams that she is driving and getting into an accident with many other cars. The message seems to confirm the fear: proximity is dangerous (Lingiardi et al., 2011). We, too, at PerFormat, set up two social dreaming groups during the pandemic, to which dozens of people from all over Italy took part (Tangolo & Castelluzzo, 2020). It is clear that the period of lockdown, characterized by severe uncertainty, isolation, and death anxiety, was marked by the presence of a collective adjustment disorder: There was a high prevalence in the population of anxiety states, depressed moods, conduct disorders, withdrawal, physical symptoms, as well as sleep, work or school dysfunctionality. During periods of collective tragedy such as this, we find ourselves in a very special circumstance whereby therapist and patient are having similar experiences, are immersed in the same condition. It is important for the therapist, at times like these more than others, to take care of their own emotional experiences and traumas in order to accommodate those of others. This widespread discomfort was noticeable in the distress dreams brought into the social dreaming space. However, as dream sharing went on, what emerged was an increasingly widespread ability to produce original metaphors and identify creative solutions to daytime problems. Although the dreamer is unquestionably the owner of the dream, the owner of their own metaphors, the sharing of the dream with others was, at such a dramatic time, an enriching and therapeutic experience for each of us (for a closer look at this see Chapter 11 on dreams in group psychotherapy). Thanks to the thousands of dreams collected during the pandemic we have historical memory of the collective unconscious of a period that, in its tragic nature, divided and at the same time united the whole world.

Another collection of traumatic dreams that holds a very high human, as well as historical, value is the already mentioned book published by German journalist Charlotte Beradt, which collects the dreams of hundreds of people who lived under the Third Reich. The general picture that emerges is that of a severely distressed dreamer, overtaken by a deep sense of annihilation and helplessness. The terror is such that even the content of the dreams is censored. In these dreams the will to fight is almost completely absent; we find no narratives in which the dreamer emerges victorious. As Bettelheim writes in the afterword, "The Third Reich invades and controls even the deepest and most private recesses of our minds, until finally, even in the unconscious, only submission remains" (Beradt, 1968, pp. 155–156). It is yet another way through which the victims are profoundly dehumanized. Bettelheim further observes that in the dreams collected by Beradt emerge a series of inner conflicts that were not created by the regime but are amplified by it. This is true of all collective traumas: dramatic events go for the Achilles' heels of the victims, that is, they reopen old wounds and previous traumas. This is how they find themselves overwhelmed, unable to defend themselves. Re-traumatization destroys the ability to resist, even in imagination, even in dreams. In some traumatized populations, as much as 100% of survivors suffer from terrifying dreams during or immediately after the event. These nightmares are so dramatic that they sometimes violate the usual sleep paralysis. During such nightmares, people jerk, move, and scream. Some get confused and no longer know whether they are dreaming or not. These sleep disorders can accompany the dreamer throughout their life (Barrett, 2001). Malinowski (2021) argues that the traumatic dreaming of populations subjected to violence and abuse is a shared social nightmare. He continues:

> The war nightmares of combat veterans, the sexual molestation nightmares of abuse victims (often women and children), the chase nightmares of refugees forced to flee homes from government and other forces—these collective nightmares tell the stories of the powerless and the vulnerable in human society.
>
> (p. 82)

The most fragile groups exposed to sustained violence, trauma, and perennial re-traumatization seem to be asking what Rag'n'Bone Man articulates in the refrain of his song titled *Human*: "I'm only human after all. Don't put your blame on me." Whatever the hand that procured them, collective nightmares must be dealt with collectively. Untreated collective traumas produce traumatized generations who pass the traumas on to future generations. Children are forced to dream about their parents' nightmares. Moreover, the less the parent remembers, the greater the amount of unprocessed experience that is passed on to children (Connolly in Mucci, 2014). In the face of dehumanizing experiences, as therapists we owe it to ourselves to promote the process of humanization. And, as human beings, we have a social commitment to fulfill: To avoid acting akin to negligent parents who look the other way. It takes profound ethical wisdom and great sensitivity to distinguish staying three steps behind the patient (Berne, 1966) from being a bystander in the face of abuse. Being respectful of client autonomy is different than doing nothing, because the latter choice assigns us, in fact, an active role in perpetuating the victimization of trauma and violence (Clarkson, 1987). As Bettelheim writes, if trauma is provoked by human actions, it must be countered by equally decisive and equally human reactions, including our own.

References

American Psychiatric Association, ed. (2022). *Diagnostic and statistical manual of mental disorders*, 5th ed., Text Revision. Washington, DC: American Psychiatric Publishing.

Barrett, D. (2001). *Trauma and dreams*. Cambridge: Harvard University Press.

Barrett, D. (2020). *Pandemic dreams*. Oneiroi Press.
Beradt, C. (1968). *The Third Reich of dreams*. Chicago: Quadrangle Books.
Berne, E. (1961). *Transactional Analysis in psychotherapy*. New York: Ballantine Books.
Berne, E. (1966). *Principles of group treatment*. New York: Oxford University Press.
Borges, L. (2015). *Libro di sogni [Book of dreams]*. Milano: Adelphi (Originally published in Spanish in 1976).
Bowater, M. (2013). Fighting back. *Transactional Analysis Journal, 43*(1), 38–47.
Bromberg, P. M. (2006). *Awakening the dreamer: Clinical Journeys*. Mahwah, NJ: The Analytic Press.
Bromberg, P. M. (2011). *The shadow of the tsunami and the growth of the relational mind*. London: Routledge.
Clarkson, P. (1987). The bystander role. *Transactional Analysis Journal, 17*(3), 82–87.
Cornell, W. (2012). This edgy emotional landscape: A discussion of Stuthridge's "Traversing the fault lines". *Transactional Analysis Journal, 42*(4), 252–256.
Cornell, W. F., Hargaden, H., & Allen, J. R. (2005). *From transactions to relations: The emergence of a relational tradition in transactional analysis*. Chadlington Oxfordshire: Haddon Press.
Cornell, W. (2016). Failing to do the job. *Transactional Analysis Journal, 46*(4), 266–276.
Damasio, A. (2000). *The feeling of what happens: Body and emotion in the making of consciousness*. London: William Heinmann.
Ferenczi, S. (1933). Riflessioni sul trauma. *Opere, IV*, 101–109.
Ferenczi, S. (1955). *Final contributions to the problems and methods of psychoanalysis*. New York: Basic Books.
Fisher, J. (2017). *Healing the fragmented selves of trauma survivors: Overcoming internal self-alientation*. New York: Routledge/Taylor & Francis.
Fonagy, P., Gergely, G., Jurist, E. L., & Target, M. (2002). *Affect regulation, mentalization and the development of the self*. New York: Other Press.
Goulding, M. M. C., & Goulding, R. L. (1979). *Changing lives through redecision therapy*. New York: Grove Press.
Greenberg, J. (2019). Trauma, interpretation and the metaphor of oppression. *International Journal of Psychoanalysis, 100*(6), 1144–1153.
Hartmann, E. (1996). Outline for a theory on the nature and functions of dreaming. *Dreaming, 6*(2), 147–169.
Hartmann, E. (1998). *Dreams and nightmares: The new theory on the origin and meaning of dreams*. New York: Plenum Trade.
Herman, J. (1997). *Trauma and recovery: The aftermath of violence. From domestic abuse to political terror*. New York: Basic Books.
Howell, E. (2020). *Trauma and dissociation-informed psychotherapy*. New York: Norton.
Levi, P. (2013). *If this is a man & The truce*. London: Abacus Books (Originally published in Italian in 1963).
Levine, H. B. (2021). Trauma, process and representation. *The International Journal of Psychoanalysis, 102*(4), 794–807.
Lingiardi, V., Amadei, G., Caviglia, G., & De Bei, F. (2011). *La svolta relazionale [The relational turn]*. Milano: Raffaello Cortina Editore.

Lingiardi, V., & De Bei, F. (2008). La terapia come processo di umanizzazione: Sogno e memoria nell'analisi di una paziente traumatizzata [Therapy as a humanizing process: Dream and memory in the analysis of a traumatized patient]. In V. Caretti & G. Craparo (Eds.), *Trauma e psicopatologia. Un approccio evolutivo relazionale*. Roma: Astrolabio, pp. 308–332.

Lingiardi, V., & Mc Williams, N. (2017). *Psychodynamic diagnostic manual: PDM – 2* (2nd ed.). New York: Guilford Press.

Little, R. (2006). Ego state relational units and resistance to change. *Transactional Analysis Journal*, *36*(1), 7–19.

Little, R. (2011). Impasse clarification within the transference-countertransference matrix. *Transactional Analysis Journal*, *41*(1), 23–38.

Malinowski, J. (2021). *The psychology of dreaming*. London: Routledge.

McNamara, P. (2019). *The neuroscience of sleep and dreams*. Cambridge: Cambridge University Press.

Morena, S. (2014). Children and their monsters. *Transactional Analysis Journal*, *44*(2), 118–127.

Mucci, C. (2014). *Trauma e perdono. Una prospettiva psicoanalitica intergenerazionale [Trauma and forgiveness: An intergenerational psychoanalytic perspective]*. Milano: Raffaello Cortina.

Mucci, C. (2019). *Corpi borderline. Regolazione affettiva e clinica dei disturbi di personalità [Borderline bodies. Affective regulation and personality disorders]*. Milano: Raffaello Cortina.

Nader, K. (2001). Children's traumatic dreams. In D. Barrett (Ed.), *Trauma and dreams* (pp. 9–24). Cambridge: Harvard University Press.

Novak, E. T. (2013). Combining traditional ego state theory and relational approaches to Transactional Analysis in working with trauma and dissociation. *Transactional Analysis Journal*, *43*(3), 186–196.

Novellino, M. (2012). The shadow and the demon: The psychodynamics of nightmares. *Transactional Analysis Journal*, *42*(4), 277–284.

Ogden, T. H. (2005). *This art of psychoanalysis: Dreaming undreamt dreams and interrupted cries*. London: Routledge.

Pace-Schott, E., Germain, A., & Milad, M. (2015). Sleep and REM sleep disturbance in the pathophysiology of PTSD: The role of extinction memory. *Biology of Mood and Anxiety Disorders*, *5*(3), 1–19.

Schore, A. N. (1999). *Affect regulation and the origin of the self: The neurobiology of emotional development*. London: Routledge.

Stuthridge, J. (2006). Inside out: A Transactional Analysis model of trauma. *Transactional Analysis Journal*, *36*(4), 270–283.

Stuthridge, J. (2012). Traversing the fault lines: Trauma and enactment. *Transactional Analysis Journal*, *42*(4), 238–251.

Tangolo, A. E., & Castelluzzo, E. (2020). Sogno e Social Dreaming al tempo del coronavirus in Italia [Dreaming and Social Dreaming at the time of Covid-19 in Italy]. *Percorsi di Analisi Transazionale*, *7*(3), 38–48.

Thomson, G. (1987). Dreamwork in redecision therapy. *Transactional Analysis Journal*, *17*(4), 169–177.

Tudor, K. (2016). "We are": The fundamental life position. *Transactional Analysis Journal*, *46*(2), 164–176.

Van der Hart, O., Nijenhuis, E. R. S., & Steele, K. (2006). *Haunted self: Structural dissociation and the treatment of chronic traumatization.* New York: W. W. Norton & Co Inc.

Wittman, L., & de Dassel, T. (2015). Posttraumatic nightmares: From scientific evidence to clinical significance. In M. Kramer & M. Glucksman (Eds.), *Dream research: Contributions to clinical practice* (pp. 135–148). Routledge/Taylor & Francis Group.

Yalom, I. (2011). *I'm calling the police.* New York: Basic Books.

8
CHANGE AND TRANSFORMATION DREAMS

What change is possible?

As transactional analysts we carry with us the script theory of our master Eric Berne, who, however, has often been considered overly deterministic even by his early students and collaborators. In his work focused on the idea of the script entitled *What Do You Say After You Say Hello?*: *The Psychology of Human Destiny* (1972), Berne argues that in life the individual acts thinking they are the author of their own music—that is the well-known and already mentioned Berne's simile for the human being who, like the piano player, reproduces a melody unaware it has been composed by others. Human destiny, an expression that already appears in the book's subtitle, is largely decided by factors external to the individual. Beyond biological factors, Berne names parental programming as primarily responsible for script writing in children. Additionally, in the book's conclusion he explains "children represent a facsimile and immortality" (p. 297). According to Berne, autonomy—the goal of healing—is more of an illusion, a hope, than an existential condition achieved through the realization of the normal process of individuation. The very concept of the archaic Parent, called an "electrode" for the automatic response it gives in the child who has introjected it, is considered an expression of a rigidly mechanistic and pathologized view. To describe this process of introjection while teaching, the author [Francesca] uses the icon of the *Martyrdom of St. Sebastian*—whose perhaps most famous painting is that by the Renaissance painter Mantegna—as the evocative picture of the child as a helpless victim of messages that, like arrows, strike him and condemn him to submission for eternity. According to Berne, very specific circumstances are needed for a profound transformation to occur in the individual's psyche. Among these, he names love, school, and psychotherapy. With regards to the therapist's task, he declares toward the end of the book, "Instead of encouraging people to live bravely in an old unhappy world, it is possible to have them live happily in a brave new world" (1972, p. 272). In any case, liberation is external, which means that interpersonal support is needed in order to encourage change and free the person from their fate, which is more often tragic than "winning." As transactional analysts we have had to emancipate ourselves from this view, which is so deterministic and reductionist as to be pessimistic and, above all, far removed from the results of research carried out over the past 50 years in developmental psychology (Cornell, 1988). The Bernian view of a child growing up subject to the will of their parents makes it difficult to believe in the possibility of profound change leading to personal self-realization. In Chapter 5 we discussed the paradigm shift brought about by Daniel Stern's revolutionary studies. In the two decades following the release of *What Do You Say After You Say Hello?* and the death of its author, a number of works have been published on the subject of script theory. As early as 1976 an article by Holtby came out in the *Transactional Analysis Journal* emphasizing the active role of the child in the face of relational experiences in childhood. Along the same lines of thought came Mary and Robert Goulding. In their best-known work entitled *Changing Lives through Redecision Therapy* (1979) they assert, unlike Berne, that "the child does filter, select, make decisions for himself in response to such messages, and that he has some control over what he takes in" (p. 18). They have a very optimistic view of change, made possible and sustained by the entire therapeutic team as well as by the person of the therapist. Even more than the Gouldings, in his 1988 article Cornell proposes a more positive, structuring view of the script and only exceptionally represents it as a cage from which one must break free in order to access growth, maturity and well-being. His view—which is also found in the work of many child development scholars to whom he devotes an extensive analysis—focuses on health and resources rather than deficiencies and illness. According to Cornell, growth and change can occur at any point in life, and an unhappy childhood does not mean an equally unhappy adult life. Change and transformation have to do with freer access to conscious choice, improvisation and creativity, dimensions that recall the Bernian capacity for awareness, spontaneity and intimacy. That is, all that is at odds with the security made out of rituals and predictability offered by the script. However, structure is needed to organize and plan one's future. That is why, for Cornell (1988), the script becomes a life plan which the individual can define at any time in their life, a life plan that becomes negative only when "it involves hanging tenaciously on to certain beliefs about self and the world rather than allowing for the surprises and opportunities presented in actually living" (p. 280).

The script may represent a rough outline that helps make sense of experiences and surroundings but becomes negative when it prevents one from grasping life's surprises and unexpected opportunities. That is, when the need for security satisfied by "tenacious" adherence to an established system of reference replaces the need for exploration and prevents change and transformation. Scripts constructed in times of crisis, because of traumatic family experiences, will be more rigid and less flexible. In such cases, creativity and spontaneity, on which the Child ego state has given up out of fear, are dimensions to be recovered through the acceptance of the risk of change. Making this transition involves recovering the natural learning and developmental process of the human being in which maturity is a tension *toward* rather than a once-for-all attainable point of arrival. Embracing change means reassuring the terrified Child and moving around with one's Adult. Typical symptoms of depression such as apathy and planning immobility are in fact absence of movement of mind and body. So are obsessions, typical of various psychopathological frameworks, where continuously activating thought does not lead to movement in terms of awareness or insight but always remains the same, nailed down in its repetitiveness and intrusiveness. Even manic states, which, according to the psychoanalytic literature, are based on denial and narcissistic defenses (Lingiardi & McWilliams, 2017), although accompanied by great bodily and mental energy, temporarily produce movement that is only at times productive and constructive. It is closer to the crayfish, which, in perpetual oscillation swims forward and backward, and it is precisely backward that it ends up going in the long run.

Change and transformation in dreams

What impact does the recovery of the evolutionary transformative dimension and the acceptance of change pursued through psychotherapy have on dreams—and dream activity in general? And, at the same time, can dream activity help resume the interrupted evolutionary process? In previous chapters, we have seen that trauma nightmares and script dreams are stereotypical and recurrent. Although they vary in content, they always convey the same messages and, most importantly, leave unchanged the intensity of the emotional experience of the dreamer. In general, recurring dreams draw our attention to the dreamer's serious unresolved problems (Bowater, 2013). Ogden (2005) observes that a dreamer who cannot learn from experience "is imprisoned in the hell of an endless, unchanging world of what is" (p. 47). On the contrary, Ogden adds, only that mental phenomenon which leads to psychological growth and thus, as psychological growth by definition predicts, changes and evolves—only that can be defined as a dream. Remember the imagery suggested a few pages back of some part of the Child who, like a ghost, will continue undaunted to perturb the dreamer's nights until it has completed its mission and only then will it finally have and give peace? Lo and behold, when the Child begins to be "seen," welcomed, and heard, the dream activity changes significantly. This is among the most glaring evidence of a profound transformation taking place in the patient's psyche. Dreams change if and when the patient changes and, at the same time, they promote change (Cartwright, 2010; Ogden, 2005). In Chapter 7, too, we saw how the nightmares change as the trauma is processed. From an initial faithful reproduction of the traumatic event, the nightmares, while remaining as such, become more varied, and the emotional experience less intense. Over time, some variations on the theme are introduced that hint at some hope, which is already a hint of healing. The new dreams contemplate conclusions in which the dreamer puts up boundaries, saves themselves, perhaps takes revenge, and is generally more able to defend themselves. Changing the ending of one's nightmares is both the goal of change and the means by which it is accomplished. Renowned for her decades of research on dreams, Cartwright (2010) defines dreaming as our inner psychotherapist, capable of enabling mood regulation through the processing of emotions experienced during wakefulness. Cartwright argues that such a "nighttime therapeutic session" helps the dreamer see things in a more positive light upon waking and prepares them for a fresh start. This perspective change may require work over several dreams and several nights. It is useful, therefore, to keep note of the variation of dreams over time, in search of the feeling of refreshment that justifies their presence. After all, Bion (1962) already defined the alpha function as the function that enables us to dream, arguing that if this should fail, it is no longer possible to either dream, distinguish wakefulness from sleep, or think rationally. In line with Bion, Grinberg (1987) asserts, "It is then possible for the patient to continue learning to 'dream' his dreams in the same way that he gradually learns to 'think' his thoughts" (p. 158). Therapy can be seen as learning to dream one's dreams, and the evolution of therapy can be measured by the degree to which the patient can dream their experience on their own.

As Warner (1983) pointed out, during the course of the analysis, dreams evolve in form, content, and conclusion. Dreams change in parallel with clinical improvements. Patients with end-of-therapy dreams are more benevolent toward themselves, less critical, and less punitive, as well as showing a highly developed self-soothing capacity. A study conducted by Glucksman and Kramer (2015) confirmed Warner's findings and, in addition, showed that emotions experienced in dreams, which are primarily negative at first, become more positive over the course of psychotherapeutic treatment. In the study, the dreams of six patients who showed clear improvements in therapy were compared with those of six others whose improvements were almost nil. Kramer, who did not know the patients, acted as an independent observer. He evaluated the dreams and correctly recognized them as belonging to the two groups with a statistically significant result. The criteria by which improvements were assessed were: symptom reduction, central conflict resolution, level of functioning, ego strength, interpersonal relationships, transference resolution, affective resolution, and self-analytic ability (Luborsky et al., 1971). A second study compared the affective connotation of the first dreams brought to therapy with that of the last ones: The results show a significant shift from negative to positive emotions over the course of treatment. Moreover, negative transference appeared in 43% of the initial dreams and only 17% of the dreams at the end of therapy. The study shows how dreams change during therapy in a manner that is consistent with improvement in areas of psychological functioning.

The authors claim that: "On the basis of our studies, we believe that the MDR [Manifest Dream Report] can be used as a reliable instrument for measuring clinical progress over the course of treatment" (p. 120).

When we talk about change in dream activity, however, we can refer to different types of change depending, for example, on the patient's script. Some patients may bring fewer dreams to their sessions but nonetheless decide to use those same dreams to do sincere and courageous work on themselves. This is also true for those clients who, in the early stages of treatment, fill the room with dream accounts which take the form of defensive psychic evacuations that are more in service of avoidance than of the pursuit of intimacy. To paraphrase Ogden (2005), one can dream all one's life without any psychological work being done. Dreaming, as we shall see later, can be used in a way akin to acting out during a session. Therefore, before rushing headlong into questioning the content of the dream, it is always useful to ask what purpose it serves for the patient to have brought it (Fosshage, 1997; Segal, 1990). There are patients, as we have seen before, who defensively evacuate dreams one after another until they flood the session and cloud the therapist's mentalization. In such cases, the most significant and overriding element is the questioning of the reasons for this flooding and the exploration of the effect it has on the therapist (Segal, 1990). A change in dreams, moreover, may relate to a broader change in the dreamer's life. Major developmental milestones in an individual's life are very often accompanied by an increase in dream activity. As Bowater (2003) observes, life changes are profitable opportunities for dreaming:

> Think about what transitions are currently going on in your life. Leaving home? Entering or leaving a relationship? Becoming a parent? Losing a parent? Changing a job or location? Losing your health or your hopes? Slow transitions may be more in the background of your mind but still a source of anxiety about a change of status in your life. Dreams often bring up latent anxiety for your conscious attention.
> (pp. 39–40)

The intense emotional experiences that characterize major changes give lifeblood and creativity to the production of dreams because it is precisely through dreams that they can be processed. Long-awaited transitions are often preceded by dreams that anticipate them, as if the dream were, in a way, "a realization of reality." One of the authors (Francesca) recalls the dream she had the night before she left for Roncesvalles crossing the Pyrenees, the first mythical leg of the French Way to Santiago de Compostela. She was about to carry out a project that she had been preparing in great detail for months, and so in the dream she walked the full 27 km that separated her from her first stop. When an early alarm woke her up, she was a little tired but recharged and confident because she had verified in her dream that the route would be a happy one, free of pitfalls, and so fortunately it was. Therefore, dreams prepare the mind for great feats and anticipate the future, but also reopen, as we know, old wounds. Whether we are preparing to face joyful evolutionary changes or bereavements, all change destabilizes us, reconnecting us to our old weaknesses. As Cornell (2008) argues, "the level of protocol [...] emerge often during periods of the most intense personal growth, the most intimate stages of psychotherapy, or the deepening of our intimate relations" (p. 117).

The most delicate moments of psychotherapy are generally very rich from a dreaming perspective, and the analysis of such dreams offers a most valuable insight into the chasmic limitations of the script protocol. The theme of the dream reproduces the unconscious ghost of the script protocol following what Quinodoz (2002) calls "the individual iconography" of the dreamer (p. 26). He then explains that:

> The painter—like the dreamer—thus finds a temporary outlet for his need for reparation, in the knowledge that this process will never be completed and must be constantly renewed.
>
> (Quinodoz, 2002, p. 96)

Therefore, because it is stimulated by a profound change taking place, the appearance of distressing dreams, paradoxically, can be seen as a positive evolutionary signal, as we will find out later. An expression of transformation and change within the intersubjective field co-constructed by patient and therapist is also the appearance in the latter of countertransferential dreams, as we will further see in Chapter 12. Finally, talking *only* about dreams in therapy may be a defensive mechanism, as it might be never remembering one's dreams. From everything we have looked at so far, it is obvious that bringing one's dreams to the therapist is a clear sign of an obvious transformative process taking place. Let us now look at this very aspect in more detail.

The process of transformation in action: beginning to remember dreams

Berne's 1968 work entitled *A Layman's Guide to Psychiatry and Psychoanalysis* (first published as *Mind in Action* in 1947), in which an entire chapter is devoted to dreams and the unconscious, has already been mentioned in Chapter 3. It is so steeped in Freudian metapsychology that Freud's name has no need to appear even once in these pages, except in the bibliography where we read, "There is no substitute for Freud's work *The Interpretation of Dreams*" (p. 120). Consistent with this, Berne explains that dreams are expressions of the dreamer's unconscious desires, have a manifest and a latent content, and represent the *via regia* to the unconscious. Their function is to preserve sleep. However, in closing the paragraph devoted to the function of dreams, Berne proposes a new, original signification: Dreams help the mind to heal "after emotional wounds and distressing emotional experiences" (p. 116). In line with the latest neuroscientific hypotheses, according to Berne, dreaming promotes the processing of emotions. Emotions that if not "digested" can lead to psychopathology. Therefore, dreaming not only preserves sleep, but also the psychic health of the dreamer. What is evident in clinical experience is that psychotherapy helps to restore good sleep, develops the ability to dream and, most importantly, the ability to remember dreams. The appearance of dreams in patients who were unable to remember them thus has to do with a deeply transformative process taking place in the dreamer's mind. Because the nature of the dream is metaphorical and imaginative, its production seems to follow the acquisition and development of the capacity for mentalization, that is, the symbolic function of thought and the goal of psychotherapy according to Fonagy et al. (2002). Thinking thoughts, as well as dreaming dreams, implies taking in new, previously unknown content within oneself; it implies expanding one's mind. We saw in the chapter on dreams and trauma that in the recurring nightmare there is a *literal* repetition of the indigestible, unmetabolized traumatic experience, while in the developmental, "creative" dream, we find a symbolic representation of the traumatizing object that requires a process of working-through all thoughts and emotions attached to it. The recurring nightmare must be stopped because it is a symptom that endangers the dreamer and retraumatizes them (Bowater, 2013). On the other hand, if they are to expand their own mind, patients need therapy in order to learn to dream evolving and changing dreams. With this in mind, Ogden (2005) speaks of "dreaming undreamt dreams" and claims that:

> Undreamable experience is held in psychologically split-off states such as pockets of autism or psychosis, psychosomatic disorders and severe perversions […] To dream one's experience is to make it one's own in the process of dreaming, thinking and feeling it. The continuity of one's being—the background "hum" of being alive—is the continuous "sound" of one's dreaming oneself into being.
>
> (p. 24)

Khan (1972, in Resnik, 2005) argues that dreaming is a *capacity* precisely by virtue of the fact that it is necessary to be able to use symbolic discourse to access the dream dimension. As pointed out in a study by Grinberg, there is an inversely proportional relationship between dreaming and acting out: The inability to dream encourages acting out; the greater the number of dreams dreamed and remembered, the less recourse to acting out (1987). Therapy work stimulates the patient to remember their dreams and reappropriate parts that appear in them. In this sense, remembering one's dreams and bringing them into therapy is already a deconfusive act because the conflicts within the Child ego state are accessible and can be analyzed and integrated. The moment the dissociated parts are symbolized through dreaming, they become more available to consciousness. Ogden (2005) observes that, "To the extent that he is unable to dream his emotional experience, the individual is unable to change, or to grow, or to become anything other than who he has been" (p. 2). It is in this sense that the opposite of the dream is not the nightmare but the dream that cannot be dreamed.

The appearance of distress dreams: dreams that turn over a page

In previous chapters we have seen that dreams change as the stages of therapy progress. At crucial transitional moments in psychotherapy the patient might bring dreams that may seem to be of a regressive nature. In a longitudinal study carried out by Cartwright (2010) on a sample of people who became depressed following their divorce, it was found that the subgroup of subjects who had dreamed of their ex-partners in a dreamlike atmosphere marked by strong unpleasant emotions, such as anger and distress, were healed after one year and generally showed a healthier adjustment in life. Those who overcame grief and coped psychologically with their loss processed the negative feelings explicitly in their dream scenarios. Another study by Tousignant and colleagues (2022) on a sample of 191 subjects from a nonclinical population, showed that idiopathic nightmares predicted a significant decrease in negative emotions during the day after waking up. Thus, the data show that bad dreams have an adaptive function for the individual. They are therefore not necessarily regressive. On the contrary, to refer to those distress dreams dreamed at crucial transformative moments during one's therapeutic journey, Quinodoz (2002) uses the definition of "dreams that turn over a page." They appear as involutional dreams but are instead dreams of change because they produce a new stage of integration. The appearance of distressing content in dreams may indicate that a change has taken place, because it means that the patient unconsciously trusts that they can tolerate the representation of disturbing aspects in dreams and approach them within the therapeutic relationship. Also, this developmental aspect, if grasped, provides relief to the dreamer. Dreams that turn over a page are dreams that cause both relief and distress. The dreamer is not regressing but is able to represent misrecognized, perhaps dissociated, parts of themselves relegated up until that moment to the unconscious dimension. Quinodoz claims that such dreams are paradoxical because it is through them that the central conflict is enacted but, as the conflict is represented, it is also given meaning and can thus be integrated. The risk is, that if the transformative dimension of such dreams is not grasped by the therapist and, on the contrary, the dreams are read as regressive, they can in fact induce regression in the patient. How is it possible, then, to recognize them and distinguish them from actually regressive or traumatic bad dreams? Quinodoz explains that although upon awakening the dreamer feels distress and anxiety in relation to the dream, these unpleasant emotions disappear soon after the dream is analyzed. On the contrary, emotions experienced upon waking after nightmares of different types crystallize and remain with the dreamer. Moreover, unlike trauma nightmares that wake the dreamer up, these dreams do not interrupt sleep. Rather than distress, the author explains, it is appropriate to speak of a state of disturbance typically provoked by what lies between the familiar and the unfamiliar, which is the notion of the uncanny—this is how the German term *unheimliche* was translated into English—used by Freud (1919, in Quinodoz, 2002). Through such dreams, misrecognized parts, whether removed or split or disowned, make their way back into the self: "This gives rise to an uncanny feeling when the dreamer is confronted with the resurgence of parts of himself that are both known and unknown, but which nevertheless belong to him" (p. 12).

Dreams that turn over a page appear after a change. When the patient has evolved to what Kleinians call the depressive position, we as therapists have a better chance to stand in conflict and separation. If the therapist, instead of being frightened by dreams that turn over a page, recognizes them, they might help the patient see their transformative, evolutionary aspect. In that case, the patient calms down, and the distress and upset disappear immediately.

Dreams in psychopathology and dream psychopathology

Although there is still a long way to go in this area, we can say that Freud's (1899/2005) prophecy—"There can be no doubt that alongside of the psychology of dreams physicians will someday have to turn their attention to a psychopathology of dreams" (p. 129)—has, at least to a small extent, been fulfilled. In a study conducted by Schredl and Engelhardt (2001) on the relationship between dream activity and psychopathology, it was found that the contents of dreams are consistent with psychiatric symptoms manifested during wakefulness. With regards to the messages that dreams can offer us about the psychopathology of the dreamer, in 2013 Bowater wrote that:

> Even if there is little time to explore a dream report, a counselor can catch the essential theme by noticing what the dream ego is doing and feeling, that is, whether it is active or passive, timid or courageous, Victim or Persecutor.
>
> (p. 40)

Even earlier, analyzing the first few dreams brought to the analyst by 70 subjects over a period of five years, Saul (1940) declared that: "This experience has confirmed the generally accepted observation that the early current dreams of the analyses usually give the essence of the case" (p. 453).

If the work of dream analysis can take us into the very core of a deeper transformative work, their listening and recollection offer us information about the position from which the dreamer views the world, their coping style, their personality structure, and even their psychopathology. There is no doubt that the most extensive literature related to the relationship between dreams and psychopathology has been produced on the topic of the relationship between psychosis and depression. Psychosis and dreams have often been juxtaposed because they have many elements in common. For example, Malinowski (2020) observes that: "a hallucination during sleep is called a dream" (pp. 84–85), but there are numerous scholars among psychologists, psychiatrists, and philosophers, including Kant, Schopenhauer, and Wundt, who have provided famous juxtapositions between the psychotic and dreamlike conditions (for an extensive review on this see Freud, 1899/2005). Both, in fact, have to do with hallucinatory states; in psychosis as in REM sleep, the prefrontal cortex is deactivated and levels of dopamine—the neurotransmitter that amplifies neuronal connections—are significantly elevated. Research shows that people with psychosis and schizophrenia have more nightmares than others. Taking a one-week period into account, 70% of these patients' dreams are nightmares, compared to 10% in the general population (Malinowski, 2020). By and large, there is a very close relationship between psychosis, sleep, and dreaming. Schizophrenics have poor sleep quality, and antipsychotic drugs increase sleep duration and quality. All of us can experience psychotic symptoms after a prolonged period of insomnia (Malinowski, 2020). Among those who have explored the subject of dreams in psychotic patients is Solomon Resnik, who in 1987 published the splendid *The Theater of the Dream*, an indispensable work for those approaching studies in this field, with the expanded edition being republished in 2005. In the psychotic patient, writes Resnik, the waking life is overcome by dream elements. If the obsessive or borderline patient cannot dream, Resnik continues, the psychotic patient cannot wake up (p. 175). In psychosis, "the dream barrier breaks down," there is no longer a boundary between being awake and dreaming because dreams invade the waking space: "The dreamer—qua 'ego-centre'—corresponds partly to the psychotic ego that surrounds itself with its 'oneiroid' world, a creature that he has put into the world and totally subjected to his omnipotent, dogmatic control" (Resnik, 2005, p. 77).

The psychotic's dream is particularly bizarre, distressing and unstructured. "Pieces" of things, people, animals, figurative or abstract forms appear in it. In the early stages of the illness, it is common to find body-related anxieties such as delusional hypochondriacal fantasies or somatic hallucinations revealed through dreams. As Freud (1899/2005) writes, "The psychosis may come to life all of a sudden with the dream causing and containing the explanation for the mental disturbances, or it may slowly develop through further dreams that have yet to struggle against doubt" (p. 128).

Regardless of what the psychopathology is, it may find an opening and make its first appearance through a dream. Alternatively, the illness might keep itself to dreams without ever escaping into daytime life (Freud, 1899/2005). To work with the dreams of psychotic patients is to translate their language. The therapist is the patient's observing self that helps them gain an external perspective. From this position it is possible to extract a reading of what the dream is saying, and only through the distancing produced by this analytic operation is it possible to lower the level of anxiety that the dream carries. In the treatment of psychotic patients, even the telling of the dream is a positive, therapeutic element that bodes well from a prognostic point of view. As if the act of telling someone about the dream may lead the psychotic patient to "a 'crisis' in his dogmatic universe" (Resnik, 2005, p. 110) and to wake up. Quinodoz (2002) reports Silvano Arieti's experience with a psychotic patient. Arieti had taken the young woman into his care after an episode, characterized by delusions and hallucinations in which, in a panic, she ran through the streets of New York thinking that Russians were invading the city. After a year of treatment, the patient has a dream in which her parents chase her through the streets of the city. The conflict is thus expressed through a "psychotic way which is physiologic and available to every human being: the dream-world" (Arieti, 1963, p. 27 in Quinodoz, 2002, p. 60).

If Resnik is a key reference for the study of dreams in psychotic patients, the same can be said for Rosalind Cartwright—"the queen of dreams," as Ernst Hartmann dubbed her—in the study of the relationship between dreams and depression. Cartwright (2010) argues that the first symptom of depression, often underestimated or attributed to other medical causes, is difficulty sleeping. The sleep of depressed people is different from that of the general population. There is an overabundance of REM sleep, as well as longer, earlier, and denser stages. On the contrary, the N3 and N4 phases of sleep—the slow-wave kind, or the restorative stage of sleep—which are crucial for the consolidation of memories, are less long-lasting. However, the overabundance of REM sleep is not accompanied by an equally large production of emotionally connected dream scenarios, as one would expect (see Chapter 2). Dream recall is poor in depressed patients. Also making matters worse is the fact that the majority of depression medications reduce REM sleep. The few dreams that are remembered are either mostly connoted by negative emotions, or flat and emotionally detached, since they closely mimic waking emotions (Cartwright, 2010; Schredl & Engelhardt, 2001). Significant transitional stages in the treatment of depression consist first of all in the recovery of more waking dreams; in addition, dreams become longer, with complex plots that include several characters and scene changes.

Subsequently, we can begin to notice a higher percentage of more positive dreams before waking, which is associated with an improvement in the patient's mood the morning after (Cartwright, 2010).

Alexithymic or obsessive patients are known to have difficulty remembering their dreams. They are defined by Hartmann (1996) as people with "thick boundaries in the mind": a dimension that refers to another degree of separateness and compartmentalization in all mental functions. These people tend to keep perceptions, thoughts, and feelings distinct and separate; they keep time and space well organized; they think in value terms distinguishing in categorical terms what is right and what is wrong, what is good and what is bad; they have a clear delimited sense of self; they are very solid, well-defended, and sometimes even rigid. If we consider that dreaming is defined by Hartmann as "a thin boundary state," we can understand why such patients almost never remember their dreams, and one of the most significant pieces of evidence of an ongoing psychotherapeutic transformative process is precisely the appearance of the possibility to recall them. In contrast, patients with borderline and schizotypal personalities have very thin boundaries and their dream production is above average (Hartmann, 1996). However, these dreams do not encourage emotion-processing nor development of a symbolic mentalizing function. Grinberg (1987) calls them "evacuative dreams," and they are typically the dreams of borderline or psychotic patients but also of neurotic patients in the first stage of psychotherapy. Such dreams have the peculiarity of releasing the dreamer from unbearable affects by discharging them externally, typically onto the person of the therapist. According to the author, these dreams may follow attacks on the setting, acting out or major somatizations, and typically have parts of objects, animals, and non-human elements as content. The transformative process, encouraged by psychotherapy, produces a shift from these types of dreams to what Grinberg calls "elaborative" dreams: they stand in an inverse relationship to in-session acting out and reveal an increased capacity to integrate even previously split or dissociated psychotic aspects of one's personality. Psychotherapy, therefore, changes dreams in their quantity and quality (Warner, 1983). To be effective therapists we need to keep this in mind, since it allows us to gauge the temperature of the change taking place in our patient. Just as it is important to keep in mind that all psychotropic drugs in some way affect dreams. In REM sleep there is a decrease in the activity of biogenic amines, e.g., norepinephrine, and a rise in acetylcholine activity. Therefore, drugs that increase cholinergic activity tend to increase REM sleep and dream recall. Hypnotic drugs, such as benzodiazepines, suppress slow-wave sleep, thereby disinhibiting REM sleep and dream production, which are intense and emphasized (McNamara, 2020).

On the contrary, taking many stimulant drugs, e.g., cocaine or MDMA, increases wakefulness and inhibits REM sleep, which is disinhibited during the withdrawal period. Many scientists explain the hallucinations and nightmares typical of this phase precisely with the restoration of REM sleep. Even with alcohol intake we witness something similar: inhibition of REM sleep during intake, disinhibition during the withdrawal period. The period of abstinence is accompanied by a fertile dream production (McNamara, 2020). In this regard, Freud (1899/2005) calls the alcoholic a "paranoiac dream-equivalent" (p. 129). With regard to dream productivity, the bipolar patient often has changeable dreams, in line with their mood oscillations. If dreaming during depressive episodes reveals all the characteristics we observed above in depression, in mania or hypomania dreams are abundant, imaginative, creative, and accelerated. The writer Graham Greene, known to suffer from bipolar disorder, collected thousands of dreams in his lifetime, recording them in a notebook he kept on his bedside table ever since, at the age of 16, his analyst suggested he pick up that habit. A selection of such dreams—many of them eccentric, creative and grandiose—was published in a collection entitled *A World of My Own: A Dream Diary* (Greene, 1992). "Diagnostic" dreams in cases of bipolar disorder reveal a difference in time: During manic phases, dreams feature an acceleration of time, which undergoes a slowdown in periods of depression. As Greene writes in the introduction, "Time in the World of One's Own can move slowly or it can move very rapidly. In this case the centuries passed by me like a flash and I found myself lying on my bed" (p. 15). Moreover, dreams in mania present an upward projection—rising, flying—while in depressive dreams we usually find falling, descending, sinking (Binswanger, 1963, in Resnik, 2005). Typical of the bipolar patient is dreaming of another self or its surrogate: The personality of the bipolar patient is so split that it is sometimes represented in dreams as two different people. With the achievement of a good psychic balance, with psychological and pharmacological treatment, such a patient can have a more regular dream life, although they may continue to manifest passionate excitement and flight of ideas in their dreams (Resnik, 2005).

In the case of narcissistic patients, dream work is particularly valuable, although not easy to do. It is common to find strong resistance in these patients to the idea of bringing their dreams to therapy. As Resnik (2005) observes:

> The archaeology of the dream means precisely to recover a buried reality, which is sometimes difficult to rediscover and recognize. The analysis of narcissism is indeed painful and is not always tolerated. The dream work represents a fundamental element of analysis, which consists in deciphering, interpreting, recovering the "other language," and confronting the disillusion experienced when we realize that we are not as we would like to be.
>
> (p. 80)

Dreams, on the other hand, allow one to circumvent defenses and get directly to the deep core of pain (Little, 2011) which, if contacted without adequate preparation, stirs unbearable shame. The narcissist cannot tolerate that another person might be able to read their dreams. The narcissist—Resnik continues—"does not accept being the object of exploration, but wants to be only the subject" (p. 143). It is therefore necessary to tiptoe around and respect the boundaries of that very private space, the unconscious dream space, without provoking in the patient the feeling of being violated.

Working with transformative dreams: therapeutic stories

After years of psychotherapy and a life sheltered from intimacy with men, Maggie—a young woman who was sexually assaulted at the age of 17 by the boy she was dating, who soon afterwards left her—becomes affectively close to a man, an anesthesiologist her age, who from the beginning shows interest and involvement. He does for her what no man had done until then: picks her up to take her out to dinner, includes her in his plans, says he loves her. While not unmoved by these loving gestures toward her, Maggie cannot let go, cannot give him her trust. He goes too fast for her, and she often blames herself for not being able to give as much and relax. However, a couple of months after their first date, the man suddenly changes, disappears for days without warning, becomes elusive and abrupt in communication. Maggie is confused, chasing after him, asking for explanations, and the more she insists the more he disappears for days, then weeks. This triggers old symptoms and a brand new depressive episode in the woman. She learns from mutual acquaintances that the man who upset her so much suffers from bipolar disorder and is no stranger to such erratic behavior with women. Realizing what has happened, Maggie turns away from everyone, even from therapy, both individual and group. She feels deep shame and blames herself fiercely for what happened. What gives her no peace is that she had been blaming herself the whole time they were dating instead of realizing that there was something wrong with him: She was completely absorbed in what was happening inside her and had not really been able to "see" him. After a few months of withdrawal, running from everything, and everyone except—and not without effort—from therapy, Maggie meets another man. This time, too, he is intrigued and attracted to her. They start dating, if only sporadically. She does not trust him in the least, she lets herself go even less than before, she asks the man for an explanation for every bit of unexpected behavior, which she experiences with the same intense emotionality as a discovery of betrayal or abandonment. He is frightened in the face of such overreactivity but cares about her and forgives her; he is patient, and meets with her to talk and clarify things. In the meantime, Maggie steadily resumes her therapeutic journey, admits to the therapist that she had thought of giving up on therapy because after her breakup with the doctor she had felt unprotected. She shares her hitherto unspoken thought: "I actually don't learn anything here and I'm always exposed to the same pain." Talking about this gives her some relief; she recognizes that the pain she has felt stems from a new courage that led her to dare, to approach someone new and get involved in a relationship. Even though she has suffered and will probably still suffer for love, therapy helps her make that pain bearable. And so it is not true that she did not know how to protect herself, indeed she did: Although hurt and disappointed, she took charge of her life once again and moved away from the source of despair. This point of view sounds unexpected to her; as she listens, she takes deep breaths and falls into a contemplative silence. From that moment on, she uses her time in therapy to analyze step by step the relationship she is building with the man she is falling in love with. She brings up her fear, she expresses her doubts, she faces herself honestly and courageously: "Is it just me who sees him this way or is he really drifting away?" One day she brings a dream into the session. She dreamed of violently beating the doctor she had been seeing, who had then disappeared. Upon awakening, she is shocked by such ferocity and says of herself, "I am not like that, I am not a violent person." The first thing to point out is that this is a new dream. Maggie has never had dreams with the same theme or vehemence. Even in the daytime she has never accessed anger in an aggressive way. On the contrary, anger was usually transformed into the "parasitic" emotion of sadness and sustained by thoughts of inadequacy and guilt, or at most held back. Going beyond the content to read the symbolic message of the dream allows her to overcome the estrangement and grasp the underlying message: Maggie is attacking the one who attacked her, and the doctor represents precisely the aggressor. Etymologically, to assault means "to jump toward," meaning the opposite of what Maggie has always done: closing herself off. Through her dream Maggie expresses an anger she has never expressed before. She also acts out the power she was deprived of in the violent episode around which she has built her own rigid and limiting script (Bowater, 2013). Knowing she *has* power, knowing she is capable, is helpful in approaching a man without fear of being re-traumatized. Following the reading of this transformational dream, an expression of a profound change in her, Maggie feels reassured, anxiety and guilt fading in favor of a greater confidence in herself and especially in men.

The second case we are going to delve into is that of Milena. Milena is 40 years old and single. At the age of 20, she had a single, brief love affair. Milena is afraid. Of illness, of separating from her family of origin, of intimacy. There is no getting too close to her. Stuck in the conflict between the need to grow and individuate herself, and the fear of loneliness, she is doomed to relationship limbo: neither alone nor with someone. She loves to surround herself with "old" friends she feels safe with because they know that nothing about her personal life can be asked of her. Milena's secrecy is also physical as well as emotional: She uses clothes to hide instead of simply to cover herself, never even thinking of highlighting her shape. Given the geographical distance between Milena and the therapist, the two agree to engage in online therapy sessions. This setting fosters, rather than hinders, the alliance between therapist and patient. The therapist's screen-mediated presence cushions and mitigates the transference dimension. Moreover, the distance is reassuring: Connected from her home, Milena has more control over the situation compared to the in-presence setting in the therapist's office. Early in the process she fills the session's space with her dreams. She certainly is a fertile dreamer; moreover, she knows of the therapist's passion for dreams and so she also somehow offers something of herself that she knows is welcome. However, there comes a time when she tells the therapist nothing about her daytime life. There is a lack of "facts" on which to hook the dream analysis. As Ferenczi states, the day's residue is not the pretext of the dream, but an integral part of the dream itself (1955). A discussion with her on this very subject reveals that her dreams, like her clothes, do not uncover but conceal. After three years of therapy and numerous changes in her life, including getting a new job, joining a psychotherapy group, and falling in love again, Milena brings to therapy a very long and articulate dream. It begins with a series of encounters the dreamer has while walking through her town: There is a party with music, then some young boys who take with them a little girl, whom the dreamer, reassuringly, brings back to her parents—a happy family. Then, annoyed by the party and a group of boys who seem to engage in typical bullying behaviors, Milena decides to take a different road. She wanders off again and later makes another encounter: a dear friend who tragically died a year earlier because of a serious illness.

Here is what follows:

> *And I'm looking down as I walk, when at some point in front of me I find S. I run to her and I want to hug her, but then I think of Covid, I tell myself I can't, especially because she is fragile, but then I think she has defeated death, so if she is there she is fine. So I hug her tightly, and we cry. We start talking, she shows me that she hasn't exactly come back: Her gums are all eaten away and her teeth are wobbly, she's tired and it looks like she does not feel very well. Although from an aesthetic perspective, she's as well-dressed and elegant as she always was. We start walking and we find ourselves inside an antique store. It is beautiful, it has everything, from very old things to more modern stuff. We keep talking; in the meantime, outside, the sun is coming up. Then the store owner pops up and asks us what our intentions are. If we are interested in the things in the store or if we maybe just want to have a chat with each other, because in that case perhaps he can offer us a couple of chairs. (He was quite sarcastic). S. asks him about some magnets, and I tell him that I actually have two questions for him: First of all, I ask him if all the items in the shop are things he searches for and therefore picks and choses carefully, or if they are things that people bring to him and he accepts everything; and then I want to know if, especially in the second case, but also in the first case, he usually gets to listen to the stories behind the items as well. I tell him that I always waste so much time in antique stores because I look at every little object and imagine where it had been, in what family, where in the house, and I would like to know what's his reasoning behind all this. He doesn't answer, he looks a little annoyed, I guess I got it wrong somehow, but he says, "Do you know what is the function of all these qualitative objects? If you really want to know, I'll show you*

something." So then he takes me to the back, like the special rooms in the Vatican archives, you know, where they keep the rare books that they store them vacuum-sealed so as to preserve the paper. It takes us a while to get to this special hidden room and finally we are there. He tells me to go to the "hole." I go up the stairs which are also very strange, but I finally get up to the top and there I have to go inside this hole. It's a small entrance but inside there is a huge room. So I take off my bag, my scarf, and my shoes because I have heels on and they are bothering me; I go inside and a room opens up with a lot of broken things. There are so many broken suitcases, a section with early childhood toys and another with tools. I was expecting older things and I don't understand what I see. I was definitely not expecting this kind of stuff. The shopkeeper asks me what I see, I remain silent and he tells me there is not much to understand, but what I see and notice is that all the objects in the room involve movement. The suitcases with zippers and handles that stretch, the children's toys with pieces that move and even the kitchen utensils. This is the beginning of modernity, I say, this is when the first technology of interaction began. I feel him smile and wake up.

This is an almost "epic" dream of transformation that seems to tell the story of Milena's growth journey during therapy. Milena's dream is a journey into the depths of herself to integrate more and more recondite and conflicting elements into a mind that at the same time evolves and expands. At the beginning of the dream Milena brings a little girl back to her parents. It is as if she is relocating her Child back to its proper place. The child is not lost, nor does Milena take her with her. The dream suggests different possibilities, different "roads to take": Different realities coexist, and despite some fear, Milena decides to take a side street, a less traveled one. In the dream Milena plays an active role (Cartwright, 2010): She "takes a different road" and in doing so she meets her dead friend. S. seems to represent her dependent, fusional side—in the dream S. is interested in magnets—who is sick, tired, and no longer what it used to be. The meeting with the antique dealer symbolizes the center of the dream. It is a journey within a journey. In the meeting place there are broken things—trauma—and sacred things—vulnerable, untouchable parts, removed from the corruptibility of time. In it we find coexisting elements related to the past, present and future. Indeed, in dreams of change, old memories are combined with images of the present (Hartmann, 1996, 1998). Furthermore, she says that "all the objects in the room involve movement." Many characters appear in the dream, together with feelings of joy, discovery but also discomfort and uneasiness experienced in a clear, direct way. Milena still has a need to control the other while being attracted to them: the antiquarian, who transferentially represents the therapist, is questioned about how he works. It could be a dream about dream analysis:

The encounter between Milena and the antiquarian seems to represent the work of co-constructing meaning about the dream. A meta-dream, we might call it. Milena met the therapist-antiquarian and many open questions remained from the encounter. But she managed to take care of it all, to stay in uncertainty, to get lost in the alleys of her unconscious, to bear not knowing and to bear it with someone. As Ogden (2005) writes:

> Not knowing is a precondition for being able to imagine. The imaginative capacity in the analytic setting is nothing less than sacred. Imagination holds open multiple possibilities experimenting with them all in the form of thinking, playing, dreaming and in every other sort of creative activity.
>
> (p. 26)

Change is the beginning of modernity: Access to relation is a momentous change that does not frighten, horrify or make one fall back. It simply makes one smile.

References

Berne, E. (1968). *A layman's guide to psychiatry and psychoanalysis*. New York: Simon and Schuster.
Berne, E. (1972). *What do you say after you say hello?* New York: Bantam Books.
Bion, W. (1962). *Learning from experience*. London: W. Heinemann.
Bowater, M. (2003). Windows on your inner self: Dreamwork with Transactional Analysis. *Transactional Analysis Journal, 33*(1), 37–44.
Bowater, M. (2013). Fighting back. *Transactional Analysis Journal, 43*(1), 38–47.
Cartwright, R. (2010). *The twenty-four-hour mind: The role of sleep and dreaming in our emotional lives*. Oxford: Oxford University Press.
Cornell, W. F. (1988). Life script theory: A critical review from a developmental perspective. *Transactional Analysis Journal, 18*(4), 270–282. https://doi.org/10.1177/036215378801800402
Cornell, W. F. (2008). "My body is unhappy": Somatic foundations of script and script protocol. In Cornell, W. F., *At the interface of transactional analysis, psychoanalysis, and body psychotherapy: Clinical and theoretical perspectives*. Routledge, Taylor & Francis Group, pp. 104–117.
Ferenczi, S. (1955). *Final contributions to the problems and methods of psychoanalysis*. New York: Basic Books.
Fonagy, P., Gergely, G., Jurist, E. L., & Target, M. (2002). *Affect regulation, mentalization and the development of the self*. New York: Other Press.
Fosshage, J. L. (1997). The organizing functions of dream mentation. *Contemporary Psychoanalysis, 33*(3), 429–458.
Freud, S. (2005). *The interpretation of dreams* (D. T. O'Hara & G. M. MacKenzie, Eds.; A. A. Brill, Trans.). New York: Barnes & Noble Classics (Originally published in 1899).

Glucksman, M., & Kramer, M. (2015). The manifest dream report and clinical change. In M. Glucksman & M. Kramer (Eds.). *Dream research. Contributions to clinical practice*. New York: Routledge, pp. 106–122.

Goulding McClure, M., & Goulding, R. (1979). *Changing lives through redecision therapy*. New York: Brunner/Mazel Publisher.

Greene, G. (1992). *A world of my own: A dream diary*. New York: Viking Press.

Grinberg, L. (1987). Dreams and acting out. *The Psychoanalytic Quarterly*, *56*(1), 155–176.

Hartmann, E. (1996). Outline for a theory on the nature and functions of dreaming. *Dreaming*, *6*(2), 147–169.

Hartmann, E. (1998). *Dreams and nightmares: The new theory on the origin and meaning of dreams*. New York: Plenum Trade.

Holtby, M. (1976). The origin and insertion of script injunctions. *Transactional Analysis Journal*, *4*(4), 371–376.

Lingiardi, V. & Mc Williams, N. (2017). *Psychodynamic Diagnostic Manual: PDM – 2* (Second Edition). New York: Guilford Press.

Little, R. (2011). Impasse clarification within the transference-countertransference matrix. *Transactional Analysis Journal*, *41*(1), 23–38.

Malinowski, J. (2020). *The psychology of dreaming*. London: Routledge.

McNamara, P. (2020). *Psychopharmacology of REM sleep and dreams*. https://www.psychologytoday.com/us/blog/dream-catcher/201112/psychopharmacology-rem-sleep-and-dreams

Ogden, T. (2005). *Dreaming undreamt dreams and interrupted cries*. London: Routledge.

Quinodoz, J. M. (2002). *Dreams that turn over a page: Paradoxical dreams in psychoanalysis*. Hove: East Suxxes; New York: Brunner-Routledge.

Resnik, S. (2005). *The theatre of the dream*. London: Tavistock Publications.

Saul, L. (1940). Utilization of early current dreams in formulating psychoanalytic case. *The Psychoanalytic Quarterly*, *9*(4), 453–469.

Schredl, M., & Engelhardt, H. (2001). Dreaming and psychopathology: Dream recall and dream content of psychiatric inpatients. *Sleep and Hypnosis*, *3*(1), 44–54.

Segal, H. (1990). *Dream, phantasy and art*. London: Routledge.

Tousignant, O., Glass, D., Suvak, M., & Fireman, G. (2022). Nightmares and nondisturbed dreams impact daily change in negative emotion. *Dreaming*, *32*(3), 292–313.

Warner, S. (1983). Can psychoanalytic treatment change dreams? *Journal of the American Academy of Psychoanalysis*, *11*(2), 299–316.

9
DREAMS OF HEALING

Introduction

The end of any therapy is usually decided jointly by the therapist and the patient based on the achievement of the goals defined in the initial contract. However, in some cases, termination occurs unilaterally, without agreement and without goodbyes, such as when the patient becomes dissatisfied and decides to discontinue unnecessary or even harmful treatment. Other times the termination of therapy occurs because of the onset of external events such as a relocation, family problems, or death itself.

How things end, how one says goodbye is a key part of either a script change or confirmation. For some people, disappearing without saying goodbye or thank you is part of a script—characterized by the theme of envy and conflict—that they do not want to leave behind.

For other people, delaying the conclusion of therapy is like delaying seizure of their autonomy in order to stay close to their parents and the securities of childhood.

A mature goodbye and a peaceful ending stage of therapy is a valuable confirmation that we have done a good job. We will use the terms *healing* and *maturing* as synonyms. The term *healing* contains an explicit reference to curing, repairing the wounds of the soul, and therefore is the one we favored.

Healing, growing, maturing

To heal means, for most people, to grow up, to abandon childish pretensions and illusions, and to be able to get by in the world of "grown-ups" on one's own strength and with the help of others, help offered and received on the basis of a principle of reciprocity. This reciprocity is characteristic of relationships in which giving and having are balanced, within the framework of free choice, openness to gifts, and acceptance of life's limitations.

Berne wrote that

> The therapist should remember that while death is a tragedy, life is a comedy. (Furthermore, even one's own death is not always a tragedy as such; it may only become tragic in its effects on others.) Curiously enough, many patients reverse this dramatic principle, and treat life like a tragedy and death like a comedy. The therapist who follows them is once more a party to a *folie à deux*.
>
> (1966, p. 289)

There is no one way to be mentally healthy, mature or "healed." The healing we seek thus does not correspond to homologation to a social model but to the achievement of a dynamic balance, different for each person, that makes each individual serene and able to live in the world.

Gabbard writes "In psychodynamic therapy, the therapist pursues a uniquely subjective truth for each patient. The therapist seeks to recognize and validate the true self of the patient" (2004, p. 14). Berne (1972) would add, as has already been mentioned, that therapy aims to make the frog a prince, and to do this it must "turn upside down" the script process, bring the patient out of the script and into the real world.

Script antithesis is the powerful message the therapist gives the patient when the latter is ready to re-decide, to "turn themselves upside down," to transform themselves from a patient into a "real person eager to go into the world." According to Berne, all this, at least theoretically, can take place in a single dialectical exchange, provided that at that moment the patient is ready to receive the message with the intensity necessary for it to penetrate deeply within them and to be held within themselves as a permission and a blessing. Actually, much more often, healing messages need to grow in soil that has been made fertile, cleansed of poisons and defilements, and in order for them to be received, understood and internalized, it takes time.

We call this process *deconfusion of the Child* and we are aware that this work is complex and layered. In therapy, the process that accompanies deconfusion is long and complex but, at the same time, it is characterized by some simple experiences shared by therapist and patient. For the patient it is generally a journey of discovery of new options, new emotions being released, different perspectives from which one begins to look at oneself, others and life. For the therapist it is a matter of guiding their patient into new territories, being careful of deviations, setbacks, and personal redefinitions that would push a person to restore previous balances. Guiding someone to give up the safety of the script is both an exciting and a difficult and dangerous experience, because we often do not know how many emotional resources our patient has available to handle the stress of change.

Dreams sometimes anticipate the process of deconfusion and healing. Imagery often appears in them that guides the path of therapy and accompanies the patient's journey in an enlightening way. As we have already said, analyzed dreams are a great resource, a second therapist.

Fanny, toward the end of therapy

Fanny is coming to the end of her training as a psychotherapist and of her individual analysis. She is a young woman in her 30s who is starting a new job in a new city. She brings the following dream to therapy:

> *I am in Pisa, going in to work to share the joys and excitement of the conference* [a success in public speaking]. *I arrive and find a very dark environment. The office is an immense loft on a harbor. The structure is crumbling, I see Emanuela all energetic and I do not want to be seen, afraid that she might think me cumbersome. I stand next to Ilaria, who is working and pays no attention to me.*
>
> *Then Andrea arrives and gives me a guided tour, there is an all-windows corner and I look out. The sky is gray, the water in the harbor is still and putrid. On a terrace I see many old desks lined up and I think they are exposed to the elements. On one of them is Emanuela's purse. Andrea takes me to a hallway and I realize it is made of old and new tiles, all placed next to each other, all different.*
>
> *I ask the reason for that mosaic, and Andrea tells me that they put new tiles in where they were missing, but the ones that were still there were kept in place. I don't think it's a very a good job, but Andrea shrugs, disagreeing with me.*

In the analysis session, what emerges is the theme of Fanny's ambivalence toward the conclusion of her therapeutic journey: not everything is new, not everything is perfect. In the dream, Fanny reacts anxiously to the professional success she experienced thanks to a successful speech at a conference. There is still some transference toward therapist Emanuela, who appears twice in the dream and by whom Fanny has a desire to be seen, together with a fear of being "too cumbersome" in her eyes. Other lateral transference toward colleagues or patients in her group such as Ilaria and Andrea appear: Ilaria does not pay attention to her while Andrea acts as her guide in the new world and explains to her that the mosaic of new and old tiles means finding the good in the old. Fanny does not find it "a good job," and Andrea tells her that he disagrees with her, but does not try to convince her. In Fanny's new world there are busy (Ilaria), energetic (Emanuela), serene, and open (Andrea) people, but one can be different and disagree. It is an imperfect world and Fanny needs to define how she wants to be, what she wants to accept, and what she wants to change.

The final stage of therapy

The act of ending psychotherapy contains several meanings that are not only relational. For many patients ending therapy is like getting a high school diploma or a college degree; it means successfully concluding an educational journey and achieving autonomy.

Siegel notes that in recovering patients one can observe

> This new capacity for integration—both interpersonal and internal—may create a sense of vitality and a release of creative energy and ideas, leading to an invigorating sense of personal expression. Such spontaneous and energized processes can give rise to participation in various activities, such as painting, music, dance, poetry, creative writing, or sculpture. It can also yield a deeper sense of creativity and appreciation within the "everyday" experience of life.
>
> (1999, p. 375)

These people become capable of experiencing and appreciating more articulate and stronger feelings and emotions.

It is in these particularly intense moments, in these states of dyadic resonance, that we can truly appreciate how relationships with others can nurture and heal our emotions.

Thus we proceed to rebuild secure attachment, what is technically called "earned secure attachment" (2017, p. 320) and in this regard Janina Fisher writes that

> "earned secure attachment" bestows on the human mind and body the same qualities and resources as secure attachment in childhood: an ability to tolerate closeness and distance, giving and receiving, empathic attunement and empathic failure, the ability to see shades of grey, and the ability to tolerate disappointment.
>
> (2017, p. 216)

This is thus the measure to be used to assess a successful conclusion to one's therapeutic journey. It is precisely at this stage that our patients need to be reassured and guided to learn that adult life is not perfect, but that it is the best possible life to cope with the present and to build hope for a happy future. Finding a new balance between sleep and wakefulness, desire and restlessness, and accepting life for what it has to offer is every adult's endeavor.

Luisa's journey

Luisa is a young woman in her mid-30s; she is undergoing TA psychotherapy in an individual setting. She comes from a history of adolescent depression associated with a difficulty in feeling herself, expressing herself assertively in school and work environments, and has worked in particular on her relationship with her mother figure from whom she feels she has not received security and support (she says in therapy, "My mother is a child").

This is the dream Luisa brings to therapy:

> *I am standing in line at the airport to go to Frankfurt on a school trip.*
> *I see wonderful things in the air: a contest of colorful sand castles.*
> *I arrive on layover in Paris and it is late. An odyssey begins; it's 3:45 p.m.*
> *You (therapist) are there and you tell me it's not late! I am floundering, I have many backpacks on my shoulders and various items of junk. I don't have my boarding pass, it's the wrong one.*
> *And they tell me: ID card, please. But I have my brother's.*
> *You were there and said, "I'll see you on Wednesday," reassuring me.*
> *So I leave and everyone is welcoming. I was the only one nervous. I hugged you before I left.*

This is the self-analysis of Luisa's dream:

> *I know I should take off, and I see you as a safe place; you are always at my side.*
> *Paris was my first trip abroad, on a field trip.*
> *To me Frankfurt symbolizes independence and autonomy.*
> *Wednesday is the day I was born, a good omen.*

Luisa is approaching the end of therapy. Her dream highlights the mentalization of this stage of the journey. Luisa fears departures and detachment, recalling how her adolescence was a chaotic and confusing time (backpack full of junk) in which she felt lost, not herself ("I have the wrong boarding pass, my brother's").

The meeting with the therapist in the dream allows her to anchor herself to herself, to find the day of her birth (the true Self) and thus the possibility of leaving for Frankfurt (symbol of the Adult journey, of autonomy).

Conflict and ambivalence

The therapist needs to announce that the moment of separation will occur, and they need to make the patient imagine and anticipate it in order to discuss it together, to explore the multiple and often ambivalent feelings and thoughts it arouses. This is a stage in which to analyze the process of the working-through of the transference relationship, or, as we would say in TA, the way one separates from the parent and leaves the paternal and maternal home.

In this regard, Berne writes:

> At the deepest level, the patient comes to the therapist in the hope that if he behaves in a certain way and follows the instructions of the therapist, the therapist will eventually present him with the magic orb, and in that way he will obtain its permanent possession.
>
> (1966, p. 284)

He then adds that one painful task of the therapist is to be able to tell patients that Santa Claus does not exist:

> The therapist can offer him the whole real world to replace the lost illusion—new lamps for old nostalgias, a fresh red apple for a vanished orb.
>
> (p. 285)

In the final stage of therapy these themes must be solicited by the therapist, even if they do not emerge spontaneously, not least because the fantasies and experiences regarding how patients end their journey and how they think of themselves after therapy constitute good feedback of the change they have brought about.

As we have already mentioned, Janina Fisher (2017) asserts that toward the successful conclusion of therapy, patients achieve a coherence of narratives that allows them to build an "earned secure attachment." Reflecting on Roisman et al.'s (2002) research, Fisher argues that secure-earned individuals

> The subjects in these studies reported failed or suboptimal early attachment, painful experiences with attachment figures, even traumatic experiences. Coherence reflects having come to terms with the past, repaired its worst damage, and found a way to accept the missing experiences or childhood wounding.
>
> (2017, p. 250)

We must learn to talk to ourselves in a new way, to face the fear that every change brings, especially if the changes in the past were traumatic, if we were not supported by loving and protective parents who were, however, at the same time, able to make us experience life, including breakups and repairs. Only in this way can we stay in ambivalence and handle conflicts without them destroying us or pushing us to withdraw from risk. One cannot live without accepting risk. One cannot live without exploring, learning, facing the changes taking place despite someone's mad attempt to freeze everything and stop time.

Licia toward the end of her journey

Licia, a 60-year-old bipolar patient, has had a difficult life, characterized by deep emotional imbalances, bulimia, depression, and interruption of her working life for many years. Her relationship with her body and her reflection in the mirror troubles her greatly; she does not recognize herself, often saying she sees herself as monstrous. At the end of therapy she brings the following dream to the group:

I am as I am now, but in the high school gym. My body is what it is now.
There is a gym teacher, he is a guy in his 40s. And he tells us we have to climb on the Swedish ladder.
But it's old and as I'm trying and it falls apart. Then the teacher asks us "how is your menstrual cycle? Because it is important for your health."
I want to say I'm better with menopause, but I can't talk.
Then he pulls out a guitar. And he starts playing.
I leave the gym, walk down the hallway to a classroom.
I don't fit in, I think.
I see Emanuela, also with the body and age of present day, looking at me with great intensity. I remain speechless. My whole life flashes in front of me.
A strange thing. I still feel that look.
It is not the usual going back to high school.
State of mind hard to describe, that look I feel even now, vividly.
The look of understanding. In her [the therapist's] *eyes I see my whole life, I feel deeply emotional.*

With regards to this dream, some in the group remarked that therapy is like a second formative journey and that Licia feels like a teenager again in high school, but in the dream we also find the awareness of now: her body is the current one, she knows she is in menopause and when she can see herself through the therapist's gaze, as in the gaze of a new mother, she gets excited and seems to accept the new possibilities of a present life. There is no turning back, but a new narrative of healing is being constructed.

Opportunities for rebirth are available to her if she accepts herself as she is now.

The therapist's blessing to close the journey

The therapist's attitude must be patient and encouraging when discussing the end of therapy, akin to that of a parent when a child in early adulthood has to leave home to go out into the world alone.

You are an adult and "you are OK," as we say in TA, you can make your own decisions, you can cope, your guide is within you, you no longer need external guidance.

There is the responsibility of doing it yourself, but also the pleasure of your own power that many patients experience at this stage.

The therapist working from this perspective must from the beginning "stroke" the patient who accepts responsibility.

Another one of Licia's dreams:

> *I'm with a high school friend, who I was in love with as a young girl.*
> *We walk around and meet you, Emanuela. He comes toward you and you open your arms and welcome him. I stand and watch this extraordinarily sweet embrace and think that there is a lot of tenderness in this scene.*
> *I catch myself thinking that I usually feel envy when others enjoy life like that, and this time I feel envy as a desire to indulge in such deep embraces myself. I wake up with a sense of well-being.*

The theme Licia dwells on while analyzing the dream in group is the overcoming the destructive envy that has been her steady companion like a demon for most of her life. In the present moment, Licia thinks that she can learn from people who are more capable than her of being loved and being with others. She is very satisfied that she felt tenderness before a hug that did not include her.

Final sessions, awakening, and responsibility

According to Berne, the ideal end result of script therapy is the condition of the integrated Adult, in which the helm of the boat is solidly in the hands of the Adult ego state, while the dimensions of the Parent and Child are controlled by the helmsman and acting as a harmonized rowing crew. Today, with Tudor and Summers (2014), we speak of the integrating Adult, considering the constant function of the Adult to process and digest fixed and introjected experiences.

A brilliant Spanish philosopher, Maria Zambrano (2002), speaks of three levels of awakening from sleep and dreams: the common, uncertain everyday awakening; the awakening of the awareness of being free, mere attempts, embryos of human beings; and the awakening of responsibility. She writes, "Freedom in dreams is exonerated from the responsibility that locks its up and fixes it, that makes it become word" (2002, p. 178).[1]

We can say that the end of therapy is an awakening to the responsibility of living after we have reconciled with our wounds, our illusions, our dreams.

> If dreams were not an awakening, a certain kind of awakening, they would always go unnoticed, as unnoticed go, perhaps, certain aspects

---

1 My translation.

of human life in the dream world, behind dreams or, in wakefulness, beyond the frontiers of consciousness. To dream is already to wake up.

(2002, p. 49)[2]

Aldo, the poet veterinarian

Aldo comes to therapy in his 50s when his wife suddenly decides to leave him and their two children, a boy of 14 and a girl of 10. Aldo is shocked, he does not understand the reasons for this choice that he experiences as abandonment, and finds himself caring for the children as a single parent who has to provide for them, reassuring them about the loss of their mother. He is convinced that his wife left him for another man, a gym instructor, and one night leaves the house to look for him and kill him. A friend manages to stop him and asks him to give therapy a chance; he himself is frightened by the violence he discovers within himself. From the beginning of his therapeutic journey what emerges is a deep depression, a long history of emotional deprivation (he grew up with a narcissistic mother and a very domineering father), and after a year of individual treatment he continues therapy in group. The dream he brings up in group takes place toward the end of treatment.

First scene: I am in a car, parked near the sea and a river (at sunset), the sea is rough, there is a crazy wind, a storm is coming. I am sitting and watching. People are afraid, there's a lot of tension. I say to myself, I have to leave!

Emotions associated with the first scene: annoyance, worry. This was the situation when I came to therapy, I was alone in a storm, it was dangerous, what was happening to me and what I was causing.

Second scene: I find myself on a treadmill with lots of people. I'm with E., my 10-year-old daughter. There is a narrowing, an obstacle, and you have to get over it without getting off the belt. I tell the child: let's hold hands with a stranger.

Emotions associated with the second scene: amazement at entrusting my child to a stranger. I think it's the experience of group therapy, that is like a treadmill where you hold hands with strangers and feel protected by your contact with them.

Scene three: I find myself in the garden of a stone house. I know I have to go inside; the stairs are full of brambles. In the garden I see my father and a friend named Vittorio watching me. I climb the stairs and turn around to see a huge bear in the garden.

2 My translation.

> *Emotions associated with the third scene: physical sensations in my hands, as if I'm moving the brambles out of the way to climb, surprise at seeing the bear, feeling like I'm the bear and the stone house, pleasure at seeing my father and friend supporting me. I am finding myself again.*

Aldo is now a serene man, he has managed to raise his children and bring them back to a relationship with their mother, he has a new partner and he writes poetry and short stories after attending various creative writing courses. He is a beautiful, sensitive person who deserves the emotional rewards he has found in his new life.

Follow-up dreams

We are fortunate when, as therapists, we have the opportunity to conduct some follow-up sessions with our patients, or even when after some time patients write to us and give us some news of their lives. Some people send us their dreams even a few years after the end of therapy, and it is clear that the process of analysis continues and is very fruitful. The dreamer continues their therapeutic journey and often there is great progress in the working-through of separation and mourning, which are central emotional components in stimulating the possibility of new attachments after the therapist-parent has also let us go off on our own. If any patient has felt the reactivation of abandonment in leaving the therapist, it can often be appropriate to let dreams do the work. It is not always appropriate for the therapist to turn back, to accept without first questioning the patient's request to be taken back into therapy, to simply consider that the reactivation of the fear of abandonment is to be interpreted as a need to continue the analysis that for some would be endless. Increasing one's window of tolerance requires that the patient experience rupture and repair, and while for some people the end of therapy is an experience of rupture, listening to dreams can be an important experience of repair in which the therapist appears as an internalized figure, a voice always freely available to the patient's Child.

Giulia, one year after the end of therapy

Giulia is a young woman who embarks on a therapeutic journey at the age of 27 because of great difficulty in keeping up with med school. She is from Greece, has been studying in Italy since she was 18, and has been unable to take exams for several years. Her anxiety increases more and more year after year and Giulia feels as if imprisoned by a depression that freezes her up and, no matter how much she studies every day and plans to take exams, in the end she cannot go or, if she goes, she is seized by amnesia and withdraws after a few minutes. When she comes to therapy she is really desperate because she feels like she cannot change her path but, at the same time, she cannot continue on the one she is on either. In therapy, she ends up deciding to take a shorter course of study, still in the health professions, and then proceeds to find a job and get engaged to an Italian, making the final decision to live in her adopted country and not to return to Greece. She writes to her therapist a year after completing her studies:

> Hi. The other night I dreamed of you. Strange that in all those years of therapy I did not dream of you, and instead now that I am out of the group it is already the second time. When you appear I have a good feeling. I would say of trust and recognition. This time, although I did get out of bed to write down the dream, I unfortunately found that I couldn't. Some time ago I dreamed of my mom, and I was talking/arguing with her, the reason being marriage, or something like that. Later in the dream, you appear, and we are walking together, going up a spiral staircase. You, you talk a little bit on the phone about your own business in front of me, unabashedly. Then the staircase takes us to a large space, like a hotel/convention/exhibition waiting room (it gives that impression), and we have a snack chatting, you and I, around a tall round table, the bar kind. I don't remember anything else, but I do know that the ugly feeling of the fight was transformed into one of acceptance, welcome, and serenity.

These dreams were not analyzed and discussed, but welcomed as a gift and brought by the therapist in supervision as an opportunity for reflection and feedback.

Michele, one year after the end of therapy

Michele has been in therapy for an anxiety disorder that has been with him since early adolescence and that he associates with his mother's illness. His mother, to whom he is very close, has been suffering from cancer relapse ever since Michele's birth. It's a disease that she has fought but that has come back several times throughout their lives. During therapy, his mother gets worse and dies, Michele grieves and struggles to start living again, eventually gets engaged and married, but has trouble feeling entitled to happiness. After completing treatment, he asks for a meeting with the therapist, at which he brings the following dream:

> It is the first of January. My mother died five years ago, but the funeral takes place now. We (me, my father, my brother, the whole family) are like we are now, not then. I wonder why we are having the funeral now.
> We are not in our house, we are in an American house. All on one floor, big. The funeral is also of the American type, with the reception,

the wake. We are all there and we are the whole family now. At one point I go to cut the lasagna and I find my mother next to me, cutting the lasagna herself and putting it on plates to serve. Her hair is as long as it was before the illness. She is serene, she is fine. We are next to each other, serene.

In the reprocessing of the dream during a follow-up session, the patient says that this dream was extremely moving to him. He feels turmoil, in the dream, until he sees his mother beside him intent on the act of cutting the lasagna with him. He says, "When I saw her with her long hair from when she was still well, I calmed down and was very moved, and then woke up with this positive emotion. I didn't tell anyone, I wanted to tell you first." [He kept the dream to himself for 20 days, did not talk about it with his wife or anyone else].

He said he had felt that it was as if a breakthrough had occurred in the processing of his grief: "It is difficult for me to remember dreams. Remembering her and seeing her next to me when she was well was really important."

The therapist then asks him how he felt with regard to the fact that there was food at the wake, that it was a North American kind of house, large, all on one floor. What associations did these elements arouse in him? At first the patient is uncertain, he says "I don't know." Then he thinks about it and says that it occurs to him that now the family is in a moment of giving themselves permission to celebrate again: a baby girl (his brother's daughter) was just born and they wanted to celebrate. Then, in the days around the dream, the patient and his wife were planning a vacation to the United States (these are people who usually travel very little). He says they were talking about it precisely during that time. The therapist asks when they booked the trip and he replies that it was the day after the dream.

Molly, 30 years after the end of her therapy

Molly is 61 years old, a writer and a teacher. She has very vivid memories of a period of therapy she underwent for four years when she was 27 years old, and she is still very grateful for that analysis, which helped set her on the path of professional success that fulfills her. She did not have any children, but she feels that she is a mother to many people. She reports the following dream to her then-therapist:

I am outside with other people.

Someone from my family hands me a baby girl who is only a few months old but is sitting upright. She is a little girl identical to how I was as a baby, with little black ringlets and a smart, curious face. Someone says to me, "So now you have a chance to be with her."

I think, "Is that me? Or at least she's a granddaughter who looks exactly like me."

> *I love her at first sight and hold her in front of me, sitting down, and the further I go into the dream, the more I feel that I am the baby.*
>
> *I see that she is not wearing a diaper and has a large vagina that is very visible for the small body she has. She is therefore naked on her front bottom and legs, wearing only a little T-shirt and laughing, staring at everything. I play with her with great emotion, I feel like she can stay with me forever. Then I don't know why I make her pee, and it comes out gushing like a fountain and then I go look for her clothes, shorts and diaper.*
>
> *I get up and with her in my arms I start walking.*
>
> *At some point my memory is less accurate: there is a woman who warns me that the baby is facing some kind of danger and I enter swaggering into an enclosed space. The woman reveals to me that she is the danger so I face her with a mean look and she dissolves as if melting. Then I come out of that space and I see that I'm holding some mice in my arms together with the baby, so I shake the mice off of her and we leave safely and peacefully. We are still looking for her clothes, but I know we will find them.*

Everybody has an inner healer

Many people recount dreams that are in and of themselves forms of healing and gifts that arise within their minds outside of any therapeutic context.

Hilary, a young colleague, wrote to me about a dream that gave her a sense of deep serenity:

> *The other night, to alleviate the suffering that life is throwing at me at the moment, my unconscious took care of me: in the middle of the night it gave me a happy dream!*
>
> *In the dream there were people dear to me, as well as family members, people I have met during my life who I have had rewarding connections with, and who have given me a lot of positive energy that made our moments together very happy.*
>
> *I recognized them by their smiling faces and their eyes filled with happiness.*
>
> *Their happiness was thanks to me, thanks to the mere fact that they saw me!*

Similar to this is the last dream that Sophie Scholl, the very young White Rose activist sentenced to death by the Nazis along with her brother in 1943, told her cellmate before she was executed:

> On a beautiful sunny day you brought a child in a long white dress to be baptized. The way to the church was up a steep mountain, but

you carried the child safely and firmly. Unexpectedly there opened up before you a crevice in the glacier. You had just time enough to lay the child safely on the other side before you plunged into the abyss.

(Scholl, 1983, p. 146)

And she interpreted it herself: "The child in the white dress is our idea; it will prevail in spite of all obstacles. We were permitted to be pioneers, but we must die early for the sake of that idea" (Scholl, 1983, p. 146).

Moreover, an elderly woman, Fede, often reports dreaming of paradise, where she arrives via a white train that travels through verdant valleys. On the train or in the valleys she meets her much-loved mother whom she has lost more than 30 years before. These are dreams that give her great joy and which she recounts brimming with emotion in the morning. Shortly before her death, Fede reports to her daughter that she finally dreamed of a reconciliation with her father. The dream is very vivid:

The fields in the village where the family lived when she was a child have suffered a terrible drought and are completely parched and dry. Her father is in despair because he is a farmer. Fede looks at him and says, you don't have to worry because I have stored wheat, corn and oat seeds in three glass barrels. She shows her father the barrels full of seeds, grabs a handful of corn kernels and throws them on the ground. The field suddenly turns green and the corn grows flourishing and lush. Fede sees her father happy and says to him: "See? I have done something good. Can you trust me?"

Why keep dreaming

To dream is already to wake up to an early form of consciousness, claimed Maria Zambrano (2002). She distinguishes the dreams of the psyche from the dreams of the person, and we can agree with her that, once overcome the conflicts that the script character brings to the dreams of the psyche, the latter tend to disappear, while the dreams of the person remain for life.

The dreams of the person are creative actions, deep awakenings of our being, what Zambrano always calls "creative dreams." We find accounts of these dreams in film, literature, the arts. Dreams that express the labile and permeable boundary between the intrapsychic, intersubjective world and the human creativity that generates worlds. There are people and artists who begin the creative process in dreams, where musical themes, images, poems, and stories are born.

The following poem was born in a dream had while writing this chapter and was thus transcribed exactly as it was upon waking by one of the two authors (Emanuela). It is likely a reference to the dream-telling that is done in the morning by sharing, at breakfast, the theme of our dream, with the typical relief that dawn and daylight offer to the fears and loneliness of the night.

Words
Like dewdrops
In the morning
Damp warmth
Towards daybreak
Words
Disclosing
Light and dissolving shadows
Of the night's bleak and restless dreams
Words
Like embraces
Like bridges and rainbows of colors
Tales of love and hope

References

Berne, E. (1966). *Principles of group treatment*. New York: Oxford University Press.

Berne, E. (1972). *What do you say after you say hello?* New York: Grove Press.

Fisher, J. (2017). *Healing the fragmented selves of trauma survivors: Overcoming internal self-alienation*. New York: Routledge/Taylor & Francis.

Gabbard, G. O. & American Psychiatric Association Publishing. (2004). *Long-term psychodynamic psychotherapy: A basic text* (3rd ed.). Washington DC: American Psychiatric Association Publishing.

Roisman, G. I., Padron, E., Sroufe, L. A., & Egeland, B. (2002). Earned-secure attachment status in retrospect and prospect. *Child Development*, *73*(4), 1204–1219. https://doi.org/10.1111/1467-8624.00467

Scholl, I., & Sölle, D. (1983). *The white rose: Munich, 1942–1943*. Middletown, Scranton: Wesleyan University Press.

Siegel, D. J. (1999). *The developing mind: How relationships and the brain interact to shape who we are*. New York: Guilford Press.

Tudor, K., & Summers, G. (2014). *Co-creative transactional analysis: Papers, dialogues, responses, and developments*. London: Karnac Books.

Zambrano, M. (2002). *Il sogno creatore [The creating dream]*. Milano: Bruno Mondadori.

10
TRANSFERENCE AND DREAMS

Transference in TA

When Princess Turandot, the protagonist of one of Giacomo Puccini's operas, finds herself unarmed before Prince Calaf, the brave suitor who challenges her cold and cynical detachment, she turns to him observing, "You are pale, stranger!" and the man, not at all intimidated by such a statement, replies, "Your fear sees the pallor of dawn on my face."[1] With the sweetness of such words Calaf makes Turandot realize the truth: The one who should be afraid is not him but her, the ice princess. In psychodynamic terms we could say that the pallor that Turandot glimpses on the stranger's face is a translation of her own fear. What is seen in the other comes from and actually belongs to the inner world of the beholder. This psychic mechanism is called projection and is the means by which the phenomenon of transference, that is, transfer, translation, takes place. Transference is ubiquitous, as Freud already argued and as Turandot shows, but the instance of transference that is most studied is the one that is active toward the therapist, since it is through its analysis that healing can take place. This is a belief held not only by psychoanalysts but also by transactional analysts since the 1980s. The article entitled "Ego States and Transference" published in the *TAJ* (*Transactional Analysis Journal*) in 1985 earned Carlo Moiso, the first Italian to win it, the Eric Berne Memorial Award, the most prestigious international recognition awarded to pioneering scholars of TA. In this article, which enshrines the recovery of the psychoanalytic roots of transactional analysis, the author defines transference in terms of projections of the patient's Parent ego states onto the therapist. By identifying three types of transference, Moiso specifies that parental projections onto the therapist can be of several types, more evolved or more archaic. The first type of transference is that of P_2, the Parent ego state corresponding to the introjection of significant attachment figures in childhood. By script demand such parental

---

1 https://eportfolios.macaulay.cuny.edu/smonte12/files/2012/09/Turandot.pdf

material is transferred onto the therapist, who, because of this mechanism, is not seen as a real person. So the patient makes interpretations based on the therapist's behavior and creates expectations for them in line with the traits of the inner Parent that is transferred onto them. The following comment is a classic example of this type of projection: "I know that you, doctor, will think of me as a shallow and unserious person, but I assure you that my tardiness was caused by the construction work I found on the road." This type of transference is easily detected and recognized by both therapist and patient because such projection is preconscious and therefore accessible to consciousness once the patient has learned to recognize it for what it is. A second type of transference, in contrast, is more archaic and unconscious. In this case the patient projects onto the therapist a Parent called P_1, which is composed of introjected object relations split into good objects (P_{1+}) and bad objects (P_{1-}). These types of Parent have been self-generated by the Child as a consequence of processing parental responses to their needs. They therefore represent crude interpretations that the Child provides to explain the attachment figures' reactions to their demands. When a child perceives the environment around them as responsive and nurturing they will elaborate an idea of Parent as all-powerful, idealized, affective. When, on the other hand, the environment frustrates their request for closeness and containment by responding with distraction, distance and coldness, the child will construct the image of a Parent that is frustrating, cruel, and sadistic. However, if the child's development proceeds without significant trauma, the two types of Parent, the good and the bad, are integrated to form a complete and complex image of the parental object. In the presence, on the other hand, of those developmental relational traumas that cause severe personality disorders—pre-oedipal personalities according to Moiso—the Parent images remain separate, split, and exaggerated in their Manichean segregation. An example of P_{1+} transference may be an over-idealization of the therapist, expressed through expressions such as: *Since you know everything, can you explain to me why my husband does this?* On the contrary, a fierce anger felt or acted out by the patient toward the therapist, who stands accused of being only interested in money, may be an example of P_{1-} transference. Therefore, there are three projective transferences identified by Moiso: one, the more evolved and easier to treat P_2 transference, and two more toxic and intense ones, which are the P_{1+} and P_{1-} transference, typical of patients with narcissistic or borderline personality disorders. About two decades after Moiso's work, two British authors reinvigorated transference studies in transactional analysis. These were Charlotte Sills and Helena Hargaden, who retrieved from Kohut's psychology of the self a series of introjective transferences to add to those identified by Moiso. As they themselves explain, it is the patient's personal history that anticipates which type of transference is prominent in the therapeutic relationship. This does not mean that they are mutually exclusive. On the contrary, in some cases they may coexist or, more likely, alternate, and it is easy to witness the manifestation of one and the other at different stages of the therapeutic process. In the authors' opinion, introjective transference in patients with a childhood experience of deprivation and insecurity aims to introject the therapist as a supportive figure who can support the development of the fragile self. The first transference they describe in their *Transactional Analysis: A Relational Perspective* (2002)—in which they inaugurate the relational perspective of transactional analysis—is that of mirroring. Through it, the patient seeks to satisfy that unmet narcissistic need to have a stage and an audience that listens attentively and praises them for their performance. In this case, the patient may talk during the entire time of the session, accepting with annoyance the irritating interruptions of the therapist who, perhaps solicited in their own narcissistic aspects, may find intolerable being so ignored. According to Hargaden and Sills, it is important for the therapist to tune in to the patient's needs, give them their much-desired space, and reward their coveted performance with a loving and encouraging attitude. Only in this way—the authors conclude in line with Kohut—can the patient evolve from archaic grandiosity to healthy self-esteem. The second transference is the idealizing one. When a child loses a parent early on because they are dead, ill, absent, or distant, there remains in them a need to be able to rely on a strong person capable of providing protection and security. In this case, the patient will seek in the figure of the therapist that same perfection, which is a sign of maximum protection, with which they can then identify by internalizing it. That is why it is also appropriate in this case that the therapist consciously observes this process but at the same time accepts it while avoiding confronting the patient with the reality of their own imperfection and vulnerability. The third transference is the twin transference. In this case the patient needs to be like the therapist. The two resemble each other, they belong together, there is sympathy between them. When this type of transference follows the idealizing one, there appears to be a hope on the part of the patient to become like the therapist: attractive, accomplished, and empathetic, for instance. As if to say: *if you made it, I can make it too!* Again—the authors explain—it is important for the therapist to understand what is happening without interpreting or confronting such an attitude in the patient, who may feel rejected or, even, humiliated. An interesting and innovative article by Ray Little on the ego state relational units was published on the *TAJ* in 2006. The author argues that Parent ego states and Child ego states are not just separate entities. They are connected in P–C relational units that are the introjected representation of a specific relational pattern. There will, therefore, be as many relational units as there are such relational representations. Having been recorded in implicit memory, these cannot be retrieved directly but can only be inferred through the matrix of transference and countertransference activated by the therapeutic encounter. Let us now see the various shapes that the types of transference relations can take in the dreamer's dream life.

Transference dreams

In a splendid short story, Giovanni Papini writes:

> To be an actor in a dream is not what pains me most. There are poets who have said that man's life is but the shadow of a dream, and philosophers who have hinted that all reality is but hallucination. I instead, am haunted by another thought: who is this someone who dreams me? Who is this nameless, unknown being to whom I belong, who suddenly brought me out of the darkness of his tired brain and whose awakening will just as suddenly extinguish me, like a flame in the wind?
>
> (Manguel, 1983, p. 275)

The title of the story is "The Sick Gentleman's Last Visit," as it appears in the collection *Black Water: The Anthology of Fantastic Literature* (Manguel, 1983). It is the story of this strange, fascinating character who exists only as long as there is someone who dreams of him, and sometimes they dream of him so strongly that he becomes "real" even to those awake. Talking about himself to the man who dreams of him, he says,

> In me, Shakespeare's image has become literally and tragically exact. I am *such stuff as dreams are made of!* I exist because someone is dreaming me, someone who is now asleep and dreaming and sees me act and live and move, and in this very moment is dreaming that I am saying these very words. When this *someone* began to dream of me, I began my existence. When he wakes I will cease to be. I am an imagination, a creation, a guest of his long nightly fantasies.

He continues: "But the world of watchfulness, the world of solid reality is not mine [...] My life flows slowly in the soul of my sleeping creator [...]" (p. 275). As a transference figure, the therapist is similar to the Sick Gentleman who exists in the long night fantasies of the dreamer-patient. According to Mancia, dreams are the privileged place where the therapist's transference representation is expressed. He argues in this regard, that "The dream appears today as the pictographic and symbolic representation of the transference in its entirety and in its immediate present"[2] (Mancia, 2004, p. 100). Intrapsychic dynamics are analyzed through their reactualization in the therapeutic relationship, and the dream is an open window to it. Dreams represent a bridge between past, present, and future because they contain both elements of memory and

---

2   My translation.

fantasies assimilated to projects and desires not yet realized (Mancia, 2007; Ribeiro, 2021). The transference is the clearest expression of such a bridge. In the transference we find both the past repeating itself in the present and the expectation of the future. In this sense, in the dreamworld, past and future, cease to be distinct and incompatible dimensions (Ribeiro, 2021). The past that is transferred into dreams is a past of which the dreamer has no memory. That is, it does not belong to the world of autobiographical memory, but rather to that implicit memory whose contents are so archaic that they cannot be directly recalled but can only be reconstructed precisely through reactualizations. This is how dreams make once-unthinkable experiences thinkable and verbalizable (Mancia, 2007). Through its creation, what comes to life is that part of the dreamer's otherwise unexplored inner world. The dream allows an enactment of internalized relational patterns that the therapeutic encounter prompts and actualizes. Upon awakening, the therapist, like the protagonist in Papini's story, ceases to exist as a transference symbol to become a real person again. The dream, then, is not about the therapist. Their figure is only a pretext for the dreamer's unconscious to enact the deepest dynamics with the most significant affections of their inner world, "We assume here that the child–parent relationship is recreated, not identically but with similar anxieties and defenses, in the patient–analyst encounter" (Mancia, 2007, p. 104). Mancia refers to this process by defining the dream as a theology of the mind, precisely because through dreams take shape figures defined as "sacred," that is, representative of the dreamer's most significant internal objects, which we collectively call the Parent. But, as Moiso taught us, there is more than one Parent being projected onto the therapist, whether they are "gods"—the P_{1+}—or "devils"—the G_{1-}—of their mental universe (Mancia, 2007). The therapist, because of the "total and specific" nature of the relationship they create with the analysand, is a particularly suitable figure to represent such sacredness. Indeed, the transference does not care about the differences between present and past situations, does not care about the therapist's individualities and personal characteristics; the transference simply happens. But the transference dream is not merely the photograph of a transference. It is also and above all the symbolic narrative of the dreamer's relationship with that object, of a specific relational unit between a given Parent ego state and a Child ego state (Little, 2006). The dream in this case can be a symbolic way of painting the relationship with that person, the therapeutic relationship at that precise moment in therapy. As Mancia (2002) argues in the preface to the Italian edition of Resnik's *The Theatre of the Dream*, the dream x-rays the relational state of the analytic couple. Mancia continues: "We can define the dream today as a real experience that, as a representation of the dreamer's inner world, in its immediate present expresses the transference in all its totality" (2002, p. 15). Investigating the state of the art of the patient-therapist relationship through dream analysis is always possible and useful therapeutic action. Yalom follows the same logic when asserting:

Of all the dreams offered by patients, I believe there are none more valuable to the therapy enterprise than dreams involving the therapist (or some symbolic stand-in for the therapist). These dreams represent *great potential for therapeutic payoff* [italics mine].

(2002, p. 246)

Therefore, a plausible dream analysis may consist precisely of the exploration of transference. In this sense, every dream can be read as a transference dream, a photograph of a specific internalized representation of the Parent and Child's relationship with it. Very many dreams, in fact, are emotionally connected relational vicissitudes. And in each of them can be traced, if that is our purpose, the dreamer's experience in relation to someone highly representative of their inner world. Bringing dreams into therapy also fulfills other tasks, e.g., communicating what is otherwise incommunicable, expressing unconscious desires, defensively filling the analytic space or recalling past images and anticipating the future. But, Mancia continues (in Resnik, 2002):

What must be stressed, however, is the active and irreplaceable role of the dream in the process of *dramatization* of the relationship, aimed at constituting the shared thought of the analytic couple. That is, a process of dramatizing the affects at play in the relationship in that particular fleeting transference moment.

(p. 15)

In line with this, Ferenczi states that: "Whenever the physician appears in the patient's dreams the analysis discovers with certainty signs of transference" (1952/1980, p. 40) So, as a therapist, which Parent am I representing for the patient at this specific moment in our relational history? What relational pattern is being enacted by the patient's dream chronicle at this stage of therapy? Dream analysis is crucial in answering questions that would not otherwise be answered because it uncovers elements that do not inhabit autobiographical memory, but rather implicit memory. As Bromberg claims, such recondite parts of the self cannot be re-enacted but only re-actualized through dreams or enactment (2006). Of all the questions, *Who am I to you in this moment?* is the one that the therapist has a duty to ask and to continually ask themselves in order to protect the patient from their ghosts, from their fantasies, as Cornell recommends in his illuminating article entitled *Failing To Do The Job* (2016). And to this we might add: *Can this dream tell me anything about it?* Questions that can remain in the therapist's mind or can be investigated through intersubjective inquiry. What is certain is that the therapist, Cornell warns us, risks failure in their work when, as a result of the reactivation of forgotten ego states parts, they fail to think and lose sight of the theory of mind, assuming that their own mental perspective coincides with that of the other. The meaning of everything that has to do with the therapeutic relationship, for the patient, must be appropriately investigated. As must the countertransferential response evoked in us therapists in being the object of a given projection. Here it becomes evident how the distinction we make between working on transference dreams and countertransference dreams represents more of a "didactic" straining. There is no transference without countertransference. Since the transference–countertransference matrix is unique, there is no transference without there being a corresponding response to it on the part of the therapist. The patient's dreams and the therapist's dreams belong to neither in particular but to both, Ogden urges us to keep in mind. With the affirmation of the relational model in psychotherapy, which we discussed in Chapter 5, the epistemic shift to a second-person approach implies for the therapist an active involvement in a mutual and reciprocal relationship (Tudor, 2011), whereby not only is there no transference without countertransference, but we could speak in terms of the patient's transference and the therapist's transference. As claimed by Ermann (1999):

> As part of the interactional analysis, the whole session is regarded as the expression of an unconscious transference/countertransference process and analysed accordingly. Undoubtedly, one of the prerequisites for this basic conception is to keep the structuring of the session to an absolute minimum. Interventions are no longer conceived as "neutral" or "technical." It is presumed that all events during the course of a session including interventions are potentially transference or countertransference manifestations, yielding an influence on the framework of the ongoing process.
>
> (p. 78)

Transference and countertransference dreams, as well as enactments or psychological games played in therapy, represent for both members of the therapeutic dyad a temporary regression caused by the tension of the encounter. It happens beyond the analyst's attempt to keep themselves safe, in a neutral position. The impact of the patient's projections on the therapist is never neutral. As Novellino argues in his interesting 1984 article, the only negative countertransference is that which is not recognized and analyzed. The illusion of being masters in one's own home and in control of what takes place in the intersubjective space inhibits exploration and spurs acts that are unmentalized and unknown to consciousness. The therapist must have the courage to feel lost and yet move forward.

The transference meaning of dreams brought to therapy

The first question guiding the therapist's exploratory process when faced with a dream brought into session by the patient might be: Why this dream at this time? Beyond the content of the dream—the intrapsychic messages it conveys—the act of communicating a dream to the therapist at a given moment speaks to us about the interactive and interpersonal context of the therapeutic dyad. As Fosshage (1997) states, "All dreams reported to an analyst have transferential meaning; either the *content* of the dream is applicable or the *process* of communicating the dream carries the primary meaning for the analytic relationship" (p. 450). Reinforcing the relationship between content and dream report was Ferenczi's earlier thought in the very short 1913 paper entitled "To Whom Does One Relate One's Dreams?" in which he argues: "We analysts know that one feels impelled to relate one's dream to the very person to whom the content relates" (1926, p. 349). So, while the dream content does not necessarily have a direct reference to the transference, unless the analyst appears directly or the patient associates a dream character with them, it is the very act of telling that reveals a transference meaning. The dream chronicle would be a "bilogical transaction" and would thus take on the meaning of "unconscious communication" that the therapist must decode for the patient because, in Novellino's words, they have no other way to say it (1990). In order to investigate what that ego state relational unit, protagonist of the dream, reveals about the therapeutic situation, Fosshage (1997) invites patients to ask, "I wonder if you are experiencing that here too?" (p. 451). Ermann (1999) is of the same opinion when he writes that among the possible analytic work related to dream content, what is significant in an interpersonal sense is the communication of the dream to the therapist:

> Deciding factor here is the communicative function of the dream as a symptom of transference. In other words the dream report in the "here-and-now" offers a dialogue on transference. This aspect is more important in the interactional context than the decoding of dreams and the patient's repressed wishes and expectations If viewing dream reports from this angle, the unconscious interactional dynamic forces assume priority over latent unconscious childhood wishes.
>
> (p. 79)

In addition to analyzing the contents of the dream in search of ancient memories, unconscious fantasies, and deep intrapsychic conflicts, it is appropriate, therefore, to pick up signs of transference inherent in the very act of dream narration. Remember the story of Milena presented in Chapter 8? We saw how the prolific dream narration with which Milena filled the sessions at the beginning of therapy was analyzed by attributing a transference meaning to it: The therapist was kept distant and "cornered" with so much dream material she could drown into and, at the same time, Milena remained in the relationship in a cordial and compliant, but only seemingly open and cooperative, mode. As if the unconscious communication to the therapist was something along the lines of: *Are these the dreams you want from me? Here they are, but now leave me alone!* By attributing a transferential meaning to the dream reported in therapy, a bridge to the relationship in the here-and-now is activated. In addition to the one suggested by Fosshage, it is appropriate for the therapist to ask another question: *What is the dreamer communicating about our relationship by using this dream imagery right now?*

> The question "Why a Dream right now?" has many answers. The dream Idea as a staged scene has various potential meanings, as every event has in analysis. These may be: coming close, creating intimacy, seduction, diversion, establishing continuity, submission, making a present, withdrawal and whatever. Irrespective of the specific meaning, the dream report is always a "reaction of adjustment," i.e., a change in the closeness-distance regulation.
>
> (Ermann, 1999, p. 80)

Ermann argues that often the dream reported in therapy has to do with an unconscious communication concerning the previous session(s) and that the dream chronicle is an adaptive response to relational mismatching aimed at regulating the emotional distance between the protagonists of the therapeutic dyad. Through the dream chronicle, the conflict between therapist and patient is symbolically represented in the hope that the therapist can remedy it by adjusting the emotional distance. In Ermann's words, "Very often, a patient's dream is a direct reaction to emotional injuries evoked by interventions or the behavior of the analyst, quite unbeknown to him" (p. 82). In line with this hypothesis, the author proposes an interactive dream analysis to be added to the classical one. As in Winnicott's "squiggle game," in which patient and therapist play by making marks on a sheet of paper and then interpreting them, patient and therapist create relational meanings to associate with the dream images making therapy "an ongoing enterprise" (Winnicott, in Ogden, 2005, p. 8). Mancia, in line with Ermann, writes:

> However, the fundamental events in the encounter—separations, fear, frustration, envy and jealousy, dependence, humiliation, the asymmetry of the relation—all lead to the organization of dreams representing the patient's fantasies and defenses in the face of the painful feelings awoken in the transference.
>
> (Mancia, 2007, p. 106)

The patient's dreams, according to Mancia, attune themselves to the analyst's thinking and in this way show that they represent at a preconscious level those intrapsychic and relational changes that the patient's diurnal self is still unable to grasp. The dream would, therefore, draw on the therapist's mental life as much as the patient's, and symbolization would arise precisely from their encounter. It is in this sense that, according to Mancia, dreams would even come to spell *the fate* of the therapeutic relationship. An interesting example of such an unconscious encounter between patient and therapist is the dream brought to therapy by a patient who is an amateur painter. The woman in question dreams of a beautiful villa in the countryside. In a very bright room overlooking a large garden she meets an elderly painter who shows her one of her paintings displayed on her easel. Observing the canvas, the protagonist of the dream realizes that the painting was actually originally her painting and that the painter has modified and covered it by painting over it. Working on the dream through interactive analysis, the patient discovers to her amazement that the therapist paints out of passion in her spare time, whereas the therapist was convinced that such self-disclosure had already emerged in analysis.

Transference dreams at the beginning of therapy

Even before the first meeting between patient and therapist, transferential expectations may take shape in dreams through the enactment of the script protocol, i.e., that prototypical, archaic, and phantasmal model of the unbalanced and uneven relationship that is the child's relationship with primary attachment figures. In other words, we could say that the approach to psychotherapy is itself a circumstance that causes a physiological regression, a sense of natural discomfort and vulnerability caused by being in a new situation at a time of difficulty that the person alone cannot handle. The patient's hope is that they will be able to do so with the help of the expert sitting before them. As we have read in previous chapters, reactivation of the script pattern is a defensive response to uncertain, transient moments. Therefore, it is appropriate for the therapist to be aware of the difficulty the patient experiences when first meeting with them. Sometimes this is a much anticipated and desired moment, like a gift the person is giving themselves, of finally having someone to whom they can bring their existential travails, their symptoms, their fears. By the end of the first session these people are already expressing gratitude to the therapist who so kindly listened. Sometimes, however, the anxiety of talking about oneself is discharged during the session and at the end of the meeting one part of the patient feels lightened, another gets in touch with the guilt of having betrayed familiar taboos and the shame of baring oneself before a stranger. As Tangolo (2018) writes:

> In the psychotherapy room, for weeks and weeks the patient reveals his own story, suffering, and secrets to a stranger who listens and helps the person who is narrating put back together the puzzle of events, understand reasons and the value of scattered emotions, find new paths, and express out loud the thoughts which emerge from the

confused maze, so as to finally take decisions and directions, to get out of the blocking crossroads that are sometimes encountered in life.

(p. 74)

Sometimes, moreover, people come to consultation after a long period of hesitation, perhaps encouraged by some family member hoping for a quick improvement. Such ambivalences in beginning a course of therapy are often unspoken in the narrative of the first session but many times are the subject of dream enactment. What does such a special encounter evoke in that patient's mind? Who will be the stranger they are about to meet? What Parent will they evoke? A protective Good Fairy Godmother, willing to assist and accompany them on the fascinating and at the same time frightening journey within themselves? Or perhaps an Orc, someone monstrous to be defended against, who judges and destroys? Because of the strong emotional stress and the fantasies that arise from it, transference dreams occur very frequently at the beginning of therapy and are characterized by the presence of the figure of the therapist, or of a person, object or situation that represents a surrogate for them (Glucksman & Kramer, 2015). In many dreams occurring at the beginning of therapy, the therapist is symbolically represented by institutions, people with important and powerful roles—as in a patient's dream narrated by Yalom in *The Gift of Therapy* (2002) where the therapist is dreamily represented by a Salvation Army truck. The fact that in the dream the truck repeatedly slams into the foundations of the dreamer's room expresses that typical ambivalence we have been discussing. Transferentially, the therapist is a Parent who could "save" (P_{1+}) and at the same time a Parent who assaults the patient's mind (P_{1-}), typically symbolized by their "room." The fantasies of salvation and destruction are here confused and equally represented. A clear example of such dreams is the dream Susan had at the beginning of therapy, analyzed in Chapter 5. In that case, the therapist's surrogate was the Ministry of Health that "enacted laws," an image that reminds us once again of the imbalance of power that very often characterizes the innermost fantasies related to the therapeutic relationship in the patient's mind. Let us now look at yet another example of a transference dream at the beginning of therapy. Luigi is a 35-year-old computer technician. An only child, he comes from a family with a paranoid father and a severely diabetic mother, whom he lost when he was a child. From his childhood he remembers mostly his sick mother who had to be helped moving around and medicated in her legs because of painful ulcers resulting from the disease, as well as the isolation in which he lived after her death. Luigi was never a child, but in some ways he never stopped being one. After they have children, he and his wife start having troubles. He manifests an obsessive structure on a narcissistic basis. He is very affectionate and protective of his children; he explains that for a parent to be a good parent he must be "a producer of memories," someone able to create all those happy moments of which his mind has no memory. While he is very protective of his children, he is critical and dissatisfied with his wife; she is not enough for him, and so he goes so far as to engage in an extramarital affair with a coworker. In general, he shows a strong ambivalence toward women: On the one hand, they are the targets of anger and devaluation, on the other, of a strong sense of possessions and a desire to be at the center of their world, which reveals a deep narcissistic wound. During the second session Luigi brings the following dream:

> *I am in a mine and the head of the miners gives instructions to everyone: I work with my pickax and pull out a precious stone, red, I take it out into the sunlight and the stone melts in my hands. So I think it was worthless, and I think, "I'm not a miner, I'm just a child." I see myself small again and feel ashamed for thinking I had found who knows what when in fact I feel small and inadequate in front of the head miner.*

Interactive analysis of Luigi's dream reveals unconscious concern that he is not valuable enough in the eyes of the therapist, a woman, represented dreamily by the head miner. In embarking on a course of therapy, there is an expectation to bring out of the mind, as from a mine, what inside the patient appears important, extremely valuable. However, "into the sunlight," in sharing, the richness of his finding loses value, "melts away" in his very hands. As Mancia (2007) writes, "The analyst can use the dream to recognize the splits, identifications, denials, idealizations, fears and defenses, aggressions and seductions activated by the patient" (p. 98) at the precise moment the dream is dreamed. Luigi, at the beginning of therapy, reveals with his dream the shame of discovering himself to be an impostor, someone who has no riches to reveal but is just a "child," inadequate to the expectations of the Parent-head-miner. Paying attention to early dreams offers valuable help in understanding expectations placed on therapy and the therapist as well as tracing answers to the question: *Who am I right now to this person? Someone to defend against or someone to help and support?* Perhaps someone much feared and desired to whom one can prove one's worth, as in Luigi's case. As we saw in Chapter 5, knowing such unconscious expectations enables the therapist to facilitate the passing of the test (Weiss, 1993) in order to build a solid therapeutic alliance. For example, in Luigi's, case the therapist will have to pay special attention to giving appropriate and sincere "strokes" in response to his valuable findings. In addition to the beginning of the individual therapy journey, the analytic-transactional model provides for another step that represents a second beginning for both patient and therapist: inclusion in a therapy group. As we will see in more detail in Chapter 11, which is devoted to dreams in group psychotherapy, insertion into a therapy group is a particularly delicate moment of change that allows for the exploration of the patient's internal imagery with respect to oneself in the group, what

Eric Berne has called the group imago (Tangolo & Massi, 2022). The group imago is a set of fantasies and projections onto the group resulting from the translation onto it of the primitive experiences had in the first group to which the individual ever belonged: their family. The transferences here are multiple, because to those active toward the therapist are added to the "lateral" ones, that is, those activated by other group members. To these we can add other transferences activated by the encounter with a second therapist who sometimes co-leads the group. Many times the complex emotional solicitation provoked by such a transition stimulates rich dream production in the new group member. After four meetings in the new therapeutic setting, Luigi brings the following dream to an individual session:

There are some children, one is particularly intelligent and is about to do something important, like an exam or a task he has to pass, but he can't, his mind is distracted by something and he can't concentrate. This goes on for days until his friends realize that this blockage is due to a (video)game that the child cannot finish and has given up on. They convince him to finish the game and discover that he has not yet been able to finish it because he has not yet had understood something very important. It is a science fiction game in which an alien spaceship invades the earth, the graphics are crude, the ship is like a big dog with a huge head. The child does not understand how to deal with this huge-headed enemy with two scopes coming out of its eyes. His friend's intuition is that the real alien is not what he sees but actually hides inside that machine inside the head. At that point the dream becomes first-person and I directly participate in the fight with the alien in an attempt to get inside the big robot's head. I run after it, I am excited but I am also terrified because at that point I am in control of the situation: I have him slamming into walls, which he swallows up, gaining energy and producing poop made of glowing pixels.

As in the previous dream, Luigi here also expresses the expectation of being special and intelligent and the subsequent disappointment or failure. Thanks to his friends, who could be the members of the new group experienced as allies, the child-dreamer realizes that in order to achieve his goal he must overcome a challenge with an alien enemy "invading the earth" equipped with a huge head and two telescopes coming out of its eyes. The monster to be defeated is very reminiscent of a P_1—appearing here as an archaic and ghostly version of the paranoid and controlling father. In terms of ego state relational units, the representation of the relationship that emerges from the dream is that of a persecutory Parent to a victim Child, who in the challenge feels both excitement and terror. Entering the group seems to have fostered in Luigi the enactment of a transferential relationship different from that which emerged in the first phase of individual therapy. Now the therapist is no longer the one to be seen and appreciated by, but someone potentially very dangerous to be defended against. Good thing there are friends. After a year, Luigi will decide to discontinue group therapy, revealing that he has begun dating one of his groupmates.

The evolution of transference in therapy

As therapy progresses, the therapist is no longer just a blank screen on which to project the patient's parental issues. As Hargaden and Sills (2002) argue, people do not project into a vacuum, and there is always at least a modicum of truth in any projection. Yalom relates that patients' dreams having to do with his absence or death increased in parallel with his aging (2002). If relationship, says Petruska Clarkson, is a major feature in any relevant change or "metanoia" that occurs, psychotherapy is the locus of "multiple relationships" (Clarkson, 1995). Specifically, the author argues, there are five possible modes of client-therapist relationship of which the transference and countertransference relationship are only one possibility. Among others, there is also the Person-to-Person relationship, and this relational mode will become more present as the therapeutic journey goes through its various stages and transferential dynamics are gradually resolved. Therefore, in the evolution of therapy, the interactive analysis of dreams will reveal complex relational plots, where phantasmal and projective aspects mingle with real ones, born precisely from the encounter between two persons in the here-and-now of a relationship. A clinical example can help us understand the copresence of multiple relational meanings in the exchanges between patient and therapist. A young woman expresses in therapy the pain she suffered as a child for never feeling important and "special" enough in the eyes of her parents and that she experienced as an adult every time she continues to feel neglected and excluded by all those who transferentially play a parental role toward her. In the first years of therapy, this experience evokes in the therapist a "special" caring and protective attitude toward her, but with time the pain expressed by the woman turns into a complaining and blackmailing attitude. Whenever the therapist exists in the relationship as a person bringing her own needs or requirements, e.g., interruptions of sessions due to illness or vacation, exceptional schedule changes due to external forces, the patient experiences her transferentially as abandoning and neglecting her. The therapist decides to explain such a dynamic to the patient who, when confronted with this reading, has an insight, is very reflective and says she is deeply sad and upset about not seeing the other person when the self-centered Child takes over. The following week she comes into the session saying that she felt the therapist to be distant during the previous session and that she had a dream the night immediately after the session that she thinks may have something to do with what she experienced there. In the dream, a falsely courteous pharmacist tells her that the room she rented beside the pharmacy is no longer available because a new tenant has arrived. Analysis of the dream in transferential terms reveals that the hypocritical pharmacist may represent the therapist who disavowed her countertransferential experience of fatigue and anger. It is appropriate here to recall Novellino's (1984) admonition that the only negative countertransference is the denied one. The therapist continued to offer attention and protection to the patient but to do so she had to withdraw from herself and from intimacy with her. The patient, who is very sensitive, caught her withdrawal and through the dream asked the therapist to adjust the emotional distance again after the estrangement. Ermann (1999) writes:

> This adjustment expressed in dream memorising or in dream reporting, provokes and sets in motion a distance-regulating conflict. It is like playing, which engenders creativity and autonomy, simultaneously paving the way for interaction.
>
> (p. 80)

In the dynamic analyzed above, not everything can be attributed to the patient's projections. The therapist, a person with her own history and script, played a key role here in the unraveling of the dynamic. The dream was a creative way enacted by the patient to encourage the therapist to reveal herself and to make therapeutic use of that revelation. The classic evolution of the patient's idealizing transference toward the therapist involves access to experiences of anger and disappointment toward her. One has to come down from that pedestal sooner or later! Analysis of the content of dozens of dreams collected over the years shows that a typical image of the evolution of transference in this sense is that of the patient urinating or defecating in the therapy room, or on some object that is more or less symbolically associated with the therapist.

In Cecilia's dream, which will be examined in the next chapter on dreamwork in group therapy, we shall see how the patient unconsciously expresses anger and disagreement with the entry of new people into the therapy group by evacuating in a deserted chapel, the sacred place of therapy. The dreamer also appears relieved to find more excrement hidden in the bushes that do not belong to her. She seems to say to herself through this image, "I am not the only one who is angry, so are the other domesticated long-time members of the group!"

Transference processing in end-of-therapy dreams

We could define dreams of healing as dreams of transference resolution. Processing transference allows us to integrate affective elements of the past with those of the present, and overcome the unbalanced and uneven phantasmal representation of the Parent–Child relationship in favor of an equal Adult–Adult relationship between therapist and patient. Regarding the conclusion of therapy in relation to transference, Ferenczi argues that:

It was precisely psychoanalytic research that highlighted in the relationship between doctor and patient, or even between master and pupil, or father and son, the presence of certain affective elements without which no effective collaboration is possible. However, while in suggestion all the physician's efforts are aimed at maintaining and reinforcing that active agent, that is, his own authority on the one hand and the patient's credulity and dependence on the other, psychoanalysis resorts to it only provisionally; the treatment cannot end before those transference phenomena which in suggestion are instead carefully aroused and cultivated are gradually clarified and resolved.[3]

(Ferenczi, 2002, p. 113)

The transference dimension ceases to exist when the phantasmal relationship gives way to the relationship between two people in the here-and-now. Moiso (1985) writes that healing understood as leaving the script involves the processing of transferential material and the therapist becoming a real person. The "Person-to-Person" relationship, as defined by Petruska Clarkson (1995) as one of the possible relational modes between patient and therapist, becomes the privileged mode of interaction between members of the therapeutic dyad. So, not everything about the therapist is transference. The therapist is also a real figure who belongs to the life of the individual undergoing therapy. The person of the therapist can be symbolically represented in the dream, and they must have the sensitivity and competence to accept this type of relationship. When this happens, the therapist manifests their existence and meets their patient intimately. As in the case brought up above of the patient who dreamed of the therapist as the hypocritical pharmacist, the patient no longer experiences the therapist's needs in a competitive mode toward herself. There is room for the existence of both in the relationship, albeit in the clarity of the contract under which each one has their own task and makes their own contribution to the realization of the agreed-upon goals. In dreams at the end of therapy, patients may continue to dream of the therapist, but their representation is new. At the moment of ending therapy, the therapist is that new Parent who confidently gives the patient permission to grow up and leave home to face the world. Let us recall the dream presented in Chapter 5 of the fight on a boat between Alexander and a panther, while his therapist sits serenely on the shore contemplating the horizon. Sometimes, the patient dreams of one part of themselves experiencing some difficulty and another offering them support and help. In such cases it seems that the therapist has been internalized as a reassuring and protective parental object. Therapy may end when there is no longer a need for the figure of the therapist on whom to project parts of one's own Parent. On

---

3   My translation.

the contrary, as we have just seen, the therapist has become an inner therapist. The therapeutic function has been absorbed, internalized and assimilated into the patient's Adult. A patient comes to mind, who, at a mature stage of her therapeutic journey, during a session with her therapist lets herself go into a long, silent cry triggered by the realization that the woman before her did not match the idealized image of an always empathic and present being who knows everything and never makes mistakes (P_{1+} transference). We do not remember what vulnerability the patient discerned in the therapist on that occasion, but we do remember that they both burst into thunderous laughter when the therapist said that she felt as if she were attending her own funeral. What had died in the patient's mind was her idealized idea of the therapist. Finally the latter could be a person. Sometimes, the death of the therapist becomes an evocative image of the death of the parental aspects projected onto them that is found in dreams at the end of therapy. The following is a dream that a very self-critical and self-deprecating patient with marked depressive aspects had at the end of her therapeutic journey:

I am walking down a slope and you come running from behind me and you pull me with you, you incite me to run with you, so I start to run but you are much faster than me. I try to keep up with you but I can't, and then we get to this place where my classmates are. I get to the end exhausted but happier and more relieved. I had started out walking very demoralized, very sad. But this makes me melt.

The therapist is truly a person who belongs to the patient's life and who is rooting for her, helping her to live with new energy the challenges of her day and age. Here the therapist is seen as a real human being, with all her limitations—she is too fast sometimes—and her imperfections. It is the therapist's job to make transient use of transference in a therapeutic sense and to help the patient overcome it, even if it means feeling more vulnerable, while some patients are comfortable in the position of interminable analysis; it is the therapist's job to help them grow, to leave the safe place of therapy to cross the boundaries of the script into the realm of the unknown, facing the ocean of life ahead. Thus, prematurely ending therapy or procrastinating its end beyond its time leads to the same result, that is, the failure to resolve transference and an addiction that, as Ferenczi (2002) wrote in the above passage, becomes an iatrogenic suggestion. No longer safe behind the mythical "blank screen," therapists must have the courage to be the object of transference—repeated relationship—and at the same time they must also have the courage to be themselves, to be real people—needed relationship—before they finally leave the scene. Papini ends the story quoted in the epigraph to this chapter with the following words: "The soft gloved hand shook mine, for the last time. Murmuring something very gently he left my room, and *only one person* has seen him since" (p. 278).

References

Bromberg, P. (2006). *Awakening the dreamer: Clinical journeys*. Mahwah, NJ: The Analytic Press.

Clarkson, P. (1995). *The therapeutic relationship in psychoanalysis, counselling psychology and psychotherapy*. San Diego: Singular Publishing Group.

Cornell, W. (2016). Failing to do the job. *Transactional Analysis Journal, 46*(4), 266–276.

Ermann, M. (1999). Telling dreams and transference: The interactional function of dreams as free association. *International Forum of Psychoanalysis, 8*(2), 75–86.

Ferenczi, S. (1926). *Further contributions to the theory and technique of psychoanalysis*. London: Hogarth Press & Institute of Psycho-Analysis.

Ferenczi, S. (1980). *First contributions to psycho-analysis*. London: Maresfield Reprints (Originally published in 1952).

Ferenczi, S. (2002). *Opere. Volume quarto. 1927/1933*. Milano: Raffaello Cortina Editore.

Fosshage, J. L. (1997). The organizing functions of dream mentation. *Contemporary Psychoanalysis, 33*(3), 429–458.

Glucksman, M., & Kramer, M. (2015). The manifest dream report and clinical change. In *Dream research: Contributions to clinical practice* New York: Routledge.

Hargaden, H., & Sills, C. (2002). *Transactional analysis: A relational perspective*. London: Routledge.

Little, R. (2006). Ego state relational units and resistance to change. *Transactional Analysis Journal, 36*(1), 7–19. https://doi.org/10.1177/036215370603600103

Mancia, M. (2002). Introduzione [Introduction]. In *Resnik, S. Il teatro del sogno* (M. Mancia, Trad.). Torino: Bollati Boringhieri (Originariamente pubblicato nel 1982).

Mancia, M. (2004). *Sentire le parole. Archivi sonori della memoria implicita e musicalità del transfert* [Hearing words. Sound archives of implicit memory and musicality of transference]. Torino: Bollati Boringhieri.

Mancia, M. (2007). *Feeling the words: Neuropsychoanalytic understanding of memory and the unconscious*. London: Routledge.

Manguel, A. (1983). *Black water: The anthology of fantastic literature*. New York: C.N. Potter.

Moiso, C. (1985). Ego states and transference. *Transactional Analysis Journal, 15*(3), 196–201.

Novellino, M. (1984). Self-Analysis of countertransference in integrative transactional analysis. *Transactional Analysis Journal, 14*(1), 63–67.

Novellino, M. (1990). Unconscious communication and interpretation in transactional analysis. *Transactional Analysis Journal, 20*(3), 168–172.

Ogden, T. (2005). *Dreaming undreamt dreams and interrupted cries*. London: Routledge.

Ribeiro, S. (2021). *The oracle of night: The history and science of dreams* (First American edition; D. Hahn, Trans.). New York: Pantheon Books.

Tangolo, A. E. (2018). *Psychodynamic psychotherapy with transactional analysis: Theory and narration of a living experience*. London: Routledge.

Tangolo, A. E., & Massi, A. (2022). *Group therapy in transactional analysis: Theory through practice*. London: Routledge.

Tudor, K. (2011). Empathy: A cocreative perspective. *Transactional Analysis Journal*, *41*(4), 322–335.

Weiss, J. (1993). *How psychotherapy works. Process and technique*. New York: Guilford.

Yalom, I. D. (2002). *The gift of therapy: An open letter to a new generation of therapists and their patients*. New York: HarperCollins.

SUGGESTION

Cinema and Fellini

Someone once wrote that it is no accident that cinema was born at the same time as psychoanalysis and Freud's thought on the interpretation of dreams. It is as if this contemporaneity of the birth has inextricably linked cinema to dreams from the very beginning.

We recommend that you begin this little journey with *His Prehistoric Past*, a 1914 short film written and directed by Charlie Chaplin, in which the vagabond Charlie falls asleep on a bench and dreams an amusing series of adventures until he is abruptly awakened by a policeman. An Italian filmmaker and film historian, Marco Bertozzi, has written beautiful pages on the link between early cinema and dreams. In his book *L'occhio e la pietra* (Bertozzi, 2003), he associates Meliès' *Voyage dans la lune* with the mythological theme of Icarus and the fantasy of flight. The path he proposes takes us to such small masterpieces as Porter's 1906 *The Dream of a Rarebit Fiend* in which

> a drunkard, returning home after indigestion, is seized by terrible nightmares, rendered with funny little devils rhythmically pounding his head. The dreamlike experience allows the protagonist a fantastic flight over New York hanging from his bed, before snagging the spire of a bell tower and plunging violently back into his room.[1]
>
> (p. 40)

We also suggest watching Luis Buñuel's small masterpieces *Un Chien Andalus* (1929) and *L'Age d'Or* (1930), manifestos of surrealism and enactments of the director's dreams. In his autobiography, Buñuel wrote about *Un Chien Andalus*:

> [It] came from an encounter between two dreams. When I arrived to spend a few days at Dali's house in Figueras, I told him about a dream I'd had in which a long, tapering cloud sliced the moon in half, like a razor blade slicing through an eye. Dali immediately told me that he'd

---

1 My translation.

seen a hand crawling with ants in a dream he'd had the previous night. "And what if we started right there and made a film?" he wondered aloud. Despite my hesitation, we soon found ourselves hard at work, and in less than a week we had a script. Our only rule was very simple: No idea or image that might lend itself to a rational explanation of any kind would be accepted. We had to open all doors to the irrational and keep only those images that surprised us, without trying to explain why.
(1984, pp. 103–104)

Here surrealist cinema and painting are expressions of the dreamlike process put on film and canvas. Again Buñuel, guiding us in our exploration of American cinema, also recalls how Chaplin composed the music for his films in his dreams: he would suddenly wake up whistling and write down the music (p. 134).

We then find Dali's imagery accompanying the representation of the dream in Hitchcock's *Spellbound* (1945). The plot revolves around a young psychoanalyst, played by an extraordinary Ingrid Bergman, who succeeds in proving the innocence of her patient accused of murder, played by a disturbing Gregory Peck, through a dream analysis that reveals the dreamer's traumas but also the identity of the real murderer.

The theme of dreams runs through cinema from Hitchcock to Kubrick, the latter of which would close his brilliant career precisely with *Eyes Wide Shut* (1999), a staging of Arthur Schnitzler's splendid *Dream Story*. The great Japanese director Akira Kurosawa (1910–1998) directly staged his dreams in *Yume* (*Dreams*, 1990).

Wim Wenders (b. 1945) also gave us powerfully dreamlike films such as *Wings of Desire* (1987) and *Until the End of the World* (1991), which we point out for the powerful insight of the viewer through which night dreams are transformed into filmic images.

The whole history of cinema is thus a history of dreams. Among countless examples, we still want to mention the splendid *Hugo Cabret* (2011) by the great Martin Scorsese, written by Brian Selznick. In the film, the story of the orphan Hugo, who wants to become a great illusionist by restoring the automaton built by his father, is intertwined with that of George Meliès, one of the most famous silent film directors. The film is dense with famous quotations from Fritz Lang's *Metropolis* (1927) to Meliès' *Journey to the Moon* (1902), in short, a masterpiece that invites us to rediscover the child dreamer within ourselves.

Federico Fellini

A separate treatment must be reserved for Federico Fellini (1920–1993) because his entire oeuvre is interwoven with his dreams, which anticipate his creative thinking. We find traces of these images and narratives in his *Book of Dreams*, in which he collects and, thanks to his graphic talent, masterfully illustrates, the dream inspirations related to his entire filmography, also influenced by his profound experience of Jungian analysis.

Tullio Kezich wrote of him in a preface to the Italian first edition of *The Book of Dreams*:

> The dreamer is a kind of director of the soul who in the neorealist manner calls upon this or that figure of their acquaintances to give life to fantasies, in a pure appearance of reality [...]
>
> Many years before he ventured into the dream universe with the cognitive tools suggested by his mentor, Jungian analyst Ernst Bernhard, Federico Fellini was aware of the importance of dreams. When I met him [...] he asked me almost immediately what I had dreamed.
>
> [...] Dream activity has always been part of his fantasies [...] As for cinema, although he never made a film entirely composed of dreams like his revered friend Akira Kurosawa (*Yume*, 1990), in his films Fellini often treats reality as something dreamed, such as the Kafkaesque setting of the episode *A Marriage Agency*. After all, *8 ½* opens with the very real nightmare of the traffic jam and is all suspended on the question "Am I dreaming or am I awake?" [...] *Juliet of the Spirits* interweaves a wife's reverie with the disagreements of married life [...] and if *The Voice of the Moon* is all built on a dream-like thread, his latest work is from *The Book of Dreams*.[2]
>
> (2007, pp. 10–15)

Kezich masterfully highlights Fellini's creative relationship with visual representations of dreams, which are to be welcomed as suggestions that are not quite translatable into words and other languages.

> Fellini accepted dreams as a fleeting flash of revelation about the unknown and did not ask for more. As far as I remember from our conversations, he maintained that nighttime fantasies are best when not explained to the fullest extent—an attitude that corresponded to his loathing of the attempt at explanation that were the reviews of his works, which he regarded as dreams on film.[3]
>
> (2007, p. 16)

---

[2] My translation.
[3] My translation.

In an interview with Lietta Tornabuoni, Fellini himself states:

> As a child, around the age of six, seven, I was convinced that there were two lives, one with my eyes open and one with my eyes closed. At night I would look forward to going to bed. I had christened the four corners of the bed with the names of the cinemas of Rimini, Fulgor, Savoia, Opera Nazionale Balilla and Sultano. The show would begin as soon as I closed my eyes. First a velvety darkness, deep and transparent, a darkness that entered another darkness. Then the darkness was shot through with flashes, like sometimes in the evening by the sea, when a storm threatens and the horizon line over the sea undergoes a bombardment of light […]
>
> I was standing near my studio on Corso d'Italia in Rome. I was myself, and I was also in charge of delivering an envelope. I could see my windows all closed. I was trying to ring the intercom, but instead of the intercom there was a plaque with a slot like of a letterbox, and on the plaque it did not say my name, but: *Disperso dei Dispersi* ("Lost of the Lost"). The envelope to be delivered opened, and it contained only a blank sheet of paper. When I came out in a wheelchair, thus unknown to myself, and saw the dismayed and questioning looks of the others, I understood the power of that dream and also delighted in its energy, vitality, invention and direction.[4]
>
> (2007, pp. 563–565)

About that same dream, critic and Fellini's friend Vincenzo Mollica comments:

> A few months earlier, one evening in a restaurant, he drew that dream: Fellini with his back to us, in front of a mailbox. He also wrote *Disperso dei Dispersi*, a reference to his beloved Kafka. He drew it on a paper napkin that we left on the table; neither of us liked it.[5]
>
> (2007, p. 565)

References

Bertozzi, M. (2003). *L'occhio e la pietra [The eye and the stone]*. Torino: Lindau.
Buñuel, L. (1984). *My last sigh*. New York: Vintage Books.
Fellini, F. (2007). *Il libro dei sogni [The book of dreams]* (T. Kezich & V. Boarini, Eds.). Milano: Rizzoli.

---

4 My translation.
5 My translation.

Kezich, T. Preface in Fellini, F. (2007). *Il libro dei sogni* [The book of dreams] (T. Kezich e V. Boarini, Eds.). Milano: Rizzoli.

Mollica, V., Afterword in Fellini, F. (2007). *Il libro dei sogni* [The book of dreams] (T. Kezich e V. Boarini, Eds.). Milano: Rizzoli.

11

DREAMWORK IN GROUP THERAPY

Introduction

The group therapy setting is particularly fertile for dreamwork because the group itself constitutes a dreamlike, evocative place for each participant. The group conjures up childhood experiences within the family, archetypal and primordial experiences of circles around the fire, in caves, and villages, when dream storytelling accompanied evenings and nights under the stars. Thanks to the mystery and fascination that surrounds their representations, therapy groups facilitate listening to dreams as well as dreaming together and learning from each other's dreams. Therefore, groups are very useful in stimulating interpersonal learning, emotional literacy, and motivation to encourage introspection. There are also multiple experiences of dream discussion groups in the field of research, and Lawrence's *social dreaming* also has many applications in management training.

A group is a collection of people who have a direct social exchange, a common purpose, and a well-defined structure of rules.

A group is *not* a line of people waiting for a bus, although a group experience could arise among people who meet casually if an event intervenes (e.g., a strike whereby the bus no longer arrives) forcing them to talk to each other, to self-organize in order to find a way to reach their desired destination together. It is particularly stimulating to rewatch *Waiting List*, a Cuban film by director Juan Carlos Tabio, in which several people are desperately waiting in a dilapidated Cuban transit station for the next bus to arrive. The problem is that the bus never comes. As a number of buses pass by the station, and others that are full or at the end of the line stop, it soon becomes obvious to everyone that the bus they have been waiting for has left them stranded. In the director's imagination, the awaiting people decide to turn the station into a better place to live and proceed to organize in order to do so. Thus the disorganized collection of desperate people becomes a group.

The necessary setting in psychotherapy

The setting that constitutes a psychotherapy group requires some essential conditions: a therapist, a group of patients—between four and eight if the group meets weekly or fortnightly—and a shared commitment to confidentiality. Participants are asked to be willing to give and receive feedback and to share why they agreed to participate, along with their intended goal.

The consistency of regularly cadenced meetings, the stability of the meeting place (physical or virtual room), and the precise and defined time of an hour and a half or two provide the basis for working analytically.

Other dimensions of the group are learned as we go along, particularly openness to listening, a non-judgmental attitude toward others, the gift of sharing, and learning from each other. For an overview of the way we conceive the group, we refer to *Group Therapy in Transactional Analysis* (Tangolo & Massi, 2022), in which the psychodynamic intervention model is described at length. In such a model of work, dreams emerge spontaneously from the very beginning of group formation. Indeed, for some patients, dreams are already being shared in the sessions preceding group entry because the very decision to enter an analysis group stimulates the dream process, memories of other groups such as family, school groups, and early adolescent groups. Among the dreams we collect before entering the group are some really significant ones: a boxing ring, a castle whose door remains closed, a new therapist who looks like Cruella Deville (the villain in Walt Disney's movie *The Hundred and One Dalmatians*), a school class to which we return feeling the discomfort of being excluded or mocked.

Some people, in fact, come to the group with dreams of anxiety or fear, and want to make sure whether it is indeed better to remain on guard and observe before granting their trust to strangers who, among other things, seem intent on distracting the therapist from their commitment to them.

Transactional analysis groups

Psychodynamic transactional analysis groups are centered on two levels: the establishment of the group as a whole and unique organism, and the focus on the development of each individual group member. As such, groups are structured to work both in terms of group analysis and in terms of the individual's analysis within the group. We can say that the main focus of the group is on both the observation of the transference projections (called group imago) of each participant and the guidance that the therapist discreetly offers to facilitate transformative transference leading patients to change their way of being in relation to the world.

The schema that facilitates the therapist's diagnostic understanding of their patients in groups was constructed by Berne (1966), modified by Clarkson (1995), Tudor and Summers (2014), Tangolo (2015, 2022) and Tangolo and Massi (2022).

The transactional-analytic therapist observes how different group members function with respect to the idea they have of themselves among others (group imago) and then supports the evolution of that pre-established schema so that it can be transformed into a more open model allowing for increased self-esteem and social relationships in order to better live in the world and become more capable of intimate and constructive exchanges.

The stages at which therapist and group participants can see their own growth can be recognized by the behaviors and beliefs that characterize the emotional and cognitive interpretation of social events in the therapy group itself.

There are patients who are not keen on joining a group, who are very afraid of others and express a strong distrust of the proposed group analysis. If they then agree to begin anyway, they are choosing to address their inner conflict between desire and fear—with the consequent tendency toward avoidance—by embarking on a journey that can be very productive and therapeutic. The case of Betti, a patient of Anna Emanuela's, was already previously described (Tangolo, 2016), but we believe it might be useful to mention it again here.

Betti's dream report in group: *strong feeling of helplessness*

I want to open my mouth, but it won't open. My upper jaw is lodged in the teeth below.

The bottom right canine, I can feel it rocking and dislodging, like a baby tooth. The canine is pierced, hollow because it has been broken by the teeth above. I keep smashing my molars, too, which are flaking off. "Oh God, what am I doing?" I was scared, but my jaw felt automatic, out of my control. It felt like a ceiling collapsing on me.

Betti's comments and suggestions derived from the dream

"The strange thing is that when I woke up I had no muscle pain. Since that day, however, I have had jaw and neck pains."

The symptoms of jaw pains and nighttime contraction of the mouth with teeth chattering began for Betti around age 15. At the time of the dream she was 27. She said the jaw represented her ability to be in control, to shut up and evade others. Keeping quiet and keeping her secrets, telling lies and not sharing her business with anyone was very important to her, like evading the judgment of others she feared greatly. "I always felt judged by my father, I always felt wrong in his eyes. If I don't say anything about myself, I can avoid judgment."

She then added she greatly feared other people's hostility, and that she could not defend herself except by walking away. According to her, the empty canine, as if it were a baby tooth, represented her troubles in baring her teeth, that is, showing an aggressiveness that is sometimes needed, especially in a work environment. From that moment on, Betti started speaking up more and more in group, began to manifest her emotions, and trained herself to be assertive at work, as other group members observed.

Pre-established imago

Let us imagine a patient still in individual therapy, who decides to join a group, and starts thinking about what might happen in that setting. Dreams and fantasies are typical elements of each person's script. At this stage, the patient confronts the therapist about the expectations they have regarding the group, the fears that are holding them back from accepting the proposed group entry, and the previous experiences they had. Thus, the proposal to enter a group becomes an opportunity for the patient to focus their narrative on their schooling during childhood and adolescence, to recall successes and failures in sports teams or music groups, in all those contexts in which social learning happened through group experiences. Each person in any group context usually assumes a role that we call a script role, whereby someone becomes the boss, someone else the buffoon or goofball, and someone else the submissive. In the mind of every adult person the experiences of adolescence are carved either as happy memories or relational traumas, since during that time social exposure is very high and there is a great need for recognition and belonging in order to understand oneself and define oneself in the world.

Clinical example: Anne's dreams

Anne, a young woman in her 30s, is invited by her therapist to join a group that he co-leads with a colleague. The young woman agrees to participate, but dreams that the female therapist is a kind of Cruella Deville, the villain in Walt Disney's movie *The Hundred and One Dalmatians*, a thin, cruel, sharp-witted woman willing to do anything to achieve her ends.

Provisional imago

At this stage, the patient has begun the journey of group therapy, and in the first few months they start to emotionally recognize themselves, the therapist and the group as a whole, so dreams and fantasies are projections concerning the experiences of the self-slot, the transference slot (the therapist) and the group as a whole organism. In other words, in the first few months of attending group therapy, each person experiences familiar emotions, behaves in a way that confirms beliefs about themselves and the role they usually assume in a social context, behave as if they already know what can be expected from authority (parents, bosses, and therapists) and what needs to be done to be accepted by peers. For the therapist, these early group sessions are very important to see the script in action and to compare the behavior with the narrative. For example, someone might claim to be a shy and reserved person and then actually take a lot of space to be noticed by others, intervene immediately in the conversation and thus astound the therapist, who was expecting different behavior.

More on Anne

After a few months of group therapy Anne dreams that the two therapists forget about the session and she finds herself alone among the other patients, who turn the evening into an aperitif while she is uncomfortable because she feels like the newcomer and has nothing to talk about with the others.

Temporarily adapted imago

After an initial time when the patient acts out the scripted role in the stressful context of the first insertion, once the anxiety associated with the primary need to be accepted and belong diminishes, the new group member can afford to enter the conflict stage, called *storming*.

More projective slots are being defined in the patient's experience related to the people who most call to mind figures from early competitive experiences, perhaps siblings from childhood. It is time for the consolidation of one's place in the group and the expression of early conflicts. At this stage, which is certainly developmental, the new group member begins to experience dislikes and likes that enable them to differentiate from other people and get to know them as individuals. The group is perceived as a collection of individuals and not as an undifferentiated whole, and so exchanges and confrontations in which agreement or disagreement over differing opinions can be asserted are put to the test. Initially, differentiation is more likely to occur on the basis of other projective processes, the lateral transference processes that make one recognize among the strangers in the group people who are similar to siblings, friends and enemies of their adolescence, sexual partners of the past. Attraction to some, curiosity or annoyance and repulsion toward others may be strong emotions that give rise to a period of trial confrontation and conflict.

More on Anne

After a few more months, Anne dreams of having a fierce fight with Renate, who is a rather aggressive person in the group and tends to want to impose herself in confrontations with others. In the reality of the group, Anne ignores her, but in her dreams she begins to take risks and fight her.

Operative imago

If the new group member succeeds in not running away from the first conflict stage, they then proceed to gain access to a deeper knowledge of group members and to an experience of awareness of their own as well as others' power, so they must mediate and negotiate if they are to take advantage of the opportunity to get to know themselves at another level of exchange.

Each projective slot is now well-defined in the mind of the group participant: All of the script's main characters are there, so they can express the essential themes of their own ghosts. This is the stage where the patient tries to access a deeper level of the conversation, at their own increased risk. It is the stage where games are played, understood precisely in the Bernian sense as social manifestations of the script. The group members desire is to receive love and understanding, but often their ways of asking for their needs to be met are still inadequate and defensive. In fact, the more bonding increases, the more fears of being hurt are relived and relational attachment traumas may be re-experienced.

More on Anne

Anne dreams of having sex with some of the men in the group; she thinks the therapists must absolutely not know because they would be very critical of these behaviors. In the dreams, sex is a consolation for the loneliness she is experiencing, and at the same time a forbidden pleasure.

Secondarily adapted imago

After the analysis of the earliest games and affective needs, the group member who has accepted the confrontation and remains within the therapy group even if frightened by the intensity of the exchanges, enters the most constructive stage of their journey.

This is the phase of transformation, when the person experiences new decisions and new positions in their relationships with others. It is a fruitful period of work that in transactional analysis we call *deconfusion*, an emotional return to the time when it was the dreamer who wrote the script, to use Berne's expression. Dreams are very present, tending to reveal archaic anxieties and at the same time envisage new scenarios.

More on Anne

Some script dreams resurface during this period, as repetitive as the dream of retaking one's high school finals. Anne finds herself attending her senior year of high school again, sick with anxiety at no longer remembering Ancient Greek and not having any books. Unlike in the past, however, the dream ends with the belief that she will be fine because she is now an adult and that if she graduated in the past this must also apply to the present.

Clarified imago

This is the final period of therapy, when the patient faces new expressions of self, when they begin to think about the end of therapy and detachment from the therapist and the group. We say that the imago is clarified because the person is now able to define their role in the world based on who they currently are, abandoning childhood fantasies and regrets. It is a time of re-learning and experimentation even outside the group, which provides a *holding* in offering support for any troubles with the outside world. Many of the people who were part of the patient's life may be critical of and annoyed by the new behaviors that are perhaps less symbiotic and no longer complementary to their own scripts of mutual dependence.

Finally, on Anne

Anne dreams that she is teaching a class where the students are not listening to her and are making a lot of noise. She is yelling and yelling until she almost loses her voice. Then she decides to stop, get out, and look for another job. Anne is indeed a very competent and motivated high school teacher, but she usually needs everyone to like her and gets very stressed about it. Toward the end of therapy, she is changing many aspects of her life and is freer to choose the life she wants to lead.

So, Anne, through the evolution of her dreams, initially brings to the group her distrust of the parental figures who have abandoned her, the belief that she has to replace them, the conflict with peers when they are aggressive and competitive siblings, and then finally the possibility of choice and no longer being forced into the substitute role of the parent-teacher who has to control and inhibit the inner voice of her emotional needs.

Thus, group support becomes really important in balancing the loss of strokes/recognition.

In previous studies, dreams have been listed for each of these stages (Tangolo, 2016), and we consider it useful for the therapist to combine observation of behaviors with observation of the patient's dream evolution.

Licia's dream

One evening, Licia, a client at the end of her group journey, brings a very significant dream:

I am with a high school friend and we both come to you (the therapist). He was my lover at the time and he comes to you and you open your arms to him and I watch him surrender to you, enjoying this embrace as I would not have been able to do. In the dream I watch him with tenderness and a good kind of envy and think that I, too, would like to indulge in such an embrace.

In the dream analysis Licia observes that she is very happy with the emotional leftovers of the dream: *I was not envious as I have been all my life, my envy was the desire to indulge in the affection too.*

The group tells Licia that she has changed a lot, that she has now become capable of this surrender, transforming her aggression and envy, and that this is plain for everyone to see.

The exchange ends with an emotional moment shared in an online session during the COVID-19 pandemic, when meetings could only be held remotely.

The polyphony of the dream from Käes to Friedman

Dreams are group-like by definition; they are often crowded, with people, with objects, with ghosts, with different places and times. René Käes, a French Bionian psychoanalyst, has offered a central reflection on these aspects of the relationship between dreams and groups using philosopher Bakhtin's concept of the polyphony of language, which he applies to the dream and the group (Käes, 2002). In his essay "Il racconto dei sogni come richiesta di contenimento e di elaborazione nella terapia di gruppo" (1999), Robi Friedman argues that there is a particularly relevant aspect to dreamwork within the group experience. This aspect is related to the fact that, within the group, what is truly healing is the mechanism of projective identification among group members.

Through resonating with the emotions of others, patients can get in touch with their own otherwise rejected, "unchewed" emotions.

The group functions, in this sense, like a Bionian mother: It "chews," giving you back your emotions in the form of narrative. It provides you with elements of emotional literacy.

Dreams, in this context, become relevant for at least two reasons:

1) They are no longer merely intrapsychic, but become part of a collective dream process that starts from the intrapsychic and reaches the intersubjective, and sometimes even the interpersonal dimension.

Thus, the therapy group includes elements of collective reverie, and becomes a place of re-experimentation of archaic emotions in which dreams are also included.

So, dreams belong "to the group."

2) Dreams are specifically relevant to the way in which and the reason why they are reported (not just the content). The relevance of the creative element of storytelling becomes central to this perspective. It is useful, first of all, in answering the question about the emotional purpose of the dream.

The dream is thus seen as a work of art: no longer just "property" of the author and not simply relevant for its content (subject represented) but also for the style in which the content is presented, for the "form" (assuming that the two elements—form/content—can even be separated!).

Linked to these readings is the view of dreams as a request for containment (expressed by the patient to the therapist and the group).

Friedman's invitation is thus aimed at moving beyond the more strictly interpretive paradigm (Freud), toward listening to the impact of the dream narrative's emotional resonance on everyone.

However, the group's purpose is always the integration of the most difficult emotions.

Listening to dreams

As always, the most appropriate attitude of therapist and group members toward dreams must be listening. The dream is a gift and as such should be welcomed. Each dream given to the group is an opportunity to move from a more superficial social exchange to a deeper exchange, in which the openness of one participant allows others to question their dreams, that inner world that is precluded to some because totally repressed. In his autobiography, the great filmmaker Luis Buñuel wrote an entire chapter devoted to dreams. Among them, one of his recurring dreams deserves a mention here, one we would call a "script dream," in which it is clear how the dreamer imagines his relationship with others.

> The story's always the same, although the details may vary. I'm in a train, I've no idea where I'm going, my bags are on the rack above me. Suddenly the train comes to a halt in a station.
>
> I get up to stretch my legs and have a drink at the cafe on the platform, but I'm very careful because I know that the minute I step onto the concrete, the train will leave. I know all about this trap, I'm suspicious, I place my foot very slowly onto the platform, I look right and left, I whistle casually. The train seems to have stopped dead, so I put my other foot down and then, in a split second, like a cannonball, the train roars out of the station with all my luggage on it. I swear as loudly as I can, but there I am, once again, alone on a deserted platform.
>
> (1983, p. 94)

If Buñuel were in one of our therapy groups we could discuss at length about the trap of the train and the deception he was subjected to by the others, who quietly got off leaving him alone on the platform.

Isa, one of our group patients, often brings dreams that deserve our attention. Let us now read one of her dreams from the perspective of her relationship with the group.

Isa suffers from an anxiety disorder and significant social phobia; she always blushes when someone looks at her and is unable to speak in public. She tends to avoid new situations where she has to introduce herself. As a child she suffered from epilepsy. She lived in a family where her social withdrawal was supported and encouraged. At the beginning of treatment, she is almost 40 years old and has never been in a romantic relationship; she says she is in love with a friend, but does not have the courage to try to get close. She enters the group with many reservations, but then faces the risk and opens up about herself. She is greatly supported in her sexual explorations and early experiences of flirtation and adventure.

One day she brings the following dream:

In my dreams there is always the group. At a group session, during a break, I am alone in the room and I pee, but I actually leave a pool of blood on the floor. You, therapist, come back in and benevolently scold me as you clean up on the floor. But I remain mortified and do not respond.

In therapy Isa says, "I am struck by my own suffering," and the rest of the group observes that there is a group room in the dream, but that she has made everyone leave to be alone with the therapist. The dream, then, makes explicit the conflict that Isa experiences toward groups: a desire to be there, but also fear. Isa blushes, feels ashamed, has trouble speaking up and identifying a space for herself.

Techniques for working on dreams in group

In groups, techniques for working on dreams are used somewhat differently from the context of the individual setting. First, because each material brought by an individual participant becomes comparison material for everyone. So, if every member's disclosure is a stimulus on which the therapist questions everyone and is also considered as an expression of the collective unconscious, this becomes especially true for dreaming. And it is precisely because, as we have already observed, the group is a dream place and the minds of the group members intertwine and communicate on a subliminal level more than we might imagine. As such dreams become the group's business and not just an expression of the individual, since, after being dreamed, they are then narrated and shared in that context. To work in this group dimension there are some specific technical pointers we can provide.

When someone wants to relate a dream, the therapist invites everyone to listen attentively, then has the dreamer repeat the dream twice to accommodate everyone's attention. After the dream report, the therapist invites the dreamer and other members to acknowledge the physical sensations and emotions aroused in them by the dream narrative. Everyone can intervene without interpreting, sharing their emotional dimensions and the images they found most striking in the dream. At this point, to pick up the thread of the dream's message to the dreamer, the dreamer is asked what of the suggestions they have received they feel closest to their own. The others are then told to each take back for themselves the suggestive feeling caused by the image and the emotion they felt in listening: What you feel belongs to you; sometimes we joke around saying "take back your projection!" and ask those who are willing to share what they have learned about themselves from the dreamwork. It is amazing to experience how a stimulus generously given by one participant can make all group members work.

All the observations already made in the chapter on analysis techniques also remain valid for the group setting, but at the end of a dream analysis we must always remember to ask the other participants if they sensed any personal resonances.

In any case, to share a dream is to allow the group to descend into a deeper level of intimacy making members known in their fears and vulnerabilities, and this in itself is a learning experience for everyone, a permission to live with their shadows without being overwhelmed by them. The atmosphere that is generated in the group during and after listening to a dream is in fact always intensely emotional, especially if the therapist succeeds in involving all members.

Cecilia's dream, the cemeteries' guardian

I have to go to group therapy but I need to pee so badly, so I decide I want to be late to the session, maybe because you (Emanuela) had let in three new people who were making me uncomfortable. I go into a chapel, no one is there, I squat down on a bench and pee. In front of me I see the statue of the Virgin Mary, it's like I was asking her permission. There's only a little old lady in the corner who doesn't hear nor see me. I go back to the car and then I can't find the location of the therapy studio. I go back and forth, park, walk, find a bush where I pee again. Behind the bush I find several poops, but they are not mine. They may be dogs' or cats'. I didn't poop, I just peed.

Patient's comment:

> I realized that in a previous session I had said, in a moment of emotion, that in therapy you changed my diaper: I was surprised I had used

this term to describe the group therapy experience. Why do I come up with all these kinds of images (poop, pee, and the like)? Why specifically "changing diapers" instead of, for example, "caring," "feeding," etc.? I associate it with the fact that a situation has arisen where I am managing to bring in more expressions of me, even my anger. I was actually angry at the entry of three new people into the group. This possibility of expressing my anger emerged from a conflict.

Let us now report an exchange between therapists about Cecilia's dream in an intervision group:

Emanuela: First, the patient represents herself in the act of urinating in church, in a context of sacredness within which her gesture is desecrating, transgressive: she urinates in the presence of the Virgin Mary! Then she does it in the bush, where others have defecated (she has not yet allowed herself this). In fact, the patient went through a period in which she had very intense dreams inherent in her redecision process, and in the previous session she had been moved by the fact that "her diaper had been changed" (as a metaphor for "you took me in when I was young and helped me grow up.")

Regarding the choice of the "diaper" theme, we can say that the patient expresses an obsessive and very controlling personality, and speaks, for all intents and purposes, of an "incontinence."

The patient recalled that she made the decision to enter group therapy with me when she was part of another group. Also interesting for the evolution of the group imago, is the shift from the representation of the group as a chapel to that of the group as a bush. From the dimension of solitude, isolation, verticality, with minimal differentiation (the old woman does not listen, does not see, is disinterested) to the more vivid and multiple dimensions of the bush.

Silvia: The bush is fertile, frequented (by dogs and cats), in the open, embedded in a larger context (even dangerous, if you will: It is the place of the unexpected, you don't know what may pop up.)

Emanuela: As such the imagery of changing diapers is on this same level of exchanging smells, fluids: It is a gesture that refers to coming into contact with intimate parts of others. It is a relationship that is not aseptic but corporeal, and not idealized (as the image of breastfeeding might be, for example.)

Silvia: I don't know if it is a coincidence, but earlier you (E) had referred to the group as the digestive system. In that sense I find the image of excrement to be very pertinent. Excrement as one of the products of digestion, in the assimilation/expulsion dynamic.

Francesca: I also find the use of dreams as a means of communication important. For example, the first group imago is evoked through the sacred dimension of the chapel, which is presented precisely through the "revelation" of the dream image.

The reflections of the therapists' group were then shared with the therapy group and Cecilia to enrich the exchanges we already had in the immediate aftermath of the dream report.

The matrixes of social dreaming

During the first two years of the COVID-19 pandemic, we experienced many online group sessions dedicated to social dreaming, that served to alleviate the deep feelings of isolation and distress. The online matrixes of social dreaming brought together many people who were not in therapy, and it was truly amazing to observe the connections that quickly formed between the dreams of strangers.

As mentioned in Chapter 1, social dreaming originated in the 1980s within the Tavistock Institute thanks to the work of Gordon Lawrence. Lawrence (1998) states that dreams contain fundamental information about the situation in which people are living at the time they dream.

The dreams of people living within organizations can, according to the social dreaming approach, constitute a key to accessing the most unconscious and deepest levels of social reality, which are often also the least accessible.

Within the matrixes, members are asked to share dreams, free associations, and reflections on dreams. In the second stage, what emerged in the matrix is elaborated, highlighting possible connections to the social reality being explored. Conversations allow for elaboration of what has emerged; participants are asked to identify connections and commonalities among dreams, images, and fantasies. This in turn allows for highlighting how different dreams may share commonalities.

Dreams are linked with each other. It is as if, as social dreaming matrixes evolve, an "active container" is gradually created, which tends to change the "content" by bringing out new dreams and thoughts, transferring previous dreams and thoughts.

Matrixes can be conducted by a single conductor or by a small staff. In large groups it is common for there to be a small staff of two or three conductors. Generally, members are arranged within the room in a scattered manner, or in a spiral or in a "snowflake" arrangement.

The task of the conductor, as Neri (2002) recommends, is to facilitate among the participants the achievement of the primary task by ensuring that the rules of the setting are followed. They will leave it to the participants to find meanings.

For further study we refer to Tangolo and Castelluzzo's (2020) article describing the main themes that emerged in groups that brought together hundreds of participants from all over Italy, recalling that as early as 2007 Servaas Van Beekum described the integration between the Bionian matrixes of social dreaming and transactional analysis.

During the lockdown caused by the onset of the COVID-19 pandemic, before the vaccines, we experimented with social dreaming matrixes that were also open to patients in various groups and saw how these experiences were a great comfort to them precisely because of the openness to mixed environments of therapists and patients, without distinction of roles and levels. We are all human beings and we all live with the same existential fears, and experiencing the social dreaming group in an equal setting had a decidedly therapeutic outcome for everyone.

The experiences of online groups

The health guidelines during the pandemic forced even the most reticent therapists to shift their work with patients to a virtual context. In PerFormat's clinical experience, online groups were already in place by methodological choice to allow people living in distant locations to access group therapy. Thus, it was less disruptive to transfer each group to this different setting, which has, in part, different characteristics. In online groups, body contact is given exclusively by voice and eyes, which turn out to be powerful tools of stimulation. In addition, each group participant also sees their own image, which would not be possible in an in-person group. This data, in addition to the familiar places from which one connects—often one's home, car or a bench in the park near the office—result in an intensification of the group's dream dimension and a lowering of defenses by shortening distances. It was thus easier to access a certain kind of intimacy, to see people enter strong emotional states with a decrease in social shame for crying in public or expressing strong feelings of anger. Dream narration increased. Currently, groups that had moved online because of the pandemic have returned to meeting in presence, while others continue with the online setting and in some cases mixed settings, with some people remotely connected and others present in the physical room. The flexibility of therapists and patients has greatly increased, as has the propensity to experiment.

One benefit of this openness has undoubtedly been that people in the hospital for COVID-19 or other serious illness have been able to continue therapy with a really important *holding* benefit.

The face-to-face dimension that is very powerful in the online group may recall some of Käes' thoughts on other key experiences:

> The first is that of maternal face-to-face, particularly the experiences that occurred during the time of nurturing and caring relationships, and that reactivate tactile, visual, mimicry, and olfactory modes of

archaic communication. The second is that of specular face-to-face, which solicits the specular identificatory modes and which reactivate the anxieties of fragmentation, the feeling of the uncanny with respect to the double, aggression in the face of the rival and the intruder [...] Finally, the experience of amorous seduction and mating is found reactivated with the revival of sexual and narcissistic libidinal emotions. The plural dimension of these face-to-face experiences stimulates the enactment of affects, objects and representations associated with the original phantasmatics of the primary scene, nodal in every group.[1]

(Käes, 2002, pp. 120–121)

Our clinical experience during the COVID-19 pandemic

During the early period of the COVID-19 pandemic in Italy, the lockdown was very strict, with frequent police checks on the streets. Valerio is part of a group that moved online.

This is his dream:

We are all on a central city square and we are talking without masks. A police patrol comes up to us and tells us: "You have to disband, this is a gathering!" One of the two therapists approaches the policeman and says, "But we are a family, we are conjoined."

And therefore, Valerio concludes, if we are a family we can see each other without breaking the rules.

The group members observed that Valerio is expressing the positive feeling of having been able to maintain ties and indeed deepen the feeling of cohesion and belonging during lockdown. It is also interesting to note the representation of the critical Parent in the person of the policemen objecting to "the gathering" (a term much used at the time to define behavior that was prohibited because it facilitated the spread of contagion) and the representation of the protective Parent in the words of the therapist, who provides permission to be together because they are "conjoined" (again a term used at the time in ministerial guidelines to define the family unit). Some single participants in the group say that for them the group meeting was the only time of social exchange in the whole week.

---

1   My translation.

References

Berne, E. (1966). *Principles of group treatment.* New York: Oxford University Press.
Buñuel, L. (1983). *My last sigh.* New York: Vintage Books.
Clarkson, P. (1995). *The therapeutic relationship in psychoanalysis, counselling psychology and psychotherapy.* San Diego: Singular Pub Group.
Friedman, R. (1999). Il racconto dei sogni come richiesta di contenimento e di elaborazione nella terapia di gruppo [Dream report as a request for containment and processing in group therapy]. *Funzione Gamma.* https://www.funzionegamma.it/il-racconto-dei-sogni-come-richiesta-di-contenimento-e-di-elaborazione-nella-terapia-di-gruppo/
Kaës, R. (2002). *La polyphonie du rêve: L'expérience onirique commune et partagée* [*The polyphony of dreams: The shared dream experience*]. Paris: Dunod.
Lawrence, W. G. (1998). Social Dreaming as a tool of consultancy and action research. In W. G. Lawrence (Ed.), *Social dreaming at work.* London: Karnak Books, p. 123–140.
Neri, C. (2002). Introduzione al Social Dreaming. Relazione sui workshop tenuti a Mauriburg, Raissa e Clarice Town [Introduction to Social Dreaming. Report on workshops held in Mauriburg, Raissa and Clarice Town]. *Rivista di Psicoanalisi, XLVIII*(1), 93–114.
Tangolo, A. E. (2015). Group imago and dreamwork in group therapy. *Transactional Analysis Journal, 45*(3), 179–190. https://doi.org/10.1177/0362153715597722
Tangolo, A. E., & Castelluzzo, E. (2020). Sogno e social dreaming al tempo del coronavirus in Italia [Dreaming and Social Dreaming at the time of Covid-19 in Italy]. *Percorsi, VII*(3), 38–45.
Tangolo, A. E., & Massi, A. (2018). A contemporary perspective on transactional analysis group therapy. *Transactional Analysis Journal, 48*(3), 209–223. https://doi.org/10.1080/03621537.2018.1471288
Tangolo, A. E., & Massi, A. (2022). *Group therapy in transactional analysis: Theory through Practice.* London: Routledge.
Tudor, K., & Summers, G. (2014). *Co-creative transactional analysis: Papers, responses, dialogues, and developments.* London: Karnac Books.

12
COUNTERTRANSFERENCE DREAMS

Two patients in the therapy room

As argued by Racker (1957), countertransference can be defined as the worst danger and at the same time the best tool for understanding the therapist has at their disposal. According to the author, therefore, it is necessary for the therapist to accept their own countertransference because their unconscious understands that of the patient, and their emotional reactions are closer to the patient's deep experience than their conscious observations. Already in 1957, while addressing experienced colleagues, Racker recommended in slightly paternalistic language:

> We must begin by revision of our feelings about our own countertransference and try to overcome our own infantile ideals more thoroughly, accepting more fully the fact that we are still children and neurotics even when we are adults and analysts.
>
> (1957, p. 307)

Racker also questions the distortion involving the myth of analysis, namely the idea that therapy is the interaction between a healthy person and a sick person. This is not the case: therapy is the interaction between two personalities. The only chance the therapist has is to try to grasp some form of objectivity by observing and analyzing their own subjectivity with perseverance and dedication (1957). Thirty years after this celebrated paper, Novellino's aforementioned work was published in the *TAJ*, where the father of psychodynamic transactional analysis defines countertransference analysis as an indispensable tool for gaining information about the evolution of the therapeutic relationship, and indicates as negative only that countertransference which the therapist does not recognize or even one they repress (Novellino, 1984). In order to help the patient descend into the abyss of their ego states, it is necessary for the therapist to make the same journey, and from the abyss to know in turn how to ascend, otherwise patient and therapist remain, together, but fatally mired in the welter of nonsense and psychopathology (Tangolo, 2018). The therapist's skill, therefore, lies in accepting that the encounter with the patient will force them to move from the here-and-now of the relationship to the there-and-then, where the there-and-then may be a re-actualization of the patient or the therapist or both. Summers and Tudor call the latter situation *co-transference*, a circumstance caused by the meeting of two subjectivities and the reactivation of old emotional patterns sometimes known, sometimes emerging for the first time (Summers & Tudor, 2000). Then again, what can happen when the therapist meets the patient? Racker would answer, "everything happens that can happen in one personality faced with another" (1957, p. 311). Letting such parts of ego states speak, listening to them, analyzing them, helps to return to the present and defuse the potential that could unconsciously lead to acting out and dangerous drop outs. The broader the traumatized areas that collide, the more intense will be the projective identification and emotional response in the analytic couple. As Stuthridge (2015) states, Berne defines psychological play in psychotherapy as, "The interpersonal struggle in the complex transferential tangles that are more often referred to as enactments in the current psychoanalytic literature" (p. 104). The more intense the emotional reactivation, the higher the degree of psychological play in which the two players are immersed in the therapy space. Because patient and therapist are equally affected by the process of reactualizing unconscious relational dynamics, psychological play—or enactment, according to the author—is bidirectional, inevitable, and of extreme value when analyzed. When emotions are toxic, dysregulated, and unacknowledged, they emerge with all their intensity in the relational exchange, without having given the therapist a chance to grasp countertransferential aspects whose analysis, as mentioned above, is useful for healing. As Stuthridge (2015) points out, the higher the degree of psychological play, the more difficult it is to detect countertransference. In first-degree games, in fact, the therapist is aware of countertransferential emotions and cognitions, whereas in second-degree games, countertransference concerns unacceptable thoughts and affects that reside in misrecognized parts of the therapist's self and are replaced in the setting with acting outs. Such feelings and cognitions, whose presence is inferred from a generic sense of experienced disquiet, can be brought to consciousness through associations and imagination, as well as through dreams and metaphors related to non-verbalized experiences. In the case of third-degree games, however, the emotions are toxic, dysregulated and the countertransference is expressed solely at the visceral level. Here the therapist tentatively loses their reflective function, that is, they are not aware of what about the client is resonating within themselves. As Stuthridge (2015) writes:

> Images do not always connect neatly with meanings, new meanings can be profoundly unsettling, visceral experience is always disturbing,

and identifying unsymbolized feelings usually involves an inner wrestle with part of self we do not want to know.

(p. 114)

From such a perspective, "playing along," being in the dynamics of a psychological game, is not a slip that should be dismissed as a mistake. Reactualizing typical patterns of unsatisfying or traumatizing relationships from the client's—and, alas, the therapist's—childhood is the therapist's only chance to understand a truth that the patient does not know how to say, but does know how to live (Cornell, 2016; Little, 2011; Stuthridge, 2015). The transformative potential of the Past I–Past You (Summers & Tudor, 2000) is boundless when it causes emotional change within the therapist. The latter's ability to symbolize the experience, to make sense of both internal and external emotional drives, of their reactions, will allow the client to feel safe within a new, desired and "necessary" relationship (Little, 2011). If the therapist is able to heal a little more by taking in parts of dissociated ego states brought to light by the encounter with that client, the latter will feel involved in the therapist's states of mind and be able to make the same healing journey. The heart of therapy work is negotiation between subjectivities, much more so than interpretation (Bromberg, 2006). What extraordinary work! We are encouraged to always heal a little more to support our patients in their healing. In other words, it will be the therapist's willingness to build bridges between dissociated and disowned states of their own self, stimulated by the analytic situation, that will expand the integration of their own sense of identity and thus that of the client (Bromberg, 2006). Stuthridge explains well how this process of meta-reflection on one's personal, emotional involvement is therapeutically effective:

> The honest answer often comes "unbidden," like an unexpected guest in the night rather than being something consciously sought after. At best, we can be receptive and open to the arrival of this unexpected guest. We can keep the doors unlocked and learn to welcome discomfort in this work, or at least to let it in.
>
> (Stuthridge, 2015, p. 114)

The role of the therapist so far described foregrounds the theme of vulnerability and protection, and the entire fourth issue of the *TAJ* was dedicated to this theme in 2016. As his personal contribution to the theme, in the aforementioned article Cornell analyzes the reasons that led one of his patients to abruptly stop treatment, writing, "I didn't meet her in the moments of this madness. I stepped aside" (2016, p. 270). To protect themselves from the violence of certain projections that impact blind spots in the therapist's psyche, he invites therapists to question, together with the patient, the meaning of what is happening. The internal representation of the figure of the therapist can change abruptly in the patient's mind and become in a very narrow span of time: "asshole, liberal, sadist, narcissist, father, mother, protector, lover, abuser, and savior" (Cornell, 2016, p. 270). In an intensity similar to that reported by Cornell, we recall a patient who in a single month of treatment alternately idolized us, attacked us, sexually provoked us, and rejected us, until the cancelation of the last session was justified with a WhatsApp message that read, "There is nothing more to talk about." These were her last words enfranchising herself permanently from therapy. In this case, our responsibility as therapists was to have allowed the patient to harm us and, through us, to harm herself. As Clarkson (1995) states:

> For many adults victimized as children, the psychotherapist constitutes the first legitimate target who will stand firmly in place and not blackmail them. It is a wonderful psychological opportunity to return the blow to a substitute parent or other authority figure who has hurt them in the past and who psychologically, will always be out of reach. But, whenever the client succeeds in harming the therapist in any way, they are in fact harming themselves.[1]
>
> (p. 75)

Cornell insists on this aspect and, speaking of his experience with Samantha, argues, "She was both terrified that my mind would take over hers and at the same time terrified that her mind was too powerful for mine" (p. 270). When the representation of the therapist is thus split into opposing instances, depicting them, at the same time, as the desired other (P_{1+}) and the rejecting and feared other (P_{1-}), and the therapist reacts with their own internal fractures, the relationship risks rupture. Only by giving up defense to accommodate the contradictory nature of such projections and the emotional intensity of the countertransference does the therapist help the patient symbolize the relational experience until the extensive internal fractures are overcome (Little, 2011). On the inevitability of certain clashes Bromberg insists:

> Smoothing the bumps and paving the potholes—that is, bringing the bumps and potholes from the level of enactment to the level of conscious perception and conscious thought is at best a trying job, and with some patients it is an uncomfortably sweaty mess that stretches to its limit the analyst's capacity to endure it. Why do we have to go through all this? (Sometimes when I ask myself this question what I really mean is, "Who needs it?") The answer I have arrived at after many years of climbing out of potholes is that, like it or not, an analysis without potholes is, in the final analysis, a pseudoanalysis.
>
> (2006, p. 87)

---

[1] My translation.

Enactments, understood here as psychological games played in therapy, are useful because they provide an opportunity for confrontation in a safe context such as the therapy room. Here the goal is to tolerate tension so as to process the internal conflict symbolized by the struggle between the two members of the therapeutic dyad. The change lies precisely in the possibility of tolerating such closeness, beyond the patient's magical expectations of a salvific or persecutory nature (Bromberg, 2006). And this is precisely what Little recommends when he encourages working *within* the transference and not *with* the transference (Little, 2005): the patient's script meets the therapist's script, the patient's transference drama in turn activates the therapist's transference drama. This may happen in some respects in the very early phase of therapy, when the analytic couple meets, smells each other and intuitively chooses. More often it will take time for the client to show the therapist the wounds hidden by their own script. In a desire to protect themselves from the repetition of traumatic experiences, what Little calls the core-of-pain (2011), people, whether in the role of patient or therapist, enact a number of defensive strategies that make them appear to the world as self-sufficient and rational beings. Within the therapeutic setting, as the analytic process unravels, we often witness the emergence of an impasse between what the patient wants the therapist to be—and perhaps is—and what they fear they are or are about to become, in an unconscious dialectic between the fear of a repetition of traumatic experiences and the desire for a transformative experience. When there is relational impasse, both patient and therapist feel an energy of the same intensity in both re-experiencing the repeated relational experience (*repeated relationship*) and re-experiencing the needed relational experience (*needed relationship*). To defend against the affects associated with early traumatic experiences, the patient will project them onto the therapist who will be driven to identify with the one who experiences them not only because they are emotionally solicited from outside, but also because some aspect of the therapist is similar to that projection. This is an aspect of oneself that the therapist will need to face (Little, 2011), but for therapy to be effective, it is *essential* that this process take place. The involvement of unprocessed P/C ego states relational units (Little, 2005) or, as Bromberg puts it, the activation of dissociated states of the therapist's self, is not an iatrogenic factor or even a side effect; it is the very core of therapeutic work. As therapists, we are inevitably invited to delve into the dark recesses of our minds in order to perpetuate in ourselves a healing process that activates the same process in our patient. The therapist must recognize, accept, and address the core-of-pain that the patient has touched in them, and thus represent that secure base that the patient needs to repair the trauma. The most challenging difficulty for the therapist is to be able to read what is happening within themselves at the countertransferential level and name the emotions and thoughts that work just below the level of awareness. As mentioned above, when second- and third-degree games are being played in therapy, it is not enough for the therapist to resort to conscious scouting of their own deep inner movements. What is needed is an additional space to that of therapy, a different language and a different thought than the verbal (Bucci, 2001), which allows the rise to consciousness of outcast states of the self, of P/C ego states relational units connected to intolerable experiences that have remained fixed. It is through the decoding of subconscious symbolic messages that countertransference can be read, understood and used in a therapeutic sense. Fantasies, lapses, repression, and especially dreams are just a few examples of how countertransference information can be decoded. We know that the dream experience specifically offers a glimpse of the dreamer's inner world, as well as an x-ray of the state of the art of the therapeutic relationship, and is therefore an inexhaustible source of useful information for therapy. The analysis of the client's dreams, like that of the therapist's dreams, opens up new scenarios about the patient's mind with its objects and the therapist's mind with its countertransferential affects and script. It goes without saying that if the therapist's dream activity also becomes the object of study, the possibilities of making therapeutic use of impasses and games in which the dyad can—and indeed, must—find itself harnessed are greatly increased. Let us now look at this aspect in detail.

Of love, death, and other nonsense: countertransference dreams

In the classical psychoanalytic tradition, the fact that the therapist dreamed about their patients was seen as an expression of an unresolved dynamic in the therapist, the result of an incomplete analysis that represented an obstacle in understanding the patient's transferential dynamics and, therefore, as something to be hidden from one's supervisors or simply overlooked. This may be the reason why

> The countertransference dream (CTD), a dream of the analyst in which the patient appears undisguised in the manifest content, has received little attention in the psychoanalytic literature.
>
> (Lester et al., 1989, p. 305)

Another factor that, in our opinion, has hindered and censored the study of countertransference dreams has been the use of the Freudian theoretical framework of dreams as a disguised expression of unresolved infantile desires. This reading, when universally used to explain the meanings of dreams, prevents finding the relational meaning of the dream process itself in the co-constructed intersubjective field between patient and therapist. According to this view, narrating a dream about a patient to colleagues and supervisors is equivalent to the therapist coming out with unresolved aspects of their own childhood and personal weaknesses. The therapist would even use the clinical environment to circumvent censorship and express otherwise inexpressible desires

(Heenen-Wolff, 2005). Certainly, after dreaming about a patient, the therapist may experience a certain amount of discomfort upon waking. Understandable is the feeling of having transgressed the sacred boundary of the therapeutic setting by having taken the patient to a private place such as the dreamscape, and the discomfort of having to handle in solitude the emotional experience of having shared something so intimate with the patient. In this regard, Brown (2007) argues that

> upon seeing the patient the morning after having dreamt of him or her, the analyst may feel awkward, as though a secret knowledge of the patient has been gained and cannot be revealed. Thus, the analyst may feel alone with a sense of the patient that may seem like an ill-gotten gain—something the analyst is loath to share with colleagues, a hesitation that has at least a hint of shame and a measure of guilt that might require some act of analytic contrition, such as the analyst's return to his or her own analysis.
>
> (Brown, 2007, p. 838)

Today, with the rise of two-person psychology, to think that one can distinguish what in the therapist's dream stems from their unconscious conflicts, and what belongs to the patient is considered naive and illusory. As we saw in Chapter 10, if the patient's dream is always a transference dream, the therapist's dream in which the patient or a surrogate of the patient appears is always a countertransference dream. We do not see the risk that Heenen-Wolff sees: "The content of a session or of other elements arising from the analytic situation are thus in danger of being taken up and 'used' for the analyst's own psychic purposes" (p. 1545). Instead, we agree with Brown (2007) when she says:

> In our contemporary literature, a clinical report that does not include both the yin of the patient's transference and the corresponding yang of the analyst's experience is considered incomplete.
>
> (p. 838)

Despite the internal conflicts that this may ignite in the therapist, dream analysis about a patient is more commonly regarded as something valuable because it provides information about their countertransference, and countertransference analysis is not a distraction from working with the patient. On the contrary, it is a tool through which healing can take place (Novellino, 1984). As we have seen extensively above, the idea that there may be blind spots or unexplored areas of the unconscious is no longer to be attributed to insufficient and incomplete analysis, but rather to the deep and ever-changing dynamics that arise from the encounter between two subjects in exploration. The healing process of the therapist, like that of anyone else, is potentially infinite. Countertransference, therefore, is not an obstacle at all, but rather, as Rudge argues, "the instrument of the analyst is his own unconscious" (Rudge, 1998, p. 109). The author goes on to declare:

> Not understanding is not an obstacle, but is rather the correct position of the analyst for hearing the unconscious. Immediate understanding tends to be an evidence of resistance on the part of the analyst. If this position of immediate understanding is not avoided, the analyst will always find what he already knows.
>
> (p. 109)

Already in 1949, in his famous paper "Hate in the Counter-Transference," Winnicott was very clear about this, and thus wrote, "Counter-transference phenomena will at times be the important things in the analysis" (p. 70). In the article, the author talks about a period of great fatigue in working with patients during which he realized he was making some mistake, but did not understand why. One night he had an important dream, the reading of which helped him shed light on what was happening. The second part of the dream is as such:

> I was aware that the people in the stalls were watching a play and I was now related to what was going on on the stage through them. A new kind of anxiety now developed. What I knew was that I had no right side of my body at all. This was not a castration dream. It was a sense of not having that part of the body.
>
> (p. 71)

Upon awakening Winnicott immediately associated the experience he had in the dream with the psychotic patient he had met in session the previous day, toward whom he had felt strong irritation and the height of distress on that occasion. That day the patient had asked him to have no relationship with her body and to consider her only "spirit." Winnicott interpreted his own dream as an anguished reaction to his patient's rejection of her body and continued:

> Whatever other interpretations might be made in respect of this dream the result of my having dreamed it and remembered it was that I was able to take up this analysis again and even to heal the harm done to it by my irritability [...] The analyst must be prepared to bear strain without expecting the patient to know anything about what he is doing, perhaps over a long period of time. To do this he must be easily aware of his own fear and hate.
>
> (pp. 71–72)

It is essential to ask how psychotic-type hatred and anxiety are produced in the therapist. "Only in this way can there be any hope of the avoidance of therapy that is adapted to the needs of the therapist rather than to the needs of the patient" (p. 74). Producing dreams is a way to convey and express disturbing, indigestible emotions. Interrogating the dream allows us to shed light on emotions, perceptions and thoughts that the day work has not dwelled on. Winnicott calls such dreams, which he associates with some level of difficulty with patients, "healing dreams"; such dreams are helpful, as he puts it, "although in many cases unpleasant, have each one of them marked my arrival at a new stage in emotional development" (p. 71). The dreams prompted by the encounter with the patient help the therapist reacquaint themselves with emotions dissociated from consciousness and enable them to shed light on dark spots where patient's and therapist's blindness prevents the latter from growing and healing. Rudge (1998) uses her own dream, or rather nightmare, to understand something she had overlooked about one of her patients:

> The dream called my attention to something that I had been missing—the seriousness of her condition and the risk that she would die. I had already received enough information to suspect the seriousness of what was going on, but only through the countertransference dream did I realize what I already unconsciously knew.
>
> (p. 106)

In the dream the author realizes with horror that she is breastfeeding an infant with a bottle full of bleach instead of milk. The countertransference dream is a signal that alerts the therapist that something is moving below the level of consciousness that needs to be understood and processed, although the dream itself is already a first form of processing. Heenen-Wolff also strongly affirms the importance of countertransference dreams:

> I would advance the hypothesis, against the background of Freud's dream-theory, that every analyst's dream about his or her patient comprises countertransference elements which need to be sifted out with care each time [...] This symbolization was translated into a better capacity for thinking which, moreover, was corroborated and affirmed as the analysis continued.
>
> (p. 1556)

The analysis of one's dreams should be considered by the therapist as a tool of the therapist's technique (Zwiebel in Armando & Bolko, 2017). The therapist's dream "is the emotional truth about the hour that is present in both patient and analyst" (Brown, 2007, p. 840). The knowledge of the patient that the therapist accesses through dreaming about the patient is the most profound knowledge they can access. It is the "*knowing about* experience and *knowing through* experience" of Bionian memory (2007, p. 840). The therapist can dream about a patient and through the dream identify solutions, thoughts different than those formulated when awake. The dreamer here resembles an auxiliary Adult who collaborates to understand the meaning of a given relational dynamic. Other times the therapist dreams of the patient or former patient with whom some form of identification has been activated. Another possibility is that the dream was stimulated unconsciously by the effect of projective identification on the therapist. More often, the dream reveals the coexistence of all these aspects, similar in patient and therapist, whose encounter causes a relational impasse (Little, 2011). From the elaboration of this impasse, a transformative process is triggered which leads to the knowledge of new aspects of self and other. As we have repeatedly written, dreams are an opportunity to bring out states of the self that move below the level of consciousness. The dream narrative is a transitional space into which the dreamer allows themselves to bring, in symbolic form, states of the self-containing unprocessed affective experiences (Bromberg, 2006), and such experiences, prompted by a therapist's encounter with a patient, belong to both (Zweibel in Brown, 2007). It is precisely these unprocessed experiences that need to be attended to, beyond whether the dreamer is the patient or the therapist. The dream is the instrument through which "to evoke and manage the emergence of our most secret and shame riddled 'bad selves', our own and the patient's" (Messler Davies in Little, 2011). In this sense, missed acts, resistances, blind spots, and disconnections in session are not failures of the therapist; they are opportunities that the dream encourages us to seize (Ogden, 2021). Through dreams, the therapist can activate the mental process that leads to the elaboration of unconscious, dissociated emotions into thoughts and fantasies. This is how the patient exists in the mind of the therapist. If the therapist processes their own emotional experience that emerged from the dream event, they can help the patient experience the other as a facilitating object-self (promoting the needed relationship), otherwise they remain that feared, aggressive, and rejecting object (repeated relationship). Attention must therefore be paid to the therapist's dreams in order to assess what countertransference signals it may convey. In our supervision experiences we have noticed that, despite some resistance, young therapists show a willingness to talk about themselves through dreams. Especially after they are told in the School of Psychotherapy Training that the most famous countertransference dream is undoubtedly Freud's dream of Irma:

> Thus Anzieu leaves no doubt that the dream of "Irma's injection" should be designated as the first countertransference dream in the history of psychoanalysis.
> (Heenen-Wolff, 2005, p. 1545)

Freud's dream about the "indocile" Irma is the most analyzed dream we know of. And each author who analyzes it always proposes new perspectives of meaning. However, one element remains unchanged because it is the celebrated dreamer himself who reveals it. The dream is an attempt to mitigate the sense of ineffectiveness felt in connection with the unsuccessful analysis of the patient Irma. As Freud himself admits:

> For the result of the dream is that I am not to blame for the suffering which Irma still has, and that Otto is to blame for it. Now Otto has made me angry by his remark about Irma's imperfect cure; the dream avenges me upon him by turning the reproach back upon himself. The dream acquits me of responsibility for Irma's condition.
>
> (1899/2005, p. 416)

Interestingly, such an absolution of the therapist from responsibility recurs in many countertransference dreams. Among the therapists' dreams reported in the literature, as well as those collected and analyzed as part of our research, almost all of them variously carry the theme of doubt about the competence and effectiveness of the work performed (Brown, 2007). Among the ethical and deontological questions, one of the most named is the risk of eroticization of the therapeutic relationship. With respect to this issue, we find it interesting to mention a courageous paper by Hargaden on erotic countertransference published in a collection edited by Fowlie and Sills in 2011. In it the author recognizes the fundamental importance of analyzing the therapist's dreams as a vehicle for valuable information about countertransference, and from there about the entire analytic process with a given patient. Through the reading of a dream in which a client appears, the author becomes aware of emotions felt toward them that had hitherto been relegated below the threshold of awareness. Here Brown's (2007) observation is confirmed once more, as the dream about the patient is accompanied by the sense of inadequacy experienced by the therapist:

> When I recognized their erotic nature I felt threatened by them. I wondered if I was a bad therapist because I found my client sexually attractive. When I began to realize that my feelings could be useful to the therapy I started to ponder the significance of them and wonder about what my client might be trying to communicate to me through this unconscious process.
>
> (Hargaden, 2011, p. 235)

Understanding and processing the unconscious emotional experiences that emerged thanks to the dream allows the therapist to take care of the client, themselves and their relationship, safe from the risk of dangerous acting out. However, so far we have talked much about the therapist and little about the patient. Let us also make our own Lippman's (2000) apprehension: Lippman wonders if talking about the analyst's participation in treatment runs the risk of becoming a distraction to the study of the patient's mind and an endlessly fascinating way to talk about the self. "For what purpose do we do what we do in therapy?" is a question to which the therapist must always seek answers. However, one thing is certain. Dreaming about one's patients is not for the therapist an indication of weakness, fragility or self-centeredness, but rather an act with double healing potential that requires skill and humility (Ogden, 2005b).

An example of self-analysis of countertransference dreams

The countertransference dream we are about to recount helps to understand how self-analysis can also be a direct route for unveiling unconscious countertransferential dimensions related to a therapeutic relationship. Armando and Bolko (2017) offer therapists three suggestions that we should take into account when reading our own dreams. First, it is helpful to write down the dream in a way that distances and objectifies it. Also, it may be helpful to return to the dream later in the day or the next day. Finally, it is important to connect the dream to other events that happened during the same period by looking for a connection, a nexus of thought underlying the various themes of meaning. In the case we report here, the therapist, whom we will call Erica, does not dream directly about a client, but about "a little girl who has to do with the work environment." As in the case of Winnicott's dream, through a work of free associations that the therapist herself does upon waking, she connects the coded message of the dream to a situation that had happened a few hours earlier in the context of therapy with a patient. The previous day Erica had had telephone contact with a client we will name Sara. During the conversation, Sara vehemently expresses an emotion of anger toward Erica, guilty of not answering her phone immediately, accusing her of not calling her back until many hours later. Something serious could have happened to her, she could have died, and her therapist had not cared about her at all. With violence and desperation, Sara acts out her furious anger, then hangs up. At first Erica is stunned, then she is in turn overcome with intense anger: Her patient, with whom she felt a solid alliance and toward whom she had sincere affection, had canceled without the agreed-upon notice the last two weekly sessions, and that day demanded her utmost availability. Instinctively, the therapist connects the patient's narcissistic traits to such an aggressive and omnipotent reaction, and contacts an impulsive desire to "make her pay." With these emotions and thoughts, Erica lies down and dreams:

> *I was in a house belonging to someone I knew who I thought had something to do with work [...] There was a little girl [...] Nine months old. I look for her, in the house, I see her. There is a problem,*

however: There are two of them, identical, twins apparently. But I know that actually she is just one, she has no twins. Yet there are two girls, I'm not just seeing double. Both of them are smiling and cute, they invite me to play, but I am upset because no one seems to notice, not even Mom. In the dream I think that only one of them is real. The other one is fake. Like it's someone who doesn't have—like it's a shadow, a ghost, a part—which is somehow not real anyway. They are not distinguishable, though. You have to keep both of them, I think, you can't take the risk of leaving either of them because they are absolutely identical. As I think this, I take them in my arms, following this decision, to play with both of them: but one of them is very light and I understand that it is the fake one. The real one has a completely different weight; the other one is like an empty shell. I feel a somewhat strong emotion, of—I don't know—associated with the excitement of discovery, but also with fear: I still think they should be kept together. That's how the dream ends.

The waking therapist questions the emotions experienced during the dream: With amazement she realizes that there was no anger in her during the discovery of the "empty shell," but rather excitement and enthusiasm. This analysis allows Erica to welcome and overcome her fear to realize that there are two parts of Sara with which she has come into contact: On the one hand, there is the Child who expresses strength in wanting to change, as well as a desire for intimacy and gratitude for the support she feels she is receiving from her therapist. This is the part that Erica gives weight to, the part she defines as "real." But there is also another Child, furious and desperate because she feels she has no importance or emotional "weight" in the eyes of her idolized father. This is where her core-of-pain lies. The therapist realizes through dream self-analysis that the "missed" phone call represents a valuable opportunity for the repetition in the here-and-now of a repeated relationship with the rejecting P_{1-} introjected by the patient. The intensity of the emotions experienced within the matrix of transference and countertransference leads to the activation of a second-degree game in which the therapist—at first narcissistically—refuses to take on Sara's projection—*I will make her pay!* However, this means projectively identifying with her P_{1-}, and rejecting this part of the patient means rejecting Sara herself. The decoding of the message sent to her by the Little Professor through the production of the dream allows Erica to make peace with the "aggrieved" part of the patient but also with her own wounded and angry part of herself for not being seen—the therapist's core-of-pain—and to give space, weight, to the reparative, needed therapeutic relationship. "What do you want to do, Sara? I am here and waiting for you." This is the message Erica will send to Sara. What part of Sara will respond? The therapist does not know, but in any case, she is serene. She can now hold both girls.

Using the therapist's dreams in supervision

Once we get past the idea that the countertransference dream is something to be concealed rather than revealed, it is possible to use the dream to learn about aspects of the patient and the therapeutic relationship that have remained obscure up to that point. It is interesting to note how, in line with Brown (2007), even in our supervisory experience, talking about countertransference dreams in the didactic contexts of our School of Psychotherapy or in other formative encounters such as conferences, produced an increase in colleagues' dreams about their patients. As if talking about countertransference dreams in terms of a resource and possibility for expanding knowledge and development in therapy could have been considered as permission to dream. A therapist's dream in which the patient appears can be illuminating with respect to the problem brought to supervision:

> Supervisees report dreams to their supervisors as a means of conveying highly significant perceptions and fantasies that are either entirely repressed within the supervisee, or too dangerous to communicate directly in supervision.
>
> (Langs, 1982, in Brown, 2007)

Ogden (2005) argues that dreaming about one's patients and using such dreams in supervision is a way to protect the analysis:

> A supervisee's almost complete inability to dream his experience with the patient is a far more serious matter than his being only partially able to dream what is occurring in the analysis. The supervisee who is unable to dream his experience is often unaware that there is a problem in the analysis and finds it difficult to make use of supervision [...] An inability to dream the experience being generated in the analysis may take the form of the analyst's decision to declare the analysis a success and then to unilaterally set a termination date (in an unconscious effort to evade facing an analytic impasse).
>
> (p. 1267)

Supervision, as well as the therapist's personal therapy, is a necessary tool for becoming aware of potentially damaging emotional elements, which can be accessed by freely questioning the dream message. In our supervision experience, we have often had the opportunity to listen to therapists' dreams that either featured the patient brought in for supervision or contained aspects that the therapist related back to that patient.

To better understand what we talked about, let us see the example of a dream brought to supervision by a young colleague. The 37-year-old therapist, whom we will call Rossana, dreamed of her 40-year-old unmarried patient whom she describes as alexithymic, rigid, and critical of himself and others. Antonio has been undergoing individual therapy for a year and a half, and about four months before has entered a therapy group. Since then, the setting has involved Antonio attending group and individual therapy every other week. Despite expressing a desire to experience a loving relationship for the first time, Antonio agrees to have casual sexual encounters with women but carefully avoids any emotional involvement because he is terrified of intimacy. At home he keeps taped to the refrigerator a sheet of paper in which he has listed all the traits a woman should have in order for him to fall in love with her. His "Blemish" game causes none of the women he meets to exhibit all the requirements on the list, so he finds it futile to persist in dating them. During the week before his therapist's dream, Antony uses the space of group therapy in a new way. Exceptionally, in that context, he takes up a lot of space reading a story in which a separated 40-year-old man talks about his difficulty in letting go of relationships. Through this narrative device, the vulnerable core of Antony's self is expressed and he contacts a genuine sadness for his loneliness and for the curse of which he is a victim, which leads him to constantly try to distance himself from others. On that occasion, the other members of the group participate empathetically in Antonio's grief; the group represents an affective container for him, who, by declaring his suffering over his lack of contact with others, lays the foundation for an atmosphere of respectful listening and warm intimacy. In the week following the group session, an individual session is scheduled. However, the day before the meeting, the patient called the therapist to declare his inability to attend the session due to a problem at work. The therapist, for her part, is unable to find another slot for him during the week, as, by contract, she had made herself available to do, so the session is canceled and the meeting is postponed until the following week's group session. The therapist's dream below occurs on the night between the patient's cancelation and the missed appointment.

> *It is me and the patient inside a house; after a while I realize it is his house. The dream unfolds as my patient shows me all the rooms, here I have the kitchen, here the living room, here the study. And, in this transition from one room to another, I am very uncomfortable and inside I keep asking myself, "Am I doing something ethically wrong? Am I going out of the setting? Is this okay? Is this not okay? Well, as long as I'm just visiting the house I'm not doing anything more, so it's okay." I keep telling myself, "I'm not doing anything wrong, I'm just seeing the house, it can be an important [therapeutic] tool." At one point he shows me his studio, "Look, this is a very brightly lit room, there is a window here where the sun comes in." It is very well furnished. One thing that strikes me is that it's a very big house, when in fact, I say to myself, "He told me he was staying in a studio apartment,*

but look at this house; what did he even tell me?" Frescoes on the ceiling, very pompous, almost 19th-century decor with luxurious furniture, he shows me this room with a window and a desk with all his papers and books. I am struck by this room and I think, "But look what a beautiful room he has, he never told me about it!" I keep feeling the same discomfort, I am embarrassed, I am restrained and there is no dialogue between us. Here the dream ends and in the next scene I am in bed, I have the blanket covering me up to my chin. And I say to myself, "I am doing something unprofessional now." He is standing next to the bed and he pulls out his penis. At that point I say, "No! This is unprofessional and I can't have you as a patient anymore." I feel violated. And the dream ends there.

In the following week's group session, Antonio brings up his sadness about not having a girlfriend. The group tunes into the emotions of Antonio, who for the first time expresses his fear of rejection. During the supervision meeting that is conducted in group, Rossana wants to work to understand what is happening in the relationship with Antonio that is beyond her awareness. Why did Antonio cancel the individual session and why did she herself find it so difficult to offer an alternative time within the week to meet with him? It seems that Antonio is working deeply, but using the group to do so while at the same time keeping the therapist at arm's length. What meaning can such an attitude have and what countertransference echoes does this situation generate in Rossana?

Following Fosshage's (1983) technical rules for working with dreams, we ask the therapist what emotions accompanied her during the dream. She claims that she was not upset at all and that she questioned at length upon waking the meaning of the dream. Only at this point does Rossana add that in recent months the patient has developed an erotic transference to her, but claims that she is sure that he knows the boundaries well, so she is not frightened at all. On the infinite meanings that countertransference analysis can provide, Hargaden (2011) recommends: "It's important to learn to play with possibilities, and not to get fixed on just one meaning" (p. 244). Precisely to avoid getting fixed on just one meaning, the work in the supervision group continued with the sharing of thoughts and free associations by the colleagues who had been listening up to that point. The first reflection, in agreement with Brown's (2007) observation emphasized above, concerns the therapist's doubt regarding the propriety of her own ethical and professional conduct. In addition to this, it is clear to most of them how the two parts of the dream have to do with two different representations of the same patient, or rather, of the therapist's relationship with him: What was supposed to be a one-bedroom apartment graying with emotional distance and rigid control turns out to be a succession of sun-lit rooms with luxurious furniture. The therapist is astonished to discover an inner richness that at first had remained hidden in the patient.

Here the therapist's dreaming allows for a broader and deeper understanding of the patient. As Ogden (2005b) states, the therapist dreams the patient into existence. An identification between therapist and patient is also emphasized: When Rossana is questioned about the emotions experienced during the unfolding of the dream, she denies any involvement. It is she who is now cold and distant. Going back to Rossana, her supervisor asks her if anything that has been emphasized resonates with her. Rossana acknowledges that her unfeelingness has a defensive quality to it and that instead, as is revealed by the dream, she feels threatened by an emotional closeness that she fears will harm her patient's therapeutic journey. She adds information about her own personal experience: In her family, sex is seen as something "dirty," and guilt has always been the feeling associated with it, while work is associated with self-denial, sacrifice, and toil. The therapist, with the help of the group, understands how these elements of her script were prompted by the authentic request for closeness and intimacy expressed by Antonio, who, from a certain point in therapy onward, no longer needed to defend himself from his core-of-pain by flaunting an autonomous and self-sufficient self. His core-of-pain is represented by a need for closeness and intimacy that remained unsatisfied, expressed by a vulnerable and dependent self that manifested itself in Antonio with an erotic transference toward the therapist. The relational impasse thus consists of a repeated relationship in which the patient's need for intimacy is not met by the therapist (*bad object*) because of the interference of traumatic experiences in her own childhood related to prejudice about physical closeness and sexuality, and a necessary relationship in which the therapist is willing to satisfy Antonio's desire for intimacy through a permission she can give herself (and thus her patient) to accept and share her feelings. Talking openly in therapy about what is happening to the therapeutic dyad preserves from the occurrence of destructive acting out and allows the two to continue on the tortuous and fascinating journey toward emancipation from the limitations of their own script.

Countertransference dreams in nonclinical contexts

While it is true, as we have stated so far, that countertransference dreams bring out previously unknown emotional experiences that emerged in the ongoing relationship between the dreamer and the dream protagonist, such dreams may not be the exclusive purview of the psychotherapist in relation to patients. Even in organizational contexts, for example, coaches establish a relationship of collaboration and trust with their clients, whether company managers, collaborators, or employees, with the only difference from the clinical context being that that relationship will only be implicitly a tool for problem-solving and will not become an explicit object of work. The dream we are about to report came from a business consultant who has been following the founder of a company for several months on a coaching course aimed at improving his leadership skills. After an appointment with the client, the coach has the following dream:

> *I dream that I walk into my client's office and find him at the computer opening a corporate e-mail account for me. I am initially gratified by this choice and comment, "Ah, that is so nice of you!" Then he stops, suddenly turns somber, looks at me and says, "No, I've decided I'm not opening this account for you anymore." I am hurt, I don't understand the reason for this change, and I ask him, "But what happened? What went through your mind?" He is still quite somber, and he says to me, "How haven't you figured it out yet? You still don't get what's between us?" I don't say anything but it becomes clear to me that he has feelings for me, he is falling in love, he is very much involved. And I remain silent because I also feel that I am very close to him and very much involved with a feeling of significant attraction. However, the atmosphere in the room is heavy, and I look at him and say, "Look, I think you're too cooped up in this office, maybe you should get some air. In the meantime, I'm going to go out and walk around the company building and I think you should too." I exit the room and immediately feel better, I walk around the hallways and I come to a room that looks like a company cafeteria where there are many co-workers and employees having a party. They are all very cheerful and I think, "Of course, look at what these people are doing instead of working! I bet he stays in his office all day without keeping an eye on them. It would be better if he looked around and saw what was really going on." I keep wandering around until I get out of the corporate building and see some lawns, some greenery, a nice and pleasant outdoor environment and I think again that he does not make the most of what he might see and what might happen. I decide to go back to him and tell him what I saw and found out. I go back up and enter the room and he is still at the computer. I tell him what I saw and how I immediately felt better by getting out and wandering around and that I understood what needs to be done within the company but also what the world outside the company is like, and I repeat that he should also do what I did and get out and look around.*

In supervision, the coach recounts the dream with amazement, because working with the business executive did not present particular problems at that time. We ask along with Brown (2007) and Ogden (2005b) what of the client does the coach gather through the dream that she could not gather during wakefulness? What unconscious aspects emerge from the dream content that can help overcome impasses and establish a useful and productive working alliance in contractual terms? Thanks to the dream, the coach realizes that the great understanding she has with her client is not only a facilitating element with respect to the now-ended work contract. It can also be an aspect that colludes, amplifying it, with the manager's difficulty in having authoritative and positive leadership. Locking oneself in an office working intensely and intimately for the company, but not meeting those who make up the company itself or the outside world in which it is immersed is a myopic attitude that yields malaise. Seeing and being able to think about this part of their relationship as well helped the protagonists of the dream to give a wider scope and new light to their work.

In conclusion, as we have seen so far, constantly interrogating the cognitive, emotional, and somatic reactions that arise from the therapy encounter is the direct route to opening up new avenues of meaning and new spaces for thinking. To do so requires that patient and therapist be willing to shed light on the deeper aspects of their ego states and to accept being prompted by their encounter into the most hidden and suffering parts. Therapists, too, have a script constructed to protect their vulnerability, and therapists, too, bring that vulnerability to light through dreaming. Being a therapist, we have said repeatedly, requires courage, the courage to stand in the other's pain and to face one's own pain, which the other mirrors. Having the courage to dream preserves the relationship from acting out and sudden ruptures. Not to do so is a real shame, a missed opportunity to support a double healing, that of the patient and that of the therapist.

References

Armando, L. A., & Bolko, M. (2017). *Il trauma dimenticato. L'interpretazione dei sogni nelle psicoterapie: Storia, teoria, tecnica [Forgotten trauma. Dream interpretation in psychotherapies: history, theory, technique]*. Milano: Franco Angeli.

Bromberg, P. M. (2006). *Awakening the dreamer: Clinical journeys*. Mahwah, NJ: The Analytic Press.

Brown, L. (2007). On dreaming one's patient: Reflections on an aspect of countertransference dreams. *Psychoanalytic Quarterly, 76*(3), 835–861.

Bucci, W. (2001). Toward a "Psychodynamic Science": The state of current research. *Journal of the American Psychoanalytic Association, 49*(1), 57–68.

Clarkson, P. (1995). *The therapeutic relationship in psychoanalysis, counselling psychology and psychotherapy*. San Diego: Singular Pub Group.

Cornell, W. (2016). Failing to do the job: When the client pays the price for the therapist's countertransference. *Transactional Analysis Journal, 46*(4), 266–276.

Fosshage, J. (1983). The psychological function of dreams: A revised psychoanalytic perspective. *Psychoanalysis and Contemporary Thought, 6*(4), 641–669.

Freud, S. (2005). *The interpretation of dreams* (D. T. O'Hara & G. M. MacKenzie Eds.; A. A. Brill, Trans.). New York: Barnes & Noble Classics (Originally published in 1899).

Hargaden, H. (2011). The erotic relational matrix revisited. In H. Fowlie & C. Sills (Eds.), *Relational transactional analysis. Principles in practice*. London: Karnac, pp. 233–248.

Heenen-Wolff, S. (2005). The countertransference dream. *The International Journal of Psychoanalysis, 86*(6), 1543–1558.

Lester, E. P., Jodoin, R. M., & Robertson, B. M. (1989). Countertransference dreams reconsidered: A survey. *International Review of Psychoanalysis, 16*, 305–314.

Lippmann P. (2000). *Nocturnes: on listening to dreams*. Hillsdale, N.J.: Analytic Press.

Little, R. (2005). Integrating psychoanalytic understandings in the deconfusion of primitive Child ego states. *Transactional Analysis Journal, 35*(2), 132–146.

Little, R. (2011). Impasse clarification within the transference-countertransference matrix. *Transactional Analysis Journal, 41*(1), 23–38.

Novellino, M. (1984). Self-Analysis of countertransference in integrative transactional analysis. *Transactional Analysis Journal, 14*(1), 63–67.

Ogden, T. (2005a). *Dreaming undreamt dreams and interrupted cries*. London: Routledge.

Ogden, T. (2005b). On psychoanalytic supervision. *International Journal of Psychoanalysis, 86*(5), 1265–1280.

Ogden, T. (2021). *Coming to life in the consulting room. Toward a new analytic sensibility*. London: Routledge.

Racker, H. (1957). The meanings and uses of countertransference. *The Psychoanalytic Quarterly, 26*(3), 303–357.

Rudge, A. M. (1998). A countertransference dream: An instrument to deal with a difficult transference situation. *International Forum of Psychoanalysis, 7*(2), 105–111.

Stuthridge, J. (2015). All the world's a stage: Games, enactment, and countertransference. *Transactional Analysis Journal, 45*(2), 104–116.

Summers, G., & Tudor, K. (2000). Cocreative transactional analysis. *Transactional Analysis Journal, 30*(1), 23–40.

Tangolo, A. E. (2018). *Psychodynamic psychotherapy with transactional analysis: Theory and narration of a living experience*. London: Routledge.

Winnicott, D. W. (1949). Hate in the counter-transference. *International Journal of Psycho-Analysis, 30*, 69–74.

SUGGESTION

Cinema sci-fi, anime, and graphic novels

We present below a selection of sci-fi movies, anime, and graphic novels that are considered "must-see," that we are particularly fond of and that have a special relationship with dreams. Indeed, the plots of many sci-fi movies, anime and graphic novels deal directly with dreams. However, all the images of which they are made (the evocative, dreamy scenic designs, the landscapes, the unrealistic scenes in the movies as well as in the graphic novels) possess the same evocative power as dreams. The plots of many, in fact, deal directly with them but the imagery of which they are all composed have the same evocative power as dreams. The dreams of the films we present, in fact, no longer belong to the individual, but have been "hacked" to become collective cultural heritage. It is in the name of such universality that they absolutely must be known and enjoyed.

Although it does not belong to the sci-fi genre nor can it technically be called a dystopian film, we cannot but begin with the legendary *Rashomon* (1950), a "dream on film" by the great Japanese director Akira Kurosawa. In this masterpiece, the unsettling dimension of the dream is depicted with masterful skill. Released in 1950 and a winner at the Venice Film Festival the following year, Rashomon has become a reference for all who wish to explain the copresence of multiple points of view. The film begins with a married couple walking through the forest and being attacked by a dangerous bandit who kills the man and rapes the woman. In a court of justice, before a judge whose voice we hear but never see, the protagonists take turns narrating the incident, each bringing their own truth: the bride, her deceased samurai husband who speaks through a medium, the bandit, and a woodsman who witnessed the scene. None of them tell the same story: the woman claims to have been raped by the bandit who has killed her husband, the bandit claims to have killed the man but denies raping the woman who instead consented to sexual intercourse, the samurai claims to have committed suicide after his wife was raped, and the woodsman claims to have the truth, even if we later find out he is dishonest and has taken possession of some of the victims' belongings. Kurosawa thus dismantles all our certainties: truth does not exist; it is always partial, subjective, ambiguous, and elusive. Good and evil are not clearly separated and all the protagonists end up looking alike because every one of them is ambivalent and ambiguous in their innocence and guilt. The film has been described as "oneiric." And where if not in dreams is truth so elusive, reality so "unreal" and possibilities so infinite?

The second suggestion we offer is *Solaris* (1972), the oneiric masterpiece by Russian director Andrei Tarkovsky. The film, adapted from the novel by Polish writer Stanislaw Lem, tells the story of psychologist Kris Kelvin's arrival at the space station on the planet Solaris. Solaris is surrounded by a mysterious and inscrutable gelatinous ocean "similar to a brain." Such is the mystery surrounding the planet that the set of disciplines that have in common its study is called *solaristics*. During his stay on Solaris the protagonist meets and spends time with his wife, Hari, who died by suicide ten years earlier. The ocean, in fact, has the power to extract "guests" from the consciousness of those staying on the planet and make them living persons. The stay on Solaris is thus a dream from whose sleep, we will discover as the story continues, the protagonist will never wake up again. Tarkovsky's masterpiece has been called by critics a metaphysical, philosophical film. But it is also a neuro-scientific film because the journey on Solaris is a journey into consciousness, beyond reason, through imagination and memory. Solaris, then, is the planet of dreams. "There is no Hari, Hari can only live here on the station" the protagonist declares at one point. The connection between sleep and dreaming is obvious. The extraction of the guests occurs while they are asleep. It is upon awakening from a long, deep sleep that Kris sees his dead wife beside him again. In addition, an electroencephalogram with a person in a waking state is required to interrupt the extraction of guests from consciousness. Finally, during a meeting in the library between the last three scientists living on the space station, Snaut, a colleague and friend of the protagonist, says referring to the guests, "They come at night, but one must sleep sometime. That's the problem: mankind has lost the ability to sleep." He then reads a passage from Cervantes' *Don Quixote*:

> I know only one thing, señor. When I sleep, I know no fear, no hope, no trouble, no bliss. Blessings on him who invented sleep. The common coin that purchases all things, the balance that levels shepherd and king, fool and wise man.

Ingmar Bergman's words dedicated to the Russian director are famous: "When film is not a document, it is dream. That is why Andrei Tarkovsky is the greatest of them all."

The third classic we present is *The Matrix*, a cult film of the late 1990s, directed by the Wachowski sisters, marking a real watershed in sci-fi cinema for which it is possible to distinguish a before and after *The Matrix*. Belonging to the collective imagination for all intents and purposes, "The Matrix is everywhere." The protagonist is Thomas Anderson, played masterfully by Keanu

Reeves, a software programmer but also a hacker under the pseudonym of "Neo." One night, information about the Matrix appears on his PC screen. Neo does not know if what he has seen is real or just a dream. He then meets Morpheus, who is willing to provide him with information about the Matrix. And here is one of the most famous scenes in the history of cinema. Neo must choose between a blue pill and a red pill. If he chooses the former, he will wake up the morning after in his bed, convinced he has been dreaming. If he chooses the red pill, he will discover the truth: what seems real is actually a dream, and what appears to be a dream contains the truth. Neo chooses the red pill and thus the veil falls. The protagonist discovers that what appears as the real world is actually a virtual illusion, a dream constructed to hold human beings captive. In fact, in order to begin to move again, he needs to be connected to a device capable of reactivating muscles atrophied after years of immobility. He thus becomes aware that the world at the end of the 22nd century is in the process of decay. Machines with artificial intelligence have taken over the world, and humans are harnessed to generate power inside billions of special incubators. Neo is the Chosen One, according to Morpheus, that is, the one who is tasked with "waking up" humanity and freeing it from the dominion of machines.

Paprika (2006) is an anime directed by Satoshi Kon, presented at the Venice Film Festival of the same year, and the inspiration for Nolan's *Inception*. In an unidentified future, some neuroscientists develop a top-secret tool, the DC Mini, useful for entering dreams and being able to condition them for the purpose of helping patients heal. In one scene we see the project leader, Toratarō Shima, proudly explaining the workings of the revolutionary device and offering an interesting definition of dreams in short sleep cycles as "short films." The story continues with psychotherapist Chiba Atsuko who uses the DC Mini covertly to help her patients recover from recurring nightmares by entering their dreams under the name *Paprika*. Dreams, according to Paprika, are places where the dreamer's repressed desires are expressed. Toratarō Shima discovers that three DC Minis have been stolen, and, in a panic, throws himself out the window of the research institute. He falls into a coma, and his associates enter his dreams. In the dream we see an increasingly large parade where all the people who participated in the making of the DC Mini gradually appear, thus giving rise to a collective dream from which it is difficult to escape. We finally discover that the author of the theft is the president of the project, actually a monstrous entity, who uses the DC Mini against the scientists calling himself the keeper of dreams. In his delirious speech, he talks about the arrogance of technology threatening dreams and finally states, "Science is just garbage in the face of the immensity of the dream […] Dreams are the only vestige of humanity we still have left."

Avatar, released in 2009 at the hands of James Cameron, is a magnificent metaphor for the dream world and its relation to the waking state, dense with references to mythology, Magritte's surrealist paintings, science fiction narratives, and neuroscientific stimuli. Just think of the modes of connections of living beings on Pandora that are neuronal connections and the wonderful way it depicts the intersubjectivity and co-dependence of all living things. Many of you will be familiar with it and so we doubt we are spoiling anything, since it is the highest-grossing film in the history of cinema. Pandora is a pristine planet where living beings, animals, and plants, live in perfect peace and harmony. Humans are attracted to Pandora because it is rich in a particular mineral useful for meeting Earth's energy needs. The largest deposit of this mineral is located under the Home Tree, a sacred place of a species of humanoids called the Na'vi. While scientists, including project leader Grace Augustine, are attracted to the Na'vi culture, which they study and respect, the military forces led by Colonel Miles Quaritch are only interested in the precious mineral and want to exterminate the entire species, which is considered only an obstacle to its extraction. The film's protagonist is former Marine Jake Sully, who comes into contact with the Na'vi thanks to his Avatar, a kind of scientific alter ego composed of his DNA mixed with Na'vi DNA. When the Avatar is active, the human's body lies inside a kind of capsule and appears to sleep and dream. The Na'vi begin to trust this stranger, thanks mainly to Princess Neytiri, who speaks the human language and initiates him into the culture of her world. Sully, in love with the princess and attracted to the peaceful and harmonious world of the Na'vi, experiences deep internal conflict knowing that he is actually a traitor as a human being. It seems that the pristine nature of Pandora and the interconnected lives of its inhabitants are going to yield to the brutality and to the grim, short-sighted selfishness of humans, who use technology not to indulge evolution but to destroy the planet and its inhabitants. But this will not be the case. It will be Sully himself who will lead the redemption of the Na'vi to the point of succeeding in driving the humans off Pandora. In the very year in which we are writing these pages, a sequel was released in theaters. So the interconnections and the threats to the Na'vi do not end there.

The next film we present is the unmissable *Inception* (2010), Christopher Nolan's sci-fi where dream suggestion is not only evoked, but the plot is imbued with it. In fact, dreams are the protagonist of this work of art, whose creator's works are generally true dream journeys where space and time lose their logic—as in *Memento*, which begins at the end and goes backward to the beginning and, like a thriller, reveals its meaning only at the last minute. The dream lover can indulge in the film's plot. We get lost in it, since the director enjoys making his protagonists as well as his viewers lose any temporal and spatial reference. For everything is a dream, even when it seems not to be. Mister Cobb, played by Leonardo DiCaprio, is a dream extractor. That is, together with his team, he has the ability to insinuate himself into people's subconscious minds while they are sleeping and condition their dreams. For this to be possible, a connection must be activated with a special device capable of generating a shared dream. Saito, a prominent Japanese businessman, entrusts Cobb and his team with the task of "grafting" into the mind of his recently deceased business rival's son the idea of segmenting the economic empire he inherited. To proceed with the grafting, it is not enough to enter into a shared dream, it is necessary to descend to a deeper level, a dream within a dream. But this is still not enough, it is necessary to descend to a third-level dream to be able to graft an idea into the deepest part of the young heir's subconscious. In order to go down one level, it is necessary for one companion to remain awake while the others dream, in case there is a need to get everyone back up to the previous level. Watching the film, up to a certain point it is possible to follow the plot by following the protagonists through the different and distinct levels of the dream since they all feature different sets: a getaway van for level 1, a hotel lobby for level 2, and the mountain for level 3. Thereafter, it is no longer possible to orient oneself, to distinguish reality from dream. In the finale we watch as Cobb, having successfully completed his mission, finally returns home to his children. However, as the scene draws to a close, the spectators will forever be left with the question of whether Cobb is awake or still asleep.

Our last suggestion is *Sandman*, an original comic book series created by Neil Gaiman between 1988 and 1996, which became a TV series for Netflix in 2022. Sandman has a finite length, there will be no sequel, extension, or retcon. The comic runs for 75 issues, consisting of a weave of gothic-horror style stories that go back and forth in time inspired by Greek myths and Norse folklore from which the name *Sandman*—the titular character who brings good dreams by throwing dust on the eyes of sleepers during the night—comes from. Sandman is Morpheus, one of the seven Eternals, the founding principles of the universe, who is imprisoned in 1916 by the wizard Burgess, King of Demons, leaving a dreamless humanity to live a constant nightmare. The two wars, the epidemics of Spanish flu, and lethargic encephalitis are seen as the consequences of this imprisonment of the dream god, who is freed by accident in 1988 and seeks to rebuild his ruined kingdom. To do so, he needs to regain possession of the three symbols of his power that were taken from him: the Helm, the Ruby and the precious pouch containing the Dust that enables humans to dream. However, the experience of imprisonment has changed him forever; he experiences a crisis that will involve the very nature of dreaming and lead him to leave his role and his kingdom in the hands of the heir Daniel, until he dies. The story thus ends with an awareness of the crisis and the need to face it. The saga of the Lord of Dreams, which masterfully deals with the theme of change, is considered among the best in the genre and has been a success that has far exceeded the expectations of the publisher, illustrators and author himself. "You have changed," Calliope confesses to Morpheus, her former husband, who has come from the Dream Realm to free her because she was imprisoned by humans. As Rastelli states:

Both the main plot—the story of Morpheus, Dream of the Eternals—and the several subplots following the living, the gods and more, have as their background an inescapable crisis, which requires the characters to face it, to become aware of themselves, their nature, their relationships with what is around them, their motivations and their goals.

(p. 49)

The allegorical aspect presented in the saga related to Dream is very interesting. Dream here is not considered in the same way as Desire, which in fact is personified by another of the seven Eternals. Here Dream is preparation and incubation of the human beings' vision of reality, Dream as plans and hope, we might say. What we are left with, at the end of the TV adaptation of Sandman, is the answer he gives to those who ask him why he is so insistent in searching for his lost Dust: "Why on earth? Because without it, my realm will cease to exist, and if dreams disappear, then so will humanity."

References

Cameron, J. (2009). (Director). *Avatar*. 20th Century Fox.
Gaiman, N., Heinberg, A., Goyer, D. S., & Barker, M. (2022). (Executive producers). *The Sandman*. Warner Bros. Television.
Gaiman, N., Kieth, S., & Dringenberg, M. (1989–1996). *The Sandman*. DC Comics.
Kon, S. (2006). (Director). *Paprika*. Madhouse.
Kurosawa, A. (1950). (Director). *Rashomon*. Daiei Film.
Nolan, C. (2010). (Director). *Inception*. Warner Bros Pictures.
Tarkovsky, A. (1972). (Director). *Solaris*. Mosfilm.

AFTERWORD

by Paolo Migone[1]

You cannot talk about this book if you do not first talk about the cultural climate in which it was born, which is that of PerFormat, a school of Transactional Analysis in Pisa that is a breeding ground of ideas and culture, open to all approaches, stimulating curiosity, desire, and passion to learn in a field as complex as that of helping relationships. I was lucky enough to encounter the PerFormat school more than a decade ago. I teach in several schools of psychotherapy, and I must say that I have always felt not only admiration, but also a bit of envy when I saw the cultural verve and enthusiasm of my colleagues in Pisa, in my opinion far superior to those of other schools that belong to my approach (I did not train in Transactional Analysis, although I do share a psychodynamic perspective with the authors). I was always very impressed by the amount of cultural initiatives: the numerous conferences where the most significant figures in psychotherapy and psychoanalysis at the international level were invited, the publications of books, in Italian and English, the opening of new locations in different cities, the consistently high number of students (unlike other schools, where the numbers are much more contained), and the fact that everyone was doing clinical work very early on, that is, students were assigned patients under supervision, which hardly ever happens in other schools. The credit for all this goes mainly to one of the two authors of this book, Anna Emanuela Tangolo, PerFormat's founder and tireless driving force behind this beautiful adventure.

This book, written by Emanuela Tangolo and Francesca Vignozzi (who is one of her main collaborators and teachers at the school), testifies very well to their commitment and working style. They deal with all aspects of dreams and dreamwork in depth. As the reader will have seen, the different chapters explore several issues related to dreamwork, ranging in different theories, even far from Transactional Analysis. Hereinafter I would like to outline a concise overview of the topics that have been covered, which demonstrate very well the book's richness.

---

[1] Co-chair of the journal *Psicoterapia e Scienze Umane* (www.psicoterapiaescienzeumane.it).

The first chapter examines conceptions of the dream from a historical perspective, with references to authors from different schools: from Freud (whose *The Interpretation of Dreams* [1899] is a fundamental reference for all scholars, even those who have distanced themselves from it) to Jung, Fritz Perls and Gestalt therapy, Sándor Ferenczi, Melanie Klein, Wilfred Bion, Donald Winnicott, of course Eric Berne and Transactional Analysis, then Donald Meltzer, Thomas Ogden, Heinz Kohut, James Fosshage, Stephen Mitchell, Philip Bromberg, Wilma Bucci, the Boston Change Process Study Group that was led by Daniel N. Stern, cognitivist authors, etc. Already from reading this first chapter the reader will have noticed the vast culture that the authors convey to the students. In the second chapter there is a very clear summary of the history of neuroscience regarding dreams, and I am sure the reader will have found here a very good review of this complex field of research, which is shown here, as I have experienced it, not as arduous or difficult but as a compelling field of study. The third chapter shows how dreams are theorized and used in Transactional Analysis from the contributions of Eric Berne to more recent trends. For example, it discusses the integration of Transactional Analysis and Gestalt therapy made by Bob and Mary Goulding, the integration of verbal therapy with body therapy made by William F. Cornell, then follows it with the contributions of Richard Erskine, Ray Little, Graeme Summers, and Keith Tudor. This is discussed in more detail in the fourth chapter, which tackles the method developed by the PerFormat school for working with dreams, in different settings. The fifth chapter delves into dreamwork in the individual therapy setting; and the Transactional Analysis method, ego states, and strategic stages of therapy are thoroughly described; this chapter was useful for me to better understand this approach, of which a clear and concise overview is drawn, such that I think is very useful for young students approaching it for the first time. In the sixth chapter, the Transactional Analysis approach to dreams is explored, with the analysis of the "script" through dreams (e.g., in the case of recurring dreams). The seventh chapter discusses traumatic dreams and post-traumatic nightmares seen within the framework of trauma studies, which are especially prominent and incredibly important in psychotherapy today, with a discussion of the issue of dissociation, also strongly present in contemporary psychotherapy. The eighth chapter examines "dreams of change and transformation," and is a beautiful chapter showing how dreams can anticipate change and also how sometimes distressing dreams can actually signal a turning point, a greater ability to represent past traumatic aspects as a sign of overcoming them, and a greater ability to process them. The ninth chapter discusses healing dreams, and also contains interesting reflections on the end of therapy and how it is experienced by patient and therapist. The tenth chapter follows the interesting relationship between transference and dreams. The eleventh chapter explores the technique of dreamwork in group therapy, which is much practiced in the PerFormat school, and also examines social dreaming and the experience of online groups. The twelfth chapter centers around countertransference dreams and also how to use the therapist's dreams in supervision.

As you can very well see, then, after reading this book and the summary roundup I have just given, this is truly stimulating work. I have not yet mentioned, however, that the aspect that makes it even more interesting is that it is rich in clinical examples and even simulated psychotherapeutic sessions; the reader will have noticed how useful this clinical part is in exemplifying the theoretical exposition. But there is more: it is also overflowing with cultural stimuli, because on several occasions, paths are suggested to the reader to explore the theme of dreams as cultural and artistic expressions, with the aim of making young therapists in training understand that dreams should also be observed through different languages: poetic, artistic, literary, and so on [...] I found, for example, the section on Kafka to be very interesting, full of direct quotations from his works and letters.

This book testifies well to the resurgence of interest in dreams that we have witnessed in recent decades. Indeed, since about the 1960s, dreams had lost that central place they had in the psychotherapeutic and especially psychoanalytic movement. There had been a shift of interest from the interpretation of dreams to the interpretation of behavior in daytime life, that is, to material closer to the conscious part of the patient: symptoms, missed acts, fantasies, relational patterns, personality traits, etc. It was thought that the behavior of daytime life, thanks in part to the increasing experience of psychotherapists, was in itself already very rich and interesting for the understanding of the patient, no less than the material revealed by what Freud called the "*via regia*" to the unconscious, that is, dreams.

However, that is not true anymore: dreams have once again come to have an important place in the understanding of the psychic life of patients and in the work of psychotherapists, and this book is a fine testimony to that.

INDEX

abused child (Victim) 135
abusive parent (Persecutor) 135
acting out 157
Adult 86–89; decontamination 93–94; integrated Adult 177
adult dreams, script themes 111
alexithymic patients 161–162
alpha function 11–12
alternate personalities 141
ambivalence, end of therapy 174–175
amygdala 35
André, J. 41
ANP *see* Apparently Normal Personality
antipsychotic drugs 29
anxiety dreams 113–115
Apparently Normal Personality (ANP) 140–141, 144
archaic Parent 151
archetypes of the unconscious 6–8
Arieti, S. 161
Armando, L. A. 236
Avatar (2009) 247–248
awakening 177–178

Barrett, D. 36–37, 145
basic plots of dreams 31
BCPSG *see* Boston Study Group
Beradt, C. 106, 146
Berne, E. 13, 46, 151, 156; dreaming 157; ego states model 85–88; end of therapy 96, 175; group imago 197; life scripts 104–108; psychopathology 87; transactional analysis 46–49; trauma 134
Berta 115–117
Bertozzi, M. 204
betrayal trauma 133

Bettelheim, B. 106, 146–147
bilogic transactions 52
Bion, W. R. 11–12
Bionian matrixes 221
bi-personal approach 135–136
bipolar patients 162–164
Bolko, M. 236
Boston Study Group (BCPSG) 22–23
Bowater, M. 49–50, 138; life changes 155; recurring dreams 110
brain damage, inability to dream 28–29
Bromberg, P. M. 16, 141, 228
Brown, L. 231, 235
Buber, M. 85
Bucci, W. 17–18
Buñuel, L. 204–205, 217

Cartwright, R. 154, 161
cessation of recurrent dreams 121–122
change 152–156; distress dreams 158–159; dream psychopathology 159–163; "dreams that turn over a page" 158–159; end of therapy 175; *see also* transformation
Child 86–88, 187, 189; contamination 93, 99; Creative Child 57; deconfusion 171; dreaming 88–89; empty child (Victim) 135; Frightened Child 88–89; good child (Victim) 135; transformation 153
child-parent relationships 189
children 39, 151; dreams of 34–35; nightmares 137; relational experiences 152; self-state-dreams 85; trauma 133–135; *see also* Child
cholinergic neurons 27
cinema 204–205

circumambulation 6
clarified imago 215
Clarkson, P. 198, 200, 228
co-creative: empathy 57; sloppiness 23; transactional analysis 57
cognitive psychotherapy 19–20
Coleridge, S. T. 137
collective nightmares 145–147
Complex PTSD 139
condensation 35
conflict 174–175
conscious 47
contamination 93, 99
content of dreams 30–32
continuity of dreams 30
control-mastery theory 92, 98
core-of-pain 229
Cornell, W. F. 54–55, 133, 136, 152, 156, 190, 227–228
countertransference 100, 191, 199, 225–227
countertransference dreams (CTDs) 230–236; "dreams" in nonclinical contexts 241–243; "dreams" using in supervision 238–241; self-analysis of 236–237
countertransferential reactions 92
Covid-19 pandemic 223; collective nightmares 145–146; social dreaming 221–222
Creative Child 57
creative dreams 157
CTDs see countertransference dreams
cultural dreams 104

Daldianus, A. 62
De Bei, F. 144–145
deconfusion of the Child 94–95, 171, 214
decontamination 92–94, 100
default mode network (DMN) 34
deferred action 131
depression 153, 161; depressive stage 11
developmental traumas 86–87
diagnostic dreams 163
DID see dissociative identity disorder
dissociation 87, 131, 140–142; and trauma 134–136
dissociative identity disorder (DID) 141
distress dreams 53, 158–159
DMN see default mode network
Domhoff, G. W. 30–31

dopamine-stimulating agents (L-DOPA) 29
dream analysis 141; see also therapy
The Dream and the Underworld (Hillman) 61–62
dream contents 30–32
dream disfigurement 5
dream imagery, emotions 70–71
dream interpretation 3–5
dream narration 222
The Dream of a Rarebit Fiend (1906) 204
dream plots 31
dream psychopathology 159–163
dream sharing 146
dream space, emotions 72
dream variation 38
dreaming brain 34, 39
dream-producing mind 140
"dreams that turn over a page" 158–159
dreamwork: in cognitive psychotherapy 19–20; preparing for 66–68; reasons for 65–66; settings for 68; working together 68–69
dyadic resonance 173

earned secure attachment 173, 175
ego states model 85–87, 134
ego states, psychopathology of 87–88
elaborative dreams 162
emotion schemas 17
Emotional Personality (EP) 141, 144; dream imagery 70–71; dream space 72; group therapy 216; protagonists of dreams 89; tracing back to current experiences 71–72
empowerment for clients 74–75
empty child (Victim) 135
enactment analysis 141, 229
end of therapy 96, 172, 176–177; final sessions 177–178; final stage 173; follow-up dreams 179; therapist's blessing to close the journey 176–177; transference dreams 199–201
end-of-therapy dreams 96–97, 154
environmental anomalies 109
environmental influences on dreams 104–107
EP see Emotional Personality
Ermann, M. 191–193, 199
eroticization of the therapeutic relationship 235

INDEX

Erskine, R. 55–56, 108, 122
evacuative dreams 162
evolution of transference in therapy 198–199
exploring with dreamers 71
Eyes Wide Shut (1999) 205

face-to-face experiences 222–223
failure or helplessness 109–110
Fellini, F. 6, 205–207
Ferenczi, S. 9–10, 131, 142, 190, 199–201
final sessions 173, 177–178; final stage of therapy 173
Fisher, J. 134, 173, 175
follow-up dreams 179–182
Fonagy, P. 21–22, 40
Fosshage, J. L. 14–15, 192
fragmentation 87
free association 5, 48, 52–53
Freud, S. 3–5; Irma's dream 4–5, 234–235; trauma 130–131
Friedman, R. 216–217
Frightened Child 88–89
Friston, K. J. 39
function of dreams, recent theories 36–40

Gestalt dream analysis 49–50
Gestalt theory 8–9
gnocco technique 95
good child (Victim) 135
Goulding, B. 49, 152
Goulding, M. 49, 152
Greene, G. 163
Grinberg, L. 154, 162
group imago 197
group therapy 209, 210, 212–215, 219–220; clarified imago 215; listening to dreams 217–218; operative imago 214; polyphony of dreams 216–217; pre-established imago 212; provisional imago 212–213; secondarily adapted imago 214; social dreaming 221–222; techniques for working on dreams 218–219; temporarily adapted imago 213

hallucinations 28, 160
Hall/Val de Castle scoring scale 39
Hargaden, H. 54, 186–187, 198
Hartmann, E. 35

healing 94, 135, 170–172, 182–183, 227, 231
healing dreams 233
Heenen-Wolff, S. 231, 233
Hillman, J. 61–62
hippocampus 35, 37
Hirsch, I. 15
His Prehistoric Past (1941) 204
historical influences on dreams 104–107
Hobson, J. A. 27–28, 39–40
Howell, E. 141
Hugo Cabret (2011) 205
human destiny 151
hypnagogia 33

Id energy 47
idealized Parent (Savior) 135
idealizing transference 187
Image Rehearsal Therapy (IRT) 139
inability to dream 28–29
Inception (2010) 248–249
incubus 63
inner Parent 186
Integral Adulthood 57
integrated Adult 177
The Interpretation of Dreams (Freud) 3
introjection 151
introjective transference 187
Irma's dream 4–5, 234–235
IRT *see* Image Rehearsal Therapy

Jung, C. G. 6–8, 61

Käes, R. 216, 222–223
Kafka, F. 124
Klein, M. 10–11
Kohut, H. 14
Kurosawa, A. 205, 245

Lawrence, G. 18–19
L-DOPA *see* dopamine-stimulating agents
Legrenzi, P. 40–42
Lester, E. P. 230
Levi, P. 138–139
Levin, R. 38–39
Levine, H. 133
life scripts 107–108
Ligabue, S. 50–51
Lingiardi, V. 63, 144–145

listening to dreams 65; group therapy 217–218
Little, R. 56, 187, 229

Malinowski, J. 147
Man and His Symbols (Jung) 61
Mancia, M. 41, 189–190, 193, 196
Manifest Dream Report (MDR) 155
Massini, S. 4–5
maternal reverie 12
The Matrix 246–247
McCarley, R. 27–28
McNamara, P. 37–38
Meltzer, D. 13
mentalization 21–22
Migone, P. 20–21
Milena's story 165–168, 192–193
mirroring 187
Mitchell, Stephen 15–16
Moiso, C. 51, 185–186
moment of separation 174–175
monologic transactions 52
Morena, S. 134, 138, 141–142
motivational reward 30
multiple code theory 17–18

nachtraglichkeit 130–131
narcissistic patients 163
narrative threads 31
narratives, listening to 70
negative emotions 39, 89
neglectful parent (Bystander) 135
neuroscience 26–28; recent theories on function of dreams 36–40; troubled mind-brain relationship 40–42
neurotic symptoms 6
Nielsen, T. 38–39
nightmares 36, 47, 53, 108–109, 157; collective nightmares 145–147; life scripts 107; post-traumatic nightmares 136–139; psychosis 160
norepinephrine 27, 38
Novellino, M. 50–53, 90, 199, 225
NREM sleep 27–28; *vs.* REM sleep 32–35

object relations 10–11
obsessive patients 161–162
Ogden, T. H. 13–14, 157–158, 238, 241
oneiric imagery 5
oneiric unconscious 144
Oneirocritica (Daldianus) 62

online groups 222–223
operative imago 214
The Oracle of Night: The History and Science of Dreaming (Ribeiro) 62

Panksepp, J. 29
Papini, G. 188
Paprika (2006) 247
paradoxical sleep 26
Parent 85–89, 189; archaic Parent 151; idealized Parent (Savior) 135; inner Parent 186
Parent ego states 187
parental programming 151
Parent-Child patterns, trauma 135
Parent-Child relationship 189–190, 199
Parkinson's disease 37
patient-therapist relationship 189
P/C ego states 229–230
PerFormat 57–58, 251
peri-traumatic nightmares 137
Perls, F. 8–9
person-to-person relationships 198, 200
Play Technique 10
polyphony of dreams 216–217
post-traumatic functioning 131
post-traumatic growth 142
post-traumatic nightmares 136–139
post-traumatic stress disorder (PTSD) 131
pre-established imago 212
preparing for dreamwork 66–68
principles of dreamwork 69
projection 185–186, 191
projective identification 12, 143
provisional imago 212–213
psychodynamic approach to transactional analysis 50–52
psychological games 92
psychological play 226–227
psychopathology: dreams in 159–163; of ego states 87–88
psychosis 160
psychotic patients 67–68, 160–161
PTSD *see* post-traumatic stress disorder

Quinodoz, J.-M. 156, 158–159

Racker, H. 225–226
racket-system model 108

INDEX

Rapid Eye Movement (REM) sleep 26–28, 145, 161–162; *vs.* NREM sleep 32–35
Rashomon (1950) 245–246
reasons for dreamwork 65–66
recurring dreams 7, 30; life scripts 107–108; trauma 138–139; *see also* script dreams
recurring themes 111 *see also* repetitive themes
redecision therapy 49, 134
referential cycle 17–18
referential processes 17
regressive dreams 158–159
relational attentiveness 136
relational impasse 135
relational knowing 22
relational move 22
relational psychology 15–16
relational transactional analysis 54
relationality 18–19
relationships 189–191, 198
re-learning 95–97, 101
REM *see* Rapid Eye Movement (REM) sleep
REM Sleep Behavior Disorder 37
remembering dreams 156–158
repetition principle 30
repetitive themes 109–110
Resnik, S. 67–68, 104, 160–161, 163
responsibility 177–178
re-traumatization 146–147
Ribeiro, S. 62, 108–109
Rosa, S. 62–63
Rotondo, A. 50–51
Rudge, A. M. 233

Sandman 249–250
schizophrenics, sleep quality 160
Schnitzler, A. 107
Scholl, S. 182–183
Schredl, M. 109, 121–122
Scilligo, P. 50
script antithesis 171
script beliefs 108
script dreams 48–49, 53, 104, 108–110, 217; environmental and historical influences on dreams 104–107; *see also* recurring dreams
script protocol 194
script themes, in adult dreams 111

scripts 51–52, 152; *see also* script dreams
secondarily adapted imago 214
self-analysis of, countertransference dreams (CTDs) 236–237
self-awareness 121
self-state-dreams 14, 85
Selznick, B. 205
separation, end of therapy 174–175
serotonin 27
settings for dreamwork 68
sharing dreams 67, 146, 218–219; *see also* group therapy
"The Sick Gentleman's Last Visit" (Manguel) 188
Siegel, A. 173
Sills, C. 54, 186–187, 198
sleep: depression and 161; REM *vs.* NREM 32–35; for schizophrenics 160; *see also* Rapid Eye Movement (REM) sleep
sleep consciousness 33–34
sleep deprivation 32
sleep disorders 147
sloppiness 90
social brain 34, 39
social dreaming 18–19, 221–222
social life 34
Social Stimulation Theory (SST) 39–40, 85
Solaris (1972) 246
Solms, M. 29–30
specular face-to-face 223
Spellbound (1945) 205
splitting 87
squiggle game 193
SST *see* Social Stimulation Theory
stages of therapy 90–97; dreams in stages 97–102
Stern, D. 22
Stevenson, R. L. 6
stimulant drugs, REM sleep 162
storming 213
structural work 134
Stuthridge, J. 132, 135, 226–227
subconscious fixed ideas 131
Sullivan, H. S. 15, 134
supervision, using therapist's dreams in 238–241
support for clients 74–75

techniques for working on dreams, in group therapy 218–219

temporarily adapted imago 213
therapeutic alliance 91–92
therapy work 141–142, 157
'thick boundaries in the mind' 161–162
The Third Reich of Dreams (Beradt) 106, 146
Thomson, G. 49
threat simulation 34
transactional analysis groups 210–211
transference 91, 185–187; group imago 197; idealizing transference 187; introjective transference 187; meaning of dreams brought to therapy 191–194; twin transference 187
transference dreams 53, 188–191; beginning of therapy 194–198; end of therapy 199–201; evolution of in therapy 198–199
transference dynamics 55
transformation 152–156; beginning to remember dreams 156–158; elaborative dreams 162; secondarily adapted imago 214
transitional space 12–13
trauma 35–36, 130–132, 142–145; betrayal trauma 133; centrality of 132–133; Child 87–88; collective nightmares 145–147; Complex PTSD 139; and dissociation 134–136, 140–142; post-traumatic growth 142; post-traumatic nightmares 136–139
traumatic dreaming 147
traumatic script 135
traumatolitic function of dreams 9–10
troubled mind-brain relationship 40–42
twin transference 187

Umilta, C. 40–42
Un Chien Andalus (1929) 204–205
uncanny (*unheimliche*) 159
undreamable experience 157

Vedfelt, O. 32, 37
visual dimensions of dreams 67

Waiting List 209
Wanda's dream 48–49
Weiss, J. 91–92, 98
Wenders, W. 205
we-ness 57, 136
Winnicott, D. W. 12–13, 232–233, 236
working together on dream analysis 68–69

Yalom, I. 140, 189–190, 195, 198
Yume (*Dreams*, 1990) 205

Zambrano, M. 177, 183

Taylor & Francis eBooks

www.taylorfrancis.com

A single destination for eBooks from Taylor & Francis with increased functionality and an improved user experience to meet the needs of our customers.

90,000+ eBooks of award-winning academic content in Humanities, Social Science, Science, Technology, Engineering, and Medical written by a global network of editors and authors.

TAYLOR & FRANCIS EBOOKS OFFERS:

- A streamlined experience for our library customers
- A single point of discovery for all of our eBook content
- Improved search and discovery of content at both book and chapter level

REQUEST A FREE TRIAL
support@taylorfrancis.com